SENTENCING THE SELF-CONVICTED

This book addresses the fundamental ethical and legal aspects, penal consequences and social context arising from a citizen's acceptance of guilt. The focus is upon sentencing people who have pleaded guilty; in short, post-adjudication, rather than issues arising from discussions in the pretrial phase of the criminal process.

The vast majority of defendants across all common law jurisdictions plead guilty and as a result receive a reduced sentence. Concessions by a defendant attract more lenient State punishment in all western legal systems. The concession is significant: at a stroke, a guilty plea relieves the State of the burden of proving the defendant's guilt beyond a reasonable doubt, and in open court. Plea-based sentencing has become even more visible in recent years.

The book provides insightful commentary on the following questions:

- If an individual voluntarily accepts guilt, should the State receive this plea without further investigation or any disinterested adjudication?
- Is it ethically acceptable to allow suspects and defendants to self-convict in this manner, without independent confirmation and evidence to support a conviction?
- If it is acceptable, what is the appropriate State response to such offenders?
- If the defendant is detained pretrial, the ability to secure release in return for a plea may be particularly enticing. Might it be too enticing, resulting in wrongful convictions?

Sentencing the Self-Convicted

The Ethics of Pleading Guilty

Edited by
Julian V Roberts
and
Jesper Ryberg

•HART•
OXFORD • LONDON • NEW YORK • NEW DELHI • SYDNEY

HART PUBLISHING

Bloomsbury Publishing Plc

Kemp House, Chawley Park, Cumnor Hill, Oxford, OX2 9PH, UK

1385 Broadway, New York, NY 10018, USA

29 Earlsfort Terrace, Dublin 2, Ireland

First published in Great Britain 2023

A catalogue record for this book is available from the British Library.

A catalogue record for this book is available from the Library of Congress.

Library of Congress Control Number: 2022948632

ISBN: HB: 978-1-50995-743-9
ePDF: 978-1-50995-745-3
ePub: 978-1-50995-744-6

Typeset by Compuscript Ltd, Shannon

ACKNOWLEDGEMENTS

The essays in this volume were all discussed in a seminar held at Worcester College Oxford, 25–26 March 2022. We would like to thank the Faculty of Law Research Support Fund at the University of Oxford and the Research Group for Penal Ethics at Roskilde University for supporting the event. Our thanks are also due to the authors for submitting their essays as well as the other participants attending the seminar for their feedback. Finally, we thank Carolyn Fox for copy editing the manuscript, Oisin Mag Fhogartaigh for research assistance, and Kate Whetter, Rosemarie Mearns and colleagues from Hart Bloomsbury for their help in bringing this collection into print.

Julian V Roberts
Jesper Ryberg
Oxford and Roskilde, 1 September 2022

CONTENTS

CONTRIBUTORS

Julian V Roberts is Professor of Criminology in the Faculty of Law, University of Oxford and Executive Director of the Sentencing Academy. He was the 2021 recipient of the American Society of Criminology Sellin-Glueck Award for International and Comparative scholarship. His recent books include *Paying for the Past* (with R. Frase, Oxford University Press, 2019) and *Sentencing and Artificial Intelligence* (edited with J. Ryberg, Oxford University Press, 2022).

Jesper Ryberg is Professor of Ethics and Philosophy of Law at Roskilde University, Denmark. He is head of the Research Group for Criminal Justice Ethics and member of the Royal Society for Science and Letters. He has published extensively on the philosophy of punishment and other issues within criminal justice ethics. His most recent books include *Sentencing and Artificial Intelligence* (edited with J.V. Roberts, Oxford University Press, 2022) and *Neurointerventions, Crime and Punishment: Ethical Considerations* (Oxford University Press, 2020). He is currently editing the *Oxford Handbook of the Philosophy of Punishment* (Oxford University Press, forthcoming 2023).

Thom Brooks is Professor of Law and Government at Durham University's Law School, was Dean 2016–21 and is an associate member of the Philosophy Department with past visiting appointments at Columbia, Pennsylvania, Yale and New York Universities. He is an Academic Bencher of Inner Temple, a former President of the Society of Legal Scholars and founding editor of the *Journal of Moral Philosophy.* His recent books include *Punishment*, 2nd edn (Routledge, 2021) and *The Oxford Handbook of Global Justice* (Oxford University Press, 2020). He is an adviser to the UK Labour Party and executive member of the Fabian Society and Society of Labour Lawyers.

Netanel Dagan is a lecturer at the Institute of Criminology, Faculty of Law, the Hebrew University of Jerusalem. His research interests include sentencing, prisons and parole. His recent work is published in journals such as the *British Journal of Criminology*, *Punishment & Society* and *Theoretical Criminology*.

RA Duff FBA, FRSE is Professor Emeritus of Philosophy at the University of Stirling. He was founding co-director of the Robina Institute of Criminal Law and Criminal Justice at the University of Minnesota, and founding co-editor of the journal *Criminal Law and Philosophy*. He has written widely on criminal law, criminal process and criminal punishment; his most recent book is *The Realm of the Criminal Law* (Oxford University Press, 2018).

Rebecca K Helm is the founder and director of the Evidence-Based Justice Lab at the University of Exeter. She is a current UKRI Future Leaders Fellow and is an expert in the field of psychology and law, and using empirical methodology to examine the legal system. Her work on guilty pleas has been widely cited, including by academics and courts, and in the work of non-governmental organisations.

Mike Hough is Emeritus Professor in the School of Law, Birkbeck, University of London and was previously University of London Professor of Criminal Policy from 2003 until 2016. He was the founding director of the Institute for Crime & Justice Policy Research (ICPR). He was recipient of the 2020 European Society of Criminology award for lifetime contributions to criminology and the British Society of Criminology outstanding achievement award in 2021. His most recent book is *Good Policing: Trust, Legitimacy and Authority* (Policy Press, 2021).

Jessica Jacobson is Professor of Criminal Justice and Director of the Institute for Crime & Justice Policy Research (ICPR) at Birkbeck, University of London. As ICPR Director, she oversees the institute's programme of academically grounded, policy-oriented research on justice. She is currently leading an ESRC-funded study on bereaved people's experiences of inquests. Among her most recent publications is *Participation in Courts and Tribunals: Concepts, Realities and Aspirations* (Bristol University Press, 2020, co-edited with Penny Cooper).

Adam J Kolber is Professor of Law at Brooklyn Law School and a former Laurence S. Rockefeller visiting fellow at Princeton University and visiting fellow at NYU Law School's Centre for Research in Crime and Justice. Since 2005 he has run the Neuroethics and Law Blog. Currently, he is writing a book that defends a consequentialist approach to punishment.

Marie Manikis is an Associate Professor and William Dawson Scholar at the Faculty of Law, McGill University. She is a Research Associate at the University of Oxford and an Associate Member of the International Academy of Comparative Law. She has published her work in leading peer-reviewed journals, including the *Oxford Journal of Legal Studies*, *Cambridge Law Journal* and *Public Law*.

Gabrielle Watson is the Shaw Foundation Fellow in Law at Lincoln College, Oxford and author of the award-winning *Respect and Criminal Justice* (Oxford University Press, 2020). She has held a Leverhulme Early Career Fellowship at the University of Oxford and Visiting Fellowships in Law at the Cambridge Centre for Criminal Justice and Downing College, Cambridge. In 2022 she was appointed Advisor to the Sentencing Academy.

Leo Zaibert is Andreas von Hirsch Professor of Penal Theory and Ethics at the University of Cambridge. He has written widely on punishment, forgiveness and related topics His most recent book is *Rethinking Punishment* (Cambridge University Press, 2018).

1

The Ethics of Pleading Guilty and the State Response to Self-convicting Offenders

JULIAN V ROBERTS AND JESPER RYBERG*

I. Introduction

Defendants across almost all common law jurisdictions confront a choice: plead guilty and proceed to a sentencing hearing, or plead not guilty and face a criminal trial. Civil law countries operate an analogous system whereby the accused may accept responsibility and enter into a 'penal order' (Gillieron 2019). In both contexts the defendant who pleads guilty or accepts responsibility for the crime will receive a reduced sentence. Self-conviction attracts a mitigated punishment, although the level of reduction varies widely, as do the ways in which the potential sentence reductions are communicated to defendants and the community more broadly.

Mitigating sentence for offenders who self-convict seems ethically unproblematic to many people. Provided with the evidence of their wrongdoing, some offenders accept responsibility and plead guilty. Having spared the prosecution the time and trouble of running a criminal trial, it seems not unreasonable to reward the defendant for this virtuous act. In addition, the guilty plea offers the defendant a tangible means by which to substantiate his or her remorse. Plea-based claims of remorse are likely to be far more persuasive than remorse expressed only after conviction. As noted later in the chapter, other participants in the criminal process will normally also benefit from the offender's decision to accept rather than contest conviction. Finally, the conviction itself will seem secure: if the alleged perpetrator and the prosecuting authority concur on the matter, a trial would appear unnecessary. Wherein lies the difficulty, and wherefore the academic critique of the practice?

* Our thanks to Rebecca Helm and Netanel Dagan for helpful comments on an earlier draft of this chapter.

ality, the practice of awarding a sentencing discount in return for a guilty ᵨₗₑₐ raises complex legal and ethical questions. Some of these relate to the defendant, others to the prosecuting authority, the crime victim or the wider community. Many questions require consideration of findings from empirical research; for example, the extent to which guilty plea discounts trigger wrongful convictions or exacerbate racial disproportionality in prison statistics. The central issues engage the ethical-legal aspects of a guilty plea at sentencing – for defendants, crime victims, the public and the State. This brief introductory chapter notes some of the key issues arising when defendants who plead guilty are awarded a sentence reduction and sets the stage for the diverse chapters which follow.

II. The Context

In some countries, a guilty plea can strip years off a custodial sentence, with reductions well above 50 per cent (Shaeffer 2019). In addition to a reduction in prison sentence length (or fine or length of community order), in some court systems a guilty plea can result in a prison sentence being replaced by a community punishment.[1] Elsewhere, the plea-based mitigation is more modest, although it is impossible to identify with any precision the magnitude of reductions in most jurisdictions. The reason for this is that courts enjoy wide discretion in this regard, even in the US States which operate sentencing guidelines. Few countries specify a recommended maximum plea-based reduction in statute.[2] England and Wales is the only jurisdiction where it is possible to be more precise about plea-based sentence reductions as courts must follow a guideline which stipulates a maximum sentence reduction of one-third (Sentencing Council 2017).

Most defendants in common law jurisdictions plead guilty. The plea rate in England and Wales is typical of common law jurisdictions. In 2019/20 the guilty plea rate in the lower (magistrates') courts was 79 per cent and was only slightly lower in the superior (Crown) court at 73 per cent (Gormley et al 2020). The proportion of defendants who plead guilty has changed little over the decades: Bottoms and McLean (1976) report almost identical guilty plea rates in 1960.[3] In some systems the guilty plea usually emerges following discussions or bargaining between the defendant's lawyer and the prosecuting authority. In jurisdictions

[1] There is little information on the percentage of pleas which change the nature rather than simply the quantum of sanction. One Australian study found that in one-third of a sample of guilty plea cases the sentence type changed as a result of the defendant's guilty plea (Sentencing Advisory Council of Victoria 2015).

[2] For example, in New South Wales where a 25% reduction is mandated for timely pleas (McKnight and Sprouster 2018).

[3] This stability in plea rates is significant because the magnitude of reductions has varied significantly. If the principal influence on defendants' decisions to plead guilty is the magnitude of the anticipated reduction, it would be natural to expect the plea rate to track levels of reductions awarded.

where plea negotiations are less common, the plea arises following discussions between the defendant and his or her legal adviser. In both contexts the existence of a sentence reduction for guilty plea plays a role. The sentence discount represents an incentive to plead and is one reason why defendants plead guilty.

A great deal of scholarship has addressed plea bargaining and plea negotiations – the discussions which often precede and define a guilty plea in common law systems (Langer 2021; Flynn and Freiberg 2018; Vogel 2019; Lippke 2011). The current volume, in contrast, focuses upon the ethics of a sentencing regime which rewards defendants who plead guilty, regardless of whether the plea is a consequence of negotiations between the parties. Clearly, the two subjects are related, particularly in the United States, where most pleas arise following bargaining between the defendant and the prosecutor. Yet a number of questions arise with respect to the role of a plea whether it is entered after plea discussions or spontaneously by the accused without receiving legal advice.

One of the ethical quandaries is whether defendants have an ethical duty to plead guilty if they have sufficient awareness of the case against them and knowledge of the law to conclude they are guilty. Or can defendants well aware of their legal status passively await developments, including a criminal trial? Should the State reward defendants who plead guilty by imposing less punitive punishments? In everyday life, people who accept responsibility for wrongdoing generally receive a less harsh response from the party who has been wronged. In fact, social convention expects the wronged party to acknowledge the wrongdoer's acceptance of guilt, and the mitigation represents this acknowledgement. It would be deemed churlish to ignore the individual's acceptance of his or her own wrongful conduct. To what extent should this very human reaction read across to the criminal process?

In the event that it is deemed ethically sound to reward defendants for entering a guilty plea, further questions arise. First, how should this information be communicated – directly in open court, or indirectly through the defendant's legal adviser? One approach would support clear and well-publicised sentence discounts. Without knowing about the plea-based reductions, most defendants may simply elect to be tried. And without a clear understanding of the magnitude of the reductions on offer, defendants cannot make an informed choice about plea. As noted by the Sentencing Advisory Council of Tasmania, 'requiring a judge to specify the reduction … allows offenders and their legal representatives to have a clearer understanding of the benefit of an early guilty plea' (2018: ix).

An opposing view is that the decision to plead guilty should come spontaneously from the defendant who recognises his or her guilt and elects to express this acceptance of responsibility in law. Alerting defendants to the sentence reductions, particularly if they are significant, runs the risk of eliciting wrongful pleas from innocent defendants. Better to keep them in the dark until they have arrived at a decision, at which point the benefit of the guilty plea may be revealed. In seeking to avoid or minimise wrongful convictions (by innocent defendants), this approach collides directly with the principle of transparency and the requirement for defendants to make an informed decision.

Courts offer sentence reductions in order to encourage defendants who accept their guilt to waive their right to a trial. The most obvious benefits arising when trials are avoided are utilitarian rather than deontological. The criminal justice system conserves resources at many stages, particularly in terms of court costs, but savings also benefit the police, the prosecution branch and any legal aid system. Although most scholarly commentary focuses on the fiscal savings of guilty pleas, the benefits to victims and witnesses are equally important. Victims and witnesses have much to gain from a guilty plea, particularly early pleas. Witnesses are spared the time-consuming appearances to testify. Victims are spared the same experience and have the additional benefit of knowing that their victimisation is not being contested by the defendant.[4] In addition, there are several other less obvious but equally important ethical benefits associated with sentencing rewards for defendants who plead guilty. If the defendant is convinced of his or her guilt and elects to minimise the harm of the offence by pleading guilty, this is an ethical decision that should be rewarded. At the same time, some possible unintended consequences of plea-based sentencing regimes are troubling and it is to these that we now turn.

III. The Potential Adverse Consequences of Plea-based Sentence Reductions

A. Wrongful (Self-)convictions: Convicting the Innocent

This is the most discussed potential negative consequence of awarding plea-based reductions (eg, Ashworth and Kelly 2021; Campbell, Ashworth and Redmayne 2019; Redlich, Wilford and Bushway 2017; Blume and Helm 2014; Welsh, Skinns and Sanders 2021).[5] Defendants may wrongfully plead guilty simply because they are enticed by the prospect of a significantly reduced sentence.[6] They may have pressing personal reasons to seek to escape detention (if detained in prison pre trial) or avoid future imprisonment, or they may simply fail to fully appreciate the consequences of a criminal conviction.

[4] Although it is important to acknowledge that a small minority of victims actively seek to participate in a trial. For these victims, the trial-stopping guilty plea is a cause for concern not celebration. This issue is discussed in several chapters of this volume.

[5] Academics have not always seen this as a problem. Writing at a time when plea-based sentence reductions were likely more powerful than today, Rupert Cross concluded that it was 'extremely improbable' that an accused would plead guilty simply to receive a mitigated sentence (1971: 153).

[6] The vast literature on miscarriages of justice and wrongful convictions largely overlooks the problem of wrongful *self*-conviction (see Roach (2021); Zalman and Norris (2021) for a discussion). If the defendant is coerced or unduly influenced by the sentence reduction, however, the State is as culpable as if its actors were responsible through inept or malicious prosecution. For a recent case law analysis of the factors contributing to guilty plea wrongful convictions, see Nash, Dioso-Villa and Porter 2021).

Determining how many individuals wrongfully plead guilty – the wrongful self-conviction rate – is very challenging (Wilford and Khairalla 2020). Estimates vary, but there is consensus that such false convictions occur, particularly in the United States, where prosecutors exercise considerable power over plea discussions. This power may be disproportionate when the case involves a vulnerable defendant or an unrepresented litigant. The power of a plea to affect sentencing outcomes is critical. This is particularly true in jurisdictions which employ lengthy prison sentences. If the defendant is confronted with the choice between, say, 20 years in prison if convicted following trial, and perhaps half that term following a guilty plea, the temptation to plead guilty may be very strong, regardless of whether the State has a compelling case against the accused (see Helm 2021). As a consequence, many defendants may plead guilty, despite the fact they are legally innocent. The two key dimensions, then, are the *severity* of punishments imposed, and the *magnitude* of the sentence reduction triggered by the guilty plea. Wrongful self-convictions are most likely when sentences are very severe, and the discount is very great.

A sentencing regime which greatly restricted the levels of reduction would likely reduce the number of innocent defendants who wrongfully self-convict, but may generate another problem: if very few defendants plead guilty, the court system could become even more clogged than at present. In addition, restricting or eliminating the reductions may be undesirable because it would fail to distinguish between ethically distinguishable offenders – those accepting responsibility and those unwilling to do so, but who are nevertheless convicted. For these reasons, jurisdictions attempt to achieve a balance, offering sentence reductions sufficient to elicit a guilty plea from defendants who accept their guilt, but not great enough to generate false convictions. In order to determine whether an appropriate balance has been achieved, we need to consider both empirical research on defendant decision making and the ethical aspects of plea-based reductions.

Scholars have grappled with the question of whether plea-based sentence reductions constitute an incentive or a reward. An incentive is a future benefit for which individuals may strive. It encourages people to take certain steps to secure the benefit. Absent the prospect of the benefit, these actions would be less likely. A reward is bestowed in recognition of some action which exceeded the expected norms of conduct or performance. Employers do not reward employees for showing up to work, but they may advertise an incentive for meeting specific employment-related targets. Despite this distinction, these definitions become interchangeable in the context of a criminal proceeding. The sentence reduction may be deemed an incentive for defendants who accept their guilt to plead guilty, a reward for those who do so or even as a threat for those who elect trial. It may be tempting to conclude that if the benefit is advertised well in advance of the plea decision, it constitutes an incentive, and if the reduction is only implemented after the defendant has pleaded guilty, it is a reward. But few sentencing regimes operate a 'plead guilty and then we'll see what might happen' scheme. This would be the equivalent of buying a lottery ticket without knowing what prize, if any, might follow.

The potentially coercive nature of plea-based sentence reductions troubles scholars (eg Helm, Dehaghani and Newman 2022). Whether a scheme is potentially coercive presumably depends on the magnitude of the reductions awarded. A small reduction of say 5 per cent of the custodial sentence could not reasonably be described as coercive. Discounting the sentence by half sounds more coercive, as does signalling the possibility of evading a lengthy sentence of imprisonment altogether. Some authors assume that a difference in severity of outcomes constitutes a coercive inducement. This would then support the coercion-based objection to guilty plea discounts (Holmen 2023). In a recent essay Holmen addresses the issue directly. He reviews the case for the position that plea-based discounts are coercive and concludes that 'guilty plea discounts cannot plausibly be argued to be coercive offers on the two most developed account of such proposals' (p x). Others will disagree, and the question remains contested.

The likelihood of innocents pleading guilty is presumably affected by a number of factors, including: the magnitude of the sentence reductions offered (eg Bar-Gill and Gazal Ayal 2006); whether a guilty plea can change the nature as well as the quantum of sanction (Helm, 2021); whether the defendant is in custody, and able to secure release through a guilty plea (Helm 2019); whether the defendant is vulnerable or particularly susceptible to influence in some way (Peay and Player 2018); whether the defendant has dependents whose care will be affected if a term of immediate imprisonment is imposed; whether the defendant has sufficient awareness of the prosecution case and adequate legal advice to evaluate the evidence and make an informed decision on his or her plea; and whether the defendant's lawyer advises him or her to plead guilty (eg Baldwin and McConville 1977; Lee, Jaynes and Ropp 2021). In this context the defendant's financial resources or ability to stand trial may play an important role. Some academics also regard the involvement of the judge as creating undue pressure on the defendant to plead guilty. On their view, the court should not provide any pre-trial indication of the likely benefit of pleading guilty.

The magnitude of the reductions offered to defendants who plead guilty is not the only concern. Most jurisdictions operate a sliding scale of reductions based upon the timing of the guilty plea. Under such an arrangement, the maximum reduction awarded declines the later the plea is entered (Cheng 2022). For example, defendants entering a plea at their first court appearance in England and Wales are entitled to receive a maximum reduction of one-third. The magnitude of the reduction then declines, and pleas entered on the day of trial attract a discount of only 10 per cent (Sentencing Council 2017). The purpose of the sliding scale is to encourage those defendants who intend to plead to do so early in the criminal process, when the savings for the criminal justice system will be greatest. Late guilty pleas, for example those entered on the day of trial, save little. Scholars have suggested that tying the levels of reduction to the timing of the plea contributes to the pressure on defendants (Johnston 2020). Some defendants may feel pressured to make a quick or precipitous decision against their interests. The ethical challenge here is to ensure that such a sliding scale does not also contribute to the likelihood of a wrongful plea by an innocent defendant.

B. Undermining Retributive Proportionality and Preventive Sentencing

Retributive proportionality requires sentence severity to reflect the harm caused or threatened and the offender's culpability for that harm (von Hirsch and Ashworth 2005). Most retributivists would regard the offender's plea as unrelated to the seriousness of the crime or the offender's culpability for the offence. According to their view, plea-based sentence reductions result in less than fully proportionate sentences. This is particularly true in cases of serious crimes resulting in lengthy terms of imprisonment.

Von Hirsch (2017: 55) identifies two forms of proportionality, ordinal and cardinal. A regime which operates steep plea-based sentencing discounts risks undermining the former form of proportionality.[7] Ordinal proportionality concerns how severely a crime should be punished compared to other offences of higher or lower seriousness. Crimes of similar gravity should be punished by sentences of comparable severity – what we may term retributive parity. A significant plea-based reduction may affect retributive parity at sentencing. Consider two co-accused being sentenced for a serious fraud. Offender A pleaded guilty while offender B was convicted following a trial. If the guilty plea results in offender A receiving a significantly shorter prison sentence than the other, *retributive* parity is violated, since, *ceteris paribus*, both individuals deserved a comparable sentence. A purely retributive approach would require the imposition of the same punishment on the two offenders.[8] Similarly, if an offender pleading guilty to manslaughter receives a steeply mitigated sentence, he or she may end up being punished at a level corresponding to a less serious offence such as aggravated assault (following a trial). This discrepancy would also violate ordinal proportionality since the orderly relationship between crime seriousness and sentence severity has been scrambled by the effect of the guilty plea.

Although much of the debate about plea-based mitigation focuses on the question of proportionality, other, preventive sentencing objectives may also be

[7] Cardinal proportionality refers to the overall severity of the sentencing scheme. Here desert plays 'a more restricted role' (von Hirsch 2017: 59). If the overall scheme requires a certain level of severity based on retributive considerations, and many offenders receive heavily mitigated punishments having pleaded guilty, the desired level of severity will be compromised. In this respect plea discounts may also affect cardinal proportionality.

[8] Consequentialists would be untroubled by a discrepancy in sentences for the two offenders: the offender pleading guilty has contributed to sparing resources, and the reduction awarded may encourage other defendants to plead guilty.

engaged. Deterrence advocates may oppose plea-based sentence reductions on the claim that potential offenders may see great scope to mitigate their punishment in the event of conviction, and this may undermine the deterrent power of the sentencing regime. And to the extent that the sentence contains a rehabilitation component, a steep reduction (or significant change) in sentence may impair the State's efforts to reform offenders. If the offender needs a course of treatment which requires a specific term of community supervision (or imprisonment), and this term is greatly reduced as a result of a guilty plea, the offender's rehabilitation will be compromised. This is particularly true if there is a change from a rehabilitative sanction to one less likely to encourage desistance.

C. Reduced Public and Victim Confidence in Sentencing

As noted, most people will find the practice of mitigating punishment for offenders who convict themselves acceptable. However, the public's general antipathy towards defendants emerges in reactions to the magnitude of discounts. Research generally shows only limited public support for plea-based sentence reductions (Dawes et al 2011; Gormley et al 2020; Warner et al 2020). For example, approximately 60 per cent of respondents to one nationwide survey opposed discounts in excess of one-third (Dawes et al 2011). A significant minority in all studies opposed any sentence reductions for defendants pleading guilty.[9] More substantial discounts would likely provoke public criticism, particularly if the offence is serious. The generous sentence reductions awarded in some common law jurisdictions are therefore at odds with public opinion, and may undermine confidence in the sentencing process. This may be cause for concern.[10] Some victims, too, may be demoralised to learn that an offender is able to receive years off a long custodial sentence, even if they also see the benefits to themselves and the administration of justice. The seriousness of the crime may be determinative of the victim's reaction.

D. Indirect Adverse Consequences: Racial Disparity in Sentencing Outcomes

Allowing mitigation for a guilty plea may also trigger indirect adverse consequences for sentencing. For half a century or more, research in several countries has

[9] As with all public opinion findings these trends reflect a relatively uninformed 'top of the head' reaction from respondents. Evidence of this can be found in the fact that only 2% of the sample had considered the benefits to victims and witnesses arising from a guilty plea (see Dawes et al 2011: 41). It seems likely that given more information about the benefits of a guilty plea, particularly in relation to crime victims, the public would be less opposed to sentence reductions.

[10] To the extent that the views of the public are normatively significant.

shown that visible minority defendants are less likely to plead guilty (Hood 1992; Lammy 2017). As a result, upon conviction, their prison sentences are generally longer than for White offenders. In this way guilty plea mitigation (GPM) contributes to racial disproportionality in prison admissions and populations (Johnson and Richardson 2020). For this reason, scholars consider plea discounts to represent an indirect form of sentencing discrimination, and some authors have called for the abolition of the practice (Tonry 2020). Here the challenge for sentencing regimes is to determine whether the ethical and practical advantages of awarding plea-based sentence reductions outweigh the costs in terms of ethnic disproportionality.

IV. Conclusion

To summarise, the near-ubiquitous practice across common law jurisdictions of mitigating punishment when the defendant pleads guilty creates great opportunities for administrative savings and benefits for key participants in the trial process. At the same time, the practice also carries a number of ethical and practical difficulties. Sentencing systems must tread a fine line, seeking sentence a level of mitigation which rewards defendants who accept their guilty without simultaneously eliciting wrongful self-conviction, or undermining other aspects of principled sentencing. It is not possible to draw a single general conclusion about the ethical contribution a guilty plea regime makes to the sentencing process. Systems vary greatly, and the potential for adverse consequences of awarding plea-based sentence mitigation vary accordingly. At best we can note that systems in which sentence severity levels are high, and prosecutors wield a great deal of discretionary power, are likely to see the worst adverse consequences in terms of wrongful convictions. If courts offer only modest sentence reductions, regulated by a guideline which contains sufficient safeguards for vulnerable defendants, the costs in terms of principled sentencing and justice more generally are likely to be constrained. There appears no strong consensus that abolishing pleas, or plea-based mitigation, would improve the ethicality of sentencing.[11] In addition, there is a widespread belief that without plea-based sentence reductions the number of trials would increase, clogging already crowded court systems, and for this reason alone, these regimes are unlikely to abandon the practice.

Abolition of sentence discounts seems most unlikely, but less radical reforms may well emerge. For example, regimes which operate more generous sentence reductions may consider restricting the influence of a plea on sentencing outcomes, perhaps by preventing the plea from changing the nature of the sanction.

[11] Practitioners, and in particular the judiciary, appear less convinced of some of the academic critiques of offering plea-based mitigation. See, for example, a leading judgment from the English Court of Appeal (*R v Caley* [2012] EWCA Crim 2821, [24]).

All reform proposals would need to thoroughly consider the ethical and practical consequences, whether intended or unintended. The contributors to this volume explore a range of theoretical and empirical aspects of pleading guilty. Unsurprisingly, in light of the controversial nature of the subject, authors often take conflicting positions. Our hope is that this volume contributes to promoting a better understanding of the ethical problems with the practice, and the steps necessary to address those challenges.

V. Overview of this Volume

Antony Duff opens the discussion by considering whether defendants possess a moral duty to plead guilty if they know that they are guilty. He concludes that there is such a duty: a defendant who knows that he or she is guilty owes it to his or her fellow citizens to assist the criminal law's enterprise of calling public wrongdoers to account and to answer to them for the wrongdoing. However, this duty presupposes what Duff calls 'a decent polity'. In a society that does not live up to acceptable standards for decency, defendants may have no such responsibility. But it may, within such a context, be justified to give modest sentence reductions as a reward to those who plead guilty since they have no obligation to do so.

Jesper Ryberg then explores the question of whether guilty plea discounts are consistent with a retributivist view of punishment. He considers two of the main reasons why such discounts may be at odds with a retributivist outlook, namely that discounts violate ordinal proportionality, and that they lead to the punishment of innocents. Ryberg argues that none of these reasons is persuasive. However, this conclusion is not reached by arguing that retributivism is theoretically consistent with the practice of providing such discounts. Rather, his main point is that it is theoretically unclear what retributivism implies, and that the question of the justification of plea-based discounts therefore reveals serious theoretical deficits of retributivism when it comes to providing guidance to courts at sentencing.

Zachary Hoskins focuses squarely on the concern that plea-based sentence reductions violate the commonly accepted prohibition on punishing the innocent. Hoskins concludes that significant sentence discounts do violate this key prohibition and calls for a number of reforms to mitigate the problem. These reforms include offering defendants who self-convict greater opportunity to later appeal their convictions, and a reduction in the financial burdens of trials for defendants. Although these proposals would cost time and money, Hoskins reminds us that too much conduct is currently criminalised and that lower levels of criminalisation would lead to fewer defendants. In a much smaller system, it would be possible to absorb the additional costs of ensuring that innocent defendants are never convicted and punished.

Julian Roberts and Netanel Dagan examine the issue of plea-based sentence reductions. In doing so, they provide an ethical defence of the practice of such discounts, arguing that offenders who self-convict deserve mitigation. They further argue that it would be unethical and counter-productive for the criminal justice system to deny plea-based sentence reductions for offenders who self-convict. Rather than supporting the abolition of plea-based sentence reductions, they propose a model regime, one which incorporates safeguards to ensure that sentence reductions do not elicit wrongful pleas to mitigate any adverse effects of GPM on victims.

Adam Kolber explores the relationship between pleas/verdicts and the traditional consequentialist and retributivist perspectives. He claims that the information provided by pleas and verdicts can only modestly alter moral assessments. On his view, our moral attitudes to offenders should depend on our best information about these individuals and their actions, and not purely on formal legal events such as pleas and convictions.

Gabrielle Watson discusses the statutory framework and the role of the guilty plea in the sentencing process of England and Wales. She outlines a concept of self-respect as a new conceptual tool for sentencing scholarship and means by which to deepen our understanding of the guilty plea from an ethical perspective. In principle, the guilty plea allows a defendant to take responsibility for his or her wrongdoing and emerge from the criminal process with his or her self-respect intact. Yet Watson sees good reason to be sceptical that the guilty plea regularly fulfils such a lofty aim in practice.

Thom Brooks focuses on the American model of plea-based sentence discounts. He concludes that there are strong deontological grounds for mitigating sentence for offenders who plead guilty. However, he argues that more robust judicial oversight can help to ensure that guilty pleas are both sincerely expressed and founded in fact. Guilty pleas cannot be accepted at face value in all cases, and when appropriate, they should be refused. With respect to the issue of the magnitude of discount offered, he concludes that the current sliding scale of reductions operating in England and Wales is satisfactory. However, procedural safeguards must be more robust than at present if the use of guilty plea discounts is to be justified.

Marie Manikis builds on a communicative and relational theory of punishment and proposes a dynamic and principled understanding of guilty pleas by ensuring that the assumed grounds for mitigation are (1) rooted within clear and principled sentencing rationales and (2) understood and weighed in relation to contextual grounds that justify pleas rather than formulated in abstract and predetermined assumptions. This can in part be achieved through engagement with victims, the accused, communities and the State, to ensure that the underlying assumptions that relate to victims are clear and accurate. Her proposed approach challenges current sentencing schemes that prioritise a fixed reduction based on the timing of the plea, since doing so glosses over context by assuming these underlying assumptions about pleas.

Rebecca Helm questions three assumptions that are relied on to support plea-based sentence reduction regimes: (1) that sentence reductions cannot undermine voluntariness; (2) that there is a dichotomy between incentivisation and pressure;

and (3) that giving all defendants a choice ensures equality. She suggests that legal systems need to move away from a reliance on superficial conceptions, and concludes by laying out suggested criteria for acceptable sentence reductions based on meaningful engagement with psycho-legal constructs. By drawing on these suggestions and taking these constructs seriously, states can benefit from defendant guilty pleas while providing appropriate protection for defendants in their criminal justice systems.

Mike Hough and Jessica Jacobson address the interrelationship between plea negotiation and personal mitigation in the court system in England and Wales. The authors argue that in many cases, negotiations over plea and the application of personal mitigation at sentencing can be seen as two phases of a single process in which the offending behaviour is reframed in a manner highly favourable to the offender. As such, they cumulatively and significantly reduce the severity of the sanction the court is likely to impose. This, they contend, raises questions about equity, proportionality and consistency in sentencing outcomes, and the purposes of sentencing more broadly.

In the concluding chapter, Leo Zaibert provides a critique of the practice of plea-based sentencing reductions, particularly as they operate across the United States. He begins by considering (on an abstract level) the possible reasons for thinking that a system of pleas and of plea bargaining is a good thing. After this brief exercise in abstract thinking, he explores the history of guilty pleas and plea bargaining, with particular emphasis on the different ways in which the 'adversarial' and 'inquisitorial' traditions have embraced (or shunned) these practices. In the last two sections of his chapter Zaibert discusses some specific – and disturbing – aspects of the development and implementation of the system of guilty pleas and plea bargaining in the United States.

References

Ashworth, A and Kelly, R (2021) *Sentencing and Criminal Justice*, 7th edn (Oxford, Hart Publishing).

Baldwin, J and McConville, M (1977) *Negotiated Justice: Pressures to Plead Guilty* (London, Martin Robertson).

Bar-Gill, O and Gazal Ayal, O (2006) 'Plea Bargains Only for the Guilty' 49 *The Journal of Law and Economics* 353.

Blume, JH and Helm, RK (2014) 'The Unexonerated: Factually Innocent Defendants who Plead Guilty' 100 *Cornell Law Review* 157.

Bottoms, A and McLean, J (1976) *Defendants in the Criminal Process* (London, Routledge and Kegan Paul).

Campbell, L, Ashworth, A and Redmayne, M (2019) *The Criminal Process*, 5th edn (Oxford, Oxford University Press).

Cheng, K (2022) *The Timing of Guilty Pleas: Lessons from Common Law Jurisdictions* (Cambridge, Cambridge University Press).

Cross, R (1971) *The English Sentencing System* (London, Butterworths).

Dawes, W, Harvey, P, McIntosh, B, Nunney, F and Phillips, A (2011) *Attitudes to Guilty Plea Reductions* (London, Sentencing Council).
Edkins, V and Redlich, A (eds) (2019) *A System of Pleas* (Oxford, Oxford University Press).
Flynn, A, and Freiberg, A (2018) *Plea Negotiations: Pragmatic Justice in an Imperfect World* (Cham, Palgrave Macmillan).
Gillieron, G (2019) 'Comparing Plea Bargaining and Abbreviated Trial Procedures' in D Brown, J Turner and B Weisser (eds), *The Oxford Handbook of Criminal Process* (New York, Oxford University Press).
Gormley, J, Roberts JV, Bild, J and Harris, L (2020) *Sentence Reductions for Guilty Pleas: A Review of Policy, Practice and Research* (London, Sentencing Academy).
Helm, RK (2019) 'Constrained Waiver of Trial Rights? Incentives to Plead Guilty and the Right to a Fair Trial' 46 *Journal of Law and Society* 423.
—— (2021) 'Cognition and Incentives in Plea Decisions: Categorical Differences in Outcomes as the Tipping Point for Innocent Defendants' *Psychology, Public Policy, and Law* (in press).
Helm, RK, Dehaghani, R and Newman, D (2022) 'Guilty Plea Decisions: Moving Beyond the Autonomy Myth' 85 *The Modern Law Review* 133.
Holmen, S (2023) 'Guilty Pleas' in J Ryberg (ed), *The Oxford Handbook of the Philosophy of Punishment* (New York, Oxford University Press, in press).
Hood, R (1992) *Race and Sentencing* (Oxford, Oxford University Press).
Johnson, B and Richardson, R (2020) 'Race and Plea Bargaining' in V Edkins and A Redlich (eds), *A System of Pleas* (Oxford, Oxford University Press).
Johnston, E (2020) 'The Adversarial Defence Lawyer: Myths, Disclosure and Efficiency – A Contemporary Analysis of the Role in the Criminal Procedure Rules' 24 *The International Journal of Evidence and Proof* 35.
Lammy, D (2017) *Review into the Treatment of and Outcomes for Black, Asian, and Minority Ethnic Individuals in the Criminal Justice System*, Ministry of Justice, https://assets.publishing.service.gov.uk/government/uploads/system/uploads/attachment_data/file/643001/lammy-review-final-report.pdf
Langer, M (2021) 'Plea Bargaining, Conviction Without Trial, and the Global Administratization of Criminal Convictions' 4 *Annual Review of Criminology* 35.
Lee, JG, Jaynes, C and Ropp, J (2021) 'Satisfaction, Legitimacy, and Guilty Pleas: How Perceptions and Attorneys Affect Defendant Decision-making' 38 *Justice Quarterly* 1095.
Lippke, R (2011) *The Ethics of Plea Bargaining* (Oxford, Oxford University Press).
McKnight, P and Sprouster, A (2018) 'Encouraging Early Guilty Pleas in the Criminal Justice System 30 *Judicial Officers' Bulletin* 23.
Nash, C, Dioso-Villa, R and Porter, L (2021) 'Factors Contributing to Guilty Plea Wrongful Convictions: A Quantitative Analysis of Australian Appellate Court Judgments' *Crime and Delinquency*, doi: 10.1177/00111287211054723.
Peay, J and Player, E (2018) 'Pleading Guilty: Why Vulnerability Matters' 81 *The Modern Law Review* 929.
Redlich, A, Wilford, M and Bushway, S (2017) 'Understanding Guilty Pleas Through the Lens of Social Science' 23 *Psychology, Public Policy, and Law* 458.
Roach, K (2021) *You Say You Want a Revolution? Understanding Guilty Plea Wrongful Convictions*, 18 June, https://ssrn.com/abstract=3869888 or http://dx.doi.org/10.2139/ssrn.3869888
Sentencing Council of England and Wales (2017) *Sentence Reductions for a Guilty Plea. Definitive Guideline* (London, Sentencing Council).

Sentencing Advisory Council of Tasmania (2018) *Statutory Sentencing Reductions for a Guilty Plea* (Tasmania, Sentencing Advisory Council).
Sentencing Advisory Council of Victoria (2015) *Guilty Pleas in the Higher Courts: Rates, Timing, and Discounts* (Victoria, Sentencing Advisory Council).
Shaeffer, R (2019) 'The Trial Penalty: An International Perspective' 31 *Federal Sentencing Reporter* 321.
Tonry, M (2020) *Doing Justice, Preventing Crime* (Oxford, Oxford University Press).
Vogel, M (2019) 'Plea Bargaining under the Common Law' in D Brown, J Turner and B Weisser (eds), *The Oxford Handbook of Criminal Process* (New York, Oxford University Press).
von Hirsch, A (2017) *Deserved Criminal Sentences* (Oxford, Hart Publishing).
von Hirsch, A and Ashworth, A (2005) *Proportionate Sentencing* (Oxford, Oxford University Press).
Warner, K, Spiranovich, C, Roberts, L and Gelb, K (2020) 'Juror and Community Views of the Guilty Plea Sentencing Discount: Findings from a National Australian Study' 22 *Criminology and Criminal Justice* 78.
Welsh, L, Skinns, L and Sanders, A (2021) *Sanders and Young's Criminal Justice*, 5th edn (Oxford, Oxford University Press).
Wilford, M and Khairalla, A (2020) 'Innocence and Plea Bargaining' in V Edkins and A Redlich (eds), *A System of Pleas* (Oxford, Oxford University Press).
Zalman, M and Norris, R (2021) 'Measuring Innocence: How to Think About the Rate of Wrongful Conviction' 24 *New Criminal Law Review* 601.

2

When Should We Plead Guilty?

RA DUFF*

When, if ever, should we plead guilty in a criminal court? Do we ever have a duty to plead guilty – and what could ground such a duty? Answers to these questions will depend crucially on our political and legal context: on the character and quality of the society in which we live, and of its legal system. I therefore begin by sketching two scenarios, lying near opposite ends of a spectrum. In each, I will ask what responsibilities criminal defendants might have to plead guilty or not guilty: how they should plead if they know that they are guilty, or know that they are innocent, or are not sure whether they are guilty.

I. Two Scenarios

Imagine, first, a decent democratic republic: one in which liberty, equality, fraternity are values to which its citizens and government are genuinely committed; one whose members generally treat each other, as its government treats them, with 'equal concern and respect' (Dworkin 1986: 190);[1] one whose criminal laws are democratically validated and legitimate in their scope; one whose criminal process respects the rights associated with the ideal of due process and treats defendants with respect as citizens whose law this is; one whose punishments are moderate in their severity and constructive in their intent and impact – they are punishments that citizens can impose on each other and on themselves without loss of dignity, and are followed by full restoration of civic standing. This is not a society of angels, in which there is no wrongdoing; it is a society of fallible human beings, who maintain a system of criminal law to mark and to deal appropriately with kinds of

* Grateful thanks for helpful comments to participants in the 'Pleading Guilty' workshop and in a 'Political Turns in Criminal Law Theory' seminar, and especially to Julian Roberts.

[1] To talk of 'members' or 'citizens' raises the questions of who will count as a member or citizen, and of what we can say about those who are not members or citizens but who find themselves as defendants in a criminal court. The short gesture towards an answer is that, first, a decent society welcomes new members; second, that it treats non-members with respect as guests (see Duff 2018: ch 3.3).

wrong that count as public.[2] Suppose, too, that it has a system of adversarial criminal trials in which those accused of committing such wrongs are called to formal public account.[3] In such a system, some defendants know that they are guilty of the crimes charged: should they plead guilty – or may they, without violating any civic duty, plead not guilty and leave it to the prosecution to prove their guilt if it can? Some know that they are innocent of the crimes charged, while others may be unsure whether they are guilty (whether what they know they did constitutes the crime charged): could they ever have good reason to plead guilty?

What reason they might have to plead guilty depends in part on whether in such a polity sentence severity would be affected by the defendant's plea – would there be a 'discount' for pleading guilty, or a 'trial penalty' for pleading not guilty?[4] I will argue later that we should understand such sentencing differentials as penalties for pleading not guilty, rather than as rewards for pleading guilty; but even absent such differentials, and even in a decent criminal process, there will be process costs that might motivate innocent defendants to plead guilty, especially to relatively minor charges (see, eg, Bowers 2007: 1132–34[5]). One question is whether it could ever be prudentially rational in such a system to plead guilty if sure of one's innocence, or unsure of one's guilt;[6] but my question is whether it could be ethically permissible to do so: does one who pleads guilty without being confident that he or she is guilty violate any civic responsibility?

The second scenario is less taxing on the imagination: we can envisage a polity that is to a significant degree dystopian – although not so dystopian that talk of law is nothing more than empty rhetoric. In such a polity, ideas of liberty, equality and fraternity, of equal concern and respect for all, still have *some* purchase, though as much by their absence as by their real presence: while they do partially and selectively inform the polity's institutions and its life, they function more prominently as markers for ideals that the polity radically fails to achieve – or even to pursue with serious commitment. Significant groups are effectively excluded from too many

[2] We might still ask whether what we are to imagine here is a genuine *eutopia* – a good place that does not (yet) exist but to which we can sensibly aspire; or only an *outopia* – a nowhere, a philosopher's fantasy that has no substantive relationship to our actual world. I hope that what is offered here is a *eutopia*, which instantiates ideals that do have some purchase on our existing situation – but I cannot defend that hope here.

[3] A discussion of guilty pleas presupposes a criminal process that is, at least in that respect, adversarial; but I hope that what I say about guilty pleas can be adapted to confessions in more inquisitorial systems (see further text at nn 29–30).

[4] On 'waiver rewards' as against 'trial penalties', see Lippke (2011: 12–16). The English Sentencing Council has said that 'the guilty plea reduction is in place to provide an incentive … and not a reward' (Sentencing Council 2016: 15; see Ashworth and Kelly 2021: 173–74); see further text at nn 40–41.

[5] Bowers is talking about a dystopian system; but even in a decent system there will be costs.

[6] There could be non-prudential reasons for pleading guilty when innocent – for instance to protect the guilty, whether from love or for reward. However, to plead guilty in such cases is clearly wrong, albeit a wrong that we might be reasonably tempted to commit; the question becomes harder when what recommends pleading guilty is prudence, since we must then ask how far citizens should be expected to sacrifice their own interests for the sake of the law.

of the rights and benefits – from the status – of citizenship; even if the law can claim to speak with some authority, it is unclear what authority it can claim over members of those groups (who are more likely than others to appear as defendants in its criminal courts). It might criminalise kinds of conduct that should not be criminal; the application of its laws is to a worrying extent (in effect if not in intent) discriminatory; its criminal process cannot be seen, without serious qualification, as a process through which citizens are respectfully called to answer to their peers for their alleged wrongs; its punishments are often unduly harsh and destructive; those who have been convicted face further, damaging collateral consequences that still exclude them from too many of the rights and benefits of membership.

Here again we can ask about the civic responsibilities of defendants in criminal courts. Various specific questions arise that we cannot discuss here: for instance, have they suffered such systemic injustices that the polity has lost its standing to call them to account for their alleged wrongs – at least until it has recognised and begun to address those wrongs? Do the criminal laws under which they are charged mark a serious attempt to define public wrongs to which criminalisation is an appropriate response? The general question, however, is whether in light of the background injustices that they have suffered, the inadequacy of the processes through which they are supposed to answer, and the excessive severity of the consequences of conviction, they should attend to any reasons other than those of self-interest in deciding how to plead: how far (if at all) should their knowledge of their guilt or innocence provide a normative guide for their decisions about whether to plead guilty or not guilty?

We are of course dealing here with a wide spectrum of cases, involving different kinds or degrees of injustice, which will have different implications for defendants' responsibilities; but my concern is with what kinds of difference factors such as these can properly make. To talk of making a difference implies that we should begin with the more eutopian scenario; ask what responsibilities defendants would have in that scenario; and then ask what differences are made as we move along the spectrum towards progressively more dystopian scenarios. Some might object that we should instead begin from where we are, somewhere towards the dystopian end of the spectrum, and ask from the outset what responsibilities we can have in this situation, rather than starting with what might be true of some idealised system distant from our own. I cannot defend my methodology here (the best defence is anyway to show it in practice); but I think that we can best understand the problematic features of our present practices by seeing them in the light of the values and ideals by which those practices purport to be informed, and which are instantiated in our imagined *eutopia*.

In what follows I will therefore begin, in Section II, by arguing that in a decent polity citizens who know that they are guilty have a civic responsibility to plead guilty at trial. In Section III, I will argue that in such a polity their responsibility is to plead guilty if *and only if* they know they are guilty – that those who know that they are, or might be, innocent should plead not guilty. In Section IV, I turn from *eutopia* towards relative *dystopia*, to ask whether and when it is possible for pleas to have the meaning that they have in a decent polity; and, when it is possible, what can properly be expected of defendants as they decide how to plead.

II. Pleading Guilty in a Decent System[7]

To begin, then, with pleading in the (qualifiedly) eutopian scenario, and with defendants who know that they are guilty of the crime charged. Such defendants ought to plead guilty: but that claim must be explained.

There are two reasons why those who know that they are guilty should plead guilty. First, the criminal law is their law as citizens of the polity: they therefore have a civic responsibility to make it their own, and to assist in its enterprise. Part of that enterprise is to call criminal wrongdoers to formal public account, through the criminal trial; as a citizen I must therefore be ready to assist in that enterprise. There are many questions about what kinds of assistance can be expected of lay citizens, but in a decent system they include being ready to appear as a witness, or to serve on a jury; and being ready to plead guilty if I know that I am guilty, thus serving the ends of justice, rather than seeking to hinder them by preventing the conviction of the guilty. Second, I should recognise my crime as a wrong, and thus as something for which I must answer to those whose business it is. As a public wrong, a crime is the business of the whole polity, and the criminal trial is the forum in which criminal wrongdoers are called to formal account; I therefore have a civic responsibility to answer for my crime in that forum, which I do by pleading guilty.[8]

(This duty to plead guilty is not simply an implication of a general duty of truthfulness: first, because it is a duty not just not to lie, but to speak a distinctively significant truth – to confess my guilt, rather than remaining silent; second, because it is not clear that someone who pleads not guilty while knowing that she is guilty is being untruthful, since 'Not Guilty' could be read not as a denial of guilt, but as a challenge to the prosecution to prove guilt.)

Or is that too simple-minded? It presupposes a particular view of the criminal trial (Duff et al 2007), as a process in which alleged wrongdoers are called to public account, in which one who knows himself to be guilty should therefore offer an honest account; but perhaps that view is misguided. Among the competing normative conceptions of the trial, the most relevant is that expressed by the US Supreme Court: 'The purpose of the … trial … is to prevent oppression by the Government' (*Williams v Florida* 1970: 100[9]). On this view, the trial is a process

[7] In this and the following section, I draw on Duff and Marshall (2016).

[8] What of those who know that they have committed a crime, but have not (yet) been detected: ought they to hand themselves in to the police? The quick answer is that in principle they should, for the same reasons; but see Duff and Marshall (2016: 39–43) for some necessary explanation and qualification.

[9] The Court was talking about jury trials, but the same account could be given of all trials; see Duff et al (2007: 94–96).

through which the government's charge of wrongdoing is put to the test – a test that protects citizens against oppression and injustice. One who pleads guilty waives her right to those protections, which include not only the requirement that the prosecution prove guilt, but the other safeguards of 'due process'. Such rights are waivable: we are not *required* thus to put the prosecution to the test if we prefer to plead guilty, out of remorseful recognition of our wrongdoing, or to avoid the painful process of the trial.[10] But we cannot be required to waive them, since that would undermine their significance as rights that belong to the guilty as much as to the innocent: it must be legitimate to insist on those rights, and to insist that the prosecution prove our guilt, without a confession to assist them.

It is true that even in our *eutopia* such protections against various kinds of potential state oppression are important: it is a society of fallible human beings, including fallible officials and institutions. Such protections are owed as a matter of right to the guilty as much as to the innocent: those who know that they are guilty do not enjoy them parasitically on the coattails of the innocent for whose protection they are really intended. It is also true that we should not, even in such a *eutopia*, have a *legal* duty to plead guilty if we know that we are guilty, so that someone who pleaded not guilty despite knowing himself to be guilty would commit a further offence, of dishonest pleading. A decent system of criminal justice leaves room for dissenting citizens to enact their dissent, and guards against its own fallibility. A dissenting citizen who denies the authority of the law, or of this court, might refuse to play her allotted part in the process, and refuse to enter a plea, or plead not guilty as a demand that the court nullify the law: we should not punish her for her defiance. We must remember, too, that any human system will sometimes err, and will mistakenly convict some innocents: it is bad enough that we then punish them for crimes that they did not commit; it would be even worse also to punish them for failing to confess (falsely) to those crimes.[11] Finally, we must recognise the oppressive potential of any human system of law: a legal duty to plead guilty would give even more power to the law's officials – a power that could too easily be abused.

These points do not, however, militate against the claim that offenders who know they are guilty have a *civic* responsibility (as distinct from a legal duty) to plead guilty, and not to assert their right to put the prosecution case to the test. (Civic responsibilities are owed to our fellow citizens, but lack the force of law and are enforceable only by informal persuasion from our fellows.) That responsibility might be grounded partly in the considerations that are taken to justify a guilty plea discount: pleading guilty benefits victims and those who must face the ordeal of giving evidence, and saves the resources that trials involve. But it is primarily

[10] Or might even that be denied, on the grounds that we should assist in maintaining this protective procedure? That would be plausible only if by pleading guilty I undermined others' procedural rights – which seems unlikely.

[11] Compare the wrong done to a mistakenly convicted innocent whose release on parole is delayed because he or she persists in asserting their innocence, and thus has not 'faced up to their crime'.

grounded in the responsibilities that offenders incur in a decent society.[12] If I know that I have committed a criminal wrong, I owe it to the direct victims of that wrong (if there are any) and to my fellow citizens to recognise, and make apologetic amends for, that wrong – amends to my victims for the wrong I did to them, to my fellow citizens for this violation of the values that define our civic life. I might make private amends by apologising directly to my victims: but a public, criminalised wrong requires public, formal amends as specified by the law; in a system of adversarial trials those amends consist in accepting a conviction and undertaking the legally prescribed punishment. To plead not guilty might not be to lie – it might simply be to challenge the prosecution to prove my guilt: but it is to fail to publicly recognise my guilt, and to attempt to hinder the censure that I deserve; it is therefore a failure to discharge my civic responsibilities.

This does involve waiving my rights, and the law should not demand such a waiver. But, first, it is not plausible to claim that those rights are unwaivable. Second, the idea that we should not always claim our rights is familiar: rights do not exhaust the universe of moral demands, or always serve as conclusive trumps; and we can anyway say that while I have the right to demand a trial, and to put the prosecution to the test, others (my victims, my fellow citizens) have a right that I speak the truth and formally admit my crime. Perhaps, given the dangers of social as well as legal oppression and bullying, my fellow citizens should hesitate to *demand* that I waive my rights to a trial: but I should nonetheless sometimes waive them, as a matter of my civic responsibility.

So far, I have argued that someone who knows that she is guilty of the crime charged has a civic responsibility to plead guilty. At least three further questions arise.

First, should an offender who pleads guilty receive a lighter sentence than he would have received had he been convicted after pleading not guilty? It matters here whether we should see such sentencing differentials as rewards or incentives for guilty pleas, or as penalties for not guilty pleas:[13] it is one thing to ask whether we should reward guilty pleas, quite another to ask whether we should penalise not guilty pleas. Furthermore, if sentencing should respect desert, if any significant difference in the sentences imposed on two offenders who commit similar crimes in similar circumstances is justified only if one deserves a lighter sentence, we cannot appeal only to the practical considerations that might favour such a differential: that punishing *A* less severely than similarly placed *B* would have beneficial effects (for instance, in encouraging resource-saving guilty pleas) does not show that *A* deserves a lighter sentence (or *B* a heavier one); but that is what we would need to show.

It seems more plausible to understand such a differential as a penalty for offenders who plead not guilty, than as a reward for those who plead guilty (see

[12] In penal theory it is important to ask not merely what can be done *to* offenders, but what can be demanded of them – what active responsibilities we incur in committing a crime.

[13] See n 4; also Peay and Player (2018: 935–36).

Chapter 5). One consideration is that the latter are doing no more than their civic duty: why should that entitle them to a reward? To which it might be replied that it can be appropriate to reward those who discharge their duties despite strong pressures or temptations not to do so. I am not fully persuaded by this response (paying my taxes is burdensome, and I might be very tempted to evade them: do I deserve a reward for paying them?), but there is a further consideration, connected to the presumption of innocence. Defendants are entitled to be presumed innocent by the court that tries them, until their guilt is proved. So, too, we can plausibly argue, citizens are entitled to be presumed innocent, by their fellow citizens and by the state, unless and until they show themselves not to be innocent – innocent of crimes, but also of failures to discharge their civic duties.[14] Since pleading guilty if I know that I am guilty is, in a decent society, a civic duty, our sentencing guidelines should therefore begin with the presumption that defendants who know themselves to be guilty will plead guilty: the default sentence should be one appropriate for an offender who pleads guilty; the question will then be whether that default sentence should be increased for those who do not plead guilty, as a penalty for insisting on a full trial. If that is the right question, however, the answer is 'No', for the reasons already noted for not creating a legal duty to plead guilty, and for the added reason that we should not face extra punishment for exercising our rights. This might seem an over-simplified account of a complex issue, but so long as we are talking about a (relative) *eutopia*, this simple account is plausible: the matter becomes complex only when we turn (as we will in Section IV) from a *eutopia* towards a *dystopia* in which our civic duties become more problematic.

Second, how should courts deal with guilty pleas? It matters that the plea be voluntary and informed: even if the court should (out of respect for the defendant as a presumptively responsible agent) presume voluntariness and knowledge of the plea's implications, it should investigate further if there is evidence of undue pressure or ignorance. But I will not pursue the question of what makes pleas (non-)voluntary here:[15] I want instead to consider whether informed voluntariness should be not just necessary, but sufficient for a plea to be accepted by the court without further inquiry. It might be sufficient if it should be seen simply as a 'legal fiction', which makes no real claim to truth (see Bowers 2007; Johnson 2019); if an offender who pleads guilty is playing his part in a legal drama that is not really concerned with what is true in the world, as distinct from what is pretended to be true within the drama; if a guilty plea is no more than a 'performance', or an Austinian performative (Austin 1975), analogous to 'I do' in a wedding ceremony: for such performances might not purport to assert anything that can be assessed as true or false (see Nobles and Schiff 2019[16]). But while such suggestions might

[14] On this broad construal of the (or a) presumption of innocence, see Nance (1994); Duff (2013).

[15] See, eg, Peay and Player (2018); Helm (2019); and Chapter 10 (a relative *dystopia* will face similar problems). See also Chapter 7 on the importance of the defendant's self-respect in this context.

[16] Guilty pleas 'are, in simple terms, speech acts – they execute a performance' (Nobles and Schiff 2019: 109); in criminal trials 'a commitment to autonomy … is given priority over factual accuracy' (Nobles and Schiff 2019: 123).

be plausible in more dystopian systems, they are not plausible interpretations of guilty pleas in a eutopian system. One who pleads guilty is engaged in a performance; 'Guilty' is a performative that brings about certain legal effects – it waives one's right to a trial, accepts a formal conviction and sentence. But that performance includes an assertion:[17] 'I committed the crime charged, without excuse or justification'.

It might be argued that even if guilty pleas contain an assertion of fact, the court should not question them, so long as it is satisfied that they are voluntary and informed. To question a person's guilty plea is not just to doubt her integrity (given that her plea asserts a supposed truth) but to infringe her autonomy. 'The accused … must have a complete freedom of choice whether to plead guilty or not guilty' (*R v Turner* 1970: 326[18]); but that freedom is empty if the court can reject a guilty plea. There is *some* force to this argument: questioning a guilty plea undermines the defendant's (supposed) autonomy to decide whether to maintain or to waive his rights, and a guilty plea is not just a statement, but a confession – an intimate self-revelation; to respond to someone's confession by asking 'Is that really true?' expresses an insulting doubt in her. This argument might be persuasive if the only interests at stake were the defendant's: whether or not we think that defendants should (prudentially or morally) plead guilty only if they know they are guilty, it would be a dubious kind of paternalism to interfere with their decisions. However, we need not ask whether such paternalism could be justified, since the interests of the defendant are not the only interests at stake. The interests of victims of the crime are involved: whatever vindication a conviction can bring is rendered illusory if the convicted defendant is not guilty. The interests of justice, the public interest in justice being done (and not merely being seen or seeming to be done) are at stake: a defendant who falsely pleads guilty seeks to make the court unwittingly complicit in a miscarriage of justice – the conviction and punishment of someone who is innocent of the crime charged.[19] I will say more later about why it is wrong to plead guilty if one does not know one is guilty; the crucial point here is that since other interests than those of the defendant are implicated, we cannot simply say that, from respect for her autonomy, the court should not question her plea.

We could argue, however, that respect for the defendant as a responsible agent requires a court to operate with a presumption of honesty – a relative of the presumption of innocence: it should accept a defendant's guilty plea unless there is evidence that it is not voluntary and informed, or that it is false. We could also

[17] Although Austin seemed initially to distinguish 'performatives' from 'constatives', he was clear that some performatives include assertions that can be appraised as true or false (see Longworth 2021: section 2.3).

[18] Quoted by Nobles and Schiff (2019: 121).

[19] Compare Martin (1993: 320): a prosecutor who accepts what she knows to be a false guilty plea commits 'a fraud upon the Court'; also Brockman (2010: 127): 'it is never in the public interest to convict the innocent'.

argue that a guilty plea should be accompanied by an account of the crime, of just what the defendant is formally admitting: this is not simply to make it easier for the court to assess the plea's truth, but to make the plea itself a substantive, rather than merely formal, admission of guilt; if my plea is to express my recognition of the wrong that I committed, it should be accompanied by an account of that wrong. If evidence is then presented that the plea might not be true, the court should undertake something like a *Newton* hearing,[20] whose purpose should be to determine not whether the defendant's guilt is proved beyond reasonable doubt, but whether 'there is a factual basis for the plea'.[21] There is room for argument about how strong that 'factual basis' ought to be, but from respect for the defendant's presumed honesty it perhaps need not even be enough to meet the civil 'on the balance of probabilities' standard of proof.

The third question about pleading guilty if one knows one is guilty concerns what it is to 'know one is guilty'. Two readings are possible; the complication arises when they produce different results. Knowing that I am guilty might be read simply as knowing that I am guilty *in law*: that my conduct satisfied the law's definition of an offence, and that I had no legally recognised defence for it. Or it might be taken to require knowing not just that I am guilty in law, but that I committed a genuine wrong, which demands confession and merits censure.[22] Which of these kinds of knowledge requires me to plead guilty?

It might seem that only the first kind, knowledge of legal guilt, can be relevant here: in a criminal trial, under the aegis of the criminal law, what is at stake is legal guilt; that is what the defendant must address. However, the matter is not that straightforward: for a conviction is not just a statement of fact, that the defendant's conduct satisfied the law's definition of the offence and that he had no legal defence; it condemns that conduct as a wrong, and censures the defendant for committing it. To plead guilty is to invite, to endorse, one's conviction: an honest guilty plea must therefore, like that conviction, amount not just to a statement of fact, but to a confession of wrongdoing, for which a censorial conviction is appropriate; the second reading noted above is the appropriate one. But what then should we expect of a defendant who knows that she is guilty in law, but believes that her conduct was justified, as an act of conscientious disobedience – and that the law ought to be such that she is not guilty in law? She *could* still plead guilty, but honesty would require her to explain that her plea is only a formal, factual

[20] See Ashworth and Kelly (2021: 403–05); *R v Newton* (1982). Who should present such evidence? In an adversarial system, this seems an appropriate responsibility for the prosecutor, as a 'minister of justice'.

[21] Federal Rules of Criminal Procedure, Rule 11(3); on this rule in relation to *Alford* pleas see n 25 and Shipley (1987).

[22] Anti-realists who are uneasy with talk of knowledge in this context can talk instead of belief or feeling. There might also be cases of justified but mistaken belief in one's guilt (thanks to Zach Hoskins): presumably I ought to act on such a belief in the same sense in which I ought to act on any justified, but mistaken, belief.

'plea': one that admits (or proudly asserts) legal guilt, but not wrongdoing. But we cannot say that she *ought* to plead guilty: she must be free to assert her – in her own eyes – substantive innocence, and the obvious way to do that is to plead not guilty. She must admit her legal guilt; but she must be able to make clear that she does not regard her legal guilt as genuine guilt, and to argue that the court ought to acquit her. This would be to argue that the court (the judge, the jury) ought to be able to develop the law to recognise her defence, or to nullify it by acquitting her; although she might have no real hope that such an argument will succeed, she must be allowed to make it.

This raises the question of when (if ever) judges should be willing to develop the law in this way; or whether judges or juries should ever 'nullify' the law by acquitting a defendant who is clearly guilty in law. However, that question need not detain us here: our concern is with the defendant's responsibilities rather than the court's; when I say that a defendant who knows that she is guilty ought to plead guilty, that must be read as applying only to those who know that they are normatively as well as legally guilty.

What of a defendant who admits to committing a genuine criminal wrong, but regards the law's offence label as radically unfair: I accept that my act of mercy killing was wrong, but object to it being defined as 'murder', although that is how the law labels it, and am therefore unwilling to plead guilty to a charge of murder. If there is an alternative offence that, as I see it, attaches a fairer label to my wrong, I can offer to plead to that – perhaps to plead guilty to manslaughter, but not to murder. But if there is no such alternative offence, it looks as if not guilty would be the only honest plea, unless the law can make room for a qualified 'guilty, but …' plea.[23]

What, however, of the converse case: a defendant who knows that he is not, or might not be, guilty in the law's eyes, but sees reason to plead guilty? This question takes us beyond my initial claim that (in a relative *eutopia*) I ought to plead guilty if I know that I am guilty, to the further claim that I should plead guilty *only* if I know that I am guilty.

III. Pleading Not Guilty in a Decent System

A defendant who knows or suspects that she is innocent in law of the offence charged might still, even in a relative *eutopia*, be tempted or see reason to plead guilty. The simplest case is that of someone who knows that she is innocent, but for purely prudential reasons prefers to plead guilty: the costs to her – in time, money,

[23] Thanks to Matt Matravers; see further text at nn 29–30. Of course we cannot expect the criminal law's offence definitions to capture every significant nuance of the wrongs that fall under them; but we must recognise that some labels can be radically unfair because they class together wrongs of radically different characters.

reputation – will, she thinks, be lower than those incurred by demanding a full trial (including costs that might be incurred even if she is eventually acquitted).[24] However, this case need not detain us here, since we have already seen why it is wrong to plead guilty if I know I am innocent: it is a dishonest attempt to pervert the course of justice and to make the court complicit in this perversion;[25] it frustrates the interests of justice, and thus the interests of the crime's victims, if there are any, in seeing justice done. It might be argued that *volenti non fit iniuria*: since the defendant voluntarily brings her conviction on herself, there is no injustice. There would be force in this argument if the only rights at stake were the defendant's: whether or not we can sensibly talk of wronging oneself (thus denying *volenti non fit iniuria*), a defendant who voluntarily pleads guilty is ill-placed to complain of being treated unjustly when she is then convicted. But other interests are at stake, most obviously the public interest in the course of justice; the defendant cannot consent to the violation of that interest.

Suppose the defendant is unsure whether he is legally guilty: I am not sure whether I was driving on the wrong side of the road when I collided with another car. Here too, one should plead not guilty: courts should convict only if guilt is proved beyond reasonable doubt; but my mere suspicion of my guilt does not constitute such proof. A conviction must express the claim that we, the court or the jury, know that the defendant is guilty (Duff et al 2007: 87–91); a guilty plea, which seeks a conviction, should therefore express a claim that I know I am guilty – a claim that in this case cannot be honestly made. Someone who pleads guilty while doubtful of his guilt attempts to pervert the course of justice by securing an unjustified conviction.

Suppose, however, that what is in doubt is a normative rather than a factual matter. This might be a normative issue that counts in law as a matter of 'fact': was the risk I took, or the defensive force I used, 'reasonable'; was my appropriation 'dishonest'? I might hold myself to standards stricter than those of most of my fellow citizens, stricter than the fact finder is likely to apply: I think that I took an unreasonable risk, but realise that the jury might regard it as not unreasonable; or I regard my appropriation as dishonest, though I know it would not count as dishonest 'by the standards of ordinary decent people' (see *Barton and Booth* 2020). Should I plead guilty, since I am – in my eyes – guilty of the crime as defined? No: for the criminal law is public law, and crimes are public wrongs; the question of whether a type of conduct should count as criminal is therefore not for the private conscience of the individual, but for the polity (as represented by the court). I might condemn myself morally, but as far as the criminal law is concerned, what matters is whether we citizens collectively condemn my

[24] See text at n 5; Bowers (2007).

[25] www.cps.gov.uk/legal-guidance/public-justice-offences-incorporating-charging-standard. Is it still dishonest if it is an Alford plea: 'I'm not guilty but I plead guilty' (*North Carolina v Alford* 1970)? Not strictly dishonest, but not a plea that a court should allow, since a guilty plea should be an admission of guilt.

conduct, not whether I do. To plead guilty on the basis of actions that I know the jury would not condemn as criminal is to ask that they, and thus the polity, condemn an action that they do not believe to be a criminal wrong; but that would be a perversion of justice, and of the criminal law. In *foro interno* my conscience might properly rule; but *in foro externo* I must subject myself to the judgment of my peers.

The same is true if what is in doubt is a point of law, rather than of what the law counts as fact. Suppose the defendant in *R v R* (1992), stricken by remorse after forcing sex on his wife, came to believe that his action should count in law as rape; was advised by his counsel that under the existing law this did not count as rape; but insisted on pleading guilty. Here again, a defendant who pleads guilty when the law is unclear (or, a fortiori, if it is clear that in law he is not guilty) seeks, improperly, to replace the law's judgment (the polity's public judgment) by his own private judgment.

Perhaps, however, that is too quick. A defendant who knows she is guilty in law might, as we have seen, nonetheless honestly plead not guilty: because, she will argue, she has not committed a true wrong; the court should acquit her, even if this involves nullifying the law. So why should a defendant who knows or suspects that he is not guilty in law not be allowed to plead guilty: because, he will argue, he committed a genuine criminal(isable) wrong; the court should convict him, even if that involves a kind of reverse nullification. I cannot pursue here the issues that this raises about the role of courts and juries in creating the laws that they apply,[26] but will simply note two points. First, the court should not accept such a guilty plea without further argument: the defendant should have to persuade the court to convict him. Second, what matters is whether the defendant's conduct should be defined as criminal by the law and the polity, not simply by his own conscience: he can argue that they should convict him, but that judgment is one for the court to make, not for him; the authority to determine criminal guilt is not his, but ours, as a matter of public determination of the values that our criminal law is to reflect; he must still in the end submit himself to the court's judgment.

I have argued in this section that in our relative *eutopia* defendants should plead guilty if, but only if, they know that they are guilty of the crime charged (not merely guilty in law, but guilty of a genuine wrong); one who knows or suspects that she is not guilty should plead not guilty. These ethical demands might be burdensome: a guilty defendant might hope that by pleading not guilty he could avoid conviction; an innocent defendant might find the process of going to trial more burdensome than pleading guilty even if she is acquitted. But these are burdens that, in a decent society, citizens can be expected (can expect each other) to bear: for a guilty defendant, it is the justified burden of answering for his crimes to his fellow

[26] On the jury's role, see Dzur (2012).

citizens – something that he has a civic responsibility to do. Innocent defendants cannot of course be expected to answer for their (non-existent) crimes: but they can be expected, as a matter of civic responsibility,[27] to answer to evidence-backed accusations of criminal wrongdoing,[28] thereby assisting the enterprise of the criminal law – and to do so honestly. Such expectations are justified only if defendants face a fair trial, in which they are enabled to play their part and can access adequate legal support: but these conditions are satisfied in our *eutopia*.

The discussion in this section presupposed a criminal process in which defendants are expected to enter a formal plea and have only two pleas available: guilty or not guilty.[29] It might be suggested that a more eutopian criminal process, which more adequately reflects the conception of the criminal trial on which I rely, would provide for a rather more nuanced set of answers to a criminal charge. Perhaps it would allow a third kind of plea, amounting to 'I don't know', or to some version of 'Guilty, but …'; or perhaps it would be more like some inquisitorial systems, in which rather than enter a formal plea, the accused person gives an account of what she did, and leaves it to the court to decide her guilt or innocence.[30] These suggestions certainly need further discussion, but I am initially inclined to stick to my current (albeit parochial?) guns. First, if we take the presumption of innocence seriously, we should say that a defendant who is unsure whether she is guilty ought to plead not guilty: for as far as she knows, that presumption has not been defeated by proof of her guilt; 'not guilty', whether declared by the court or by the defendant, should mean 'not proved guilty', which is to say that the presumption of innocence remains undefeated.[31] Second, it is indeed for the court to pass the final judgment on the accused's guilt or innocence, but I think there is value in a system that gives the accused person this formal role – this chance to formally confess his guilt, or formally deny it: this makes clear his role as an active participant in, rather than merely being the object of, the trial process.

It is time to turn from our relative *eutopia* towards more dystopian scenarios; but, as we will see, these require less theoretical discussion, once an account of citizens' responsibilities in a *eutopia* is established.

[27] This civic responsibility can ground a limited legal responsibility: while we should not, I have argued, be legally required to enter a plea, or to play an active role in the trial (for principled dissenters must be allowed to express their dissent by refusing to take part), we can be required to appear for trial; see Bail Act 1976, s 7.

[28] The accusation must be evidence-backed – there must be a case to answer: we should not be expected to answer to frivolous charges.

[29] I leave the *nolo contendere* plea aside here (see, eg, Bibas 2003): it sounds more like a resigned declaration of non-resistance than an active response to the charge of a kind that (in a *eutopia*) can be expected of a defendant.

[30] Thanks to Rebecca Helm and Rocío Lorca; and see text at n 23 (though we can hope that in a decent criminal law offence labels will not be radically unfair).

[31] And that is what is wrong with the Scottish 'Not Proven' verdict, as a verdict distinct from 'Not Guilty': if the defendant's guilt has not been proven, he is – as far as the court is concerned – not guilty.

IV. Pleading in a (Relative) *Dystopia*

The claim that a defendant should plead guilty if and only if he knows that he is guilty is plausible only if certain conditions are satisfied. He must live in a decent polity, in which he is treated (by his fellow citizens and by the state) with equal concern and respect, as a citizen; the law that he is accused of violating must criminalise conduct that is, or is plausibly argued to be, a public wrong; the investigative process that brought him to court, and the trial itself, must treat him with the respect due to a citizen (a respect that is due whether he is innocent or guilty, though he must be presumed to be innocent), and enable him to offer an informed and considered answer to the charge (this includes providing him with adequate legal counsel); the effects of a conviction – the formal sentence imposed, its implementation, any further collateral consequences – must be just and appropriate, as measures that a citizen can be expected to undertake or undergo without loss of dignity. We do not live in polities in which these conditions are now satisfied: what can we say to defendants in such polities?

The matter is relatively straightforward, as far as principles are concerned, if the polity is so *radically* dystopian that a guilty plea cannot have the kind of meaning that it needs to have if we are to claim that a defendant should plead guilty.[32] A defendant who knows that she is guilty should plead guilty because (and therefore if and only if) by doing so she will assist the legitimate enterprise of the criminal law – calling those who commit public wrongs to answer to their fellow citizens for those wrongs. But if she lives in a society whose criminal law (or 'criminal law') no longer pursues such an aim (if, perhaps, it is more plausibly seen as merely maintaining a ruling elite's power over an oppressed population); or whose criminal trials (or 'trials') cannot be seen as a process of calling public wrongdoers to account: then even if she wants to answer for what she recognises to be a wrong that she committed, pleading guilty is not a way of doing that, since it cannot have the appropriate public meaning (which is what matters here); it cannot constitute an acceptance of culpable responsibility that communicates to her fellow citizens her apologetic recognition of the public wrong that she committed. If the polity is not quite so radically dystopian, a guilty plea might be capable of carrying that meaning, but we might think that even a remorseful defendant need not, or even should not, plead guilty: given the injustices that pervade the polity and its laws (of which she is also a victim), it cannot plausibly be said that she owes such confessional apology to her fellow citizens; and pleading guilty would expose her to unjustly harsh penal or collateral consequences.[33]

[32] Indeed, in a radical *dystopia* it is not even clear whether we can still talk of a 'polity' at all.

[33] I should note one question that arises here. Suppose I am an advantaged member of a profoundly unjust polity: I suffer no injustice myself, but know that a large proportion of the population is unjustly oppressed (indeed, I benefit from those injustices). Those who belong to the oppressed group might have no obligation to plead guilty, as I argue here: but if I know that I have committed a crime, should I plead guilty; or should I say that in a system as corrupted as this, justice cannot be done? Much will

In such radically dystopian polities, we might say that all an unfortunate defendant can be expected to do is to look out for himself: to try to determine whether he will be better (or less harmfully) served by a guilty or by a not guilty plea. Or we might think (or he might think – we might be properly reluctant to comment on what he ought to do) that he still has duties to others – moral duties towards those who will be directly affected by his fate, political duties to his fellow sufferers – that should guide his decision; but his duties will not include a duty to answer in this forum for the public wrong that he committed. If he decides that it will be best (prudentially or ethically) to plead guilty, we might say that he engages in a legal fiction, or in a performance that has nothing to do with the truth;[34] but while these might be ways of understanding what a guilty plea can now amount to, they are also admissions of failure: we would be admitting that the criminal trial is not now what it ought to be and what it purports to be – part of an authentic criminal process that calls alleged wrongdoers to public account, in which the defendant can and should make his allotted role his own.

What, however, of less radically dystopian polities, in which guilty pleas *could* have the kind of meaning and significance that they have in a relative *eutopia*, and whose criminal law can be seen (much of the time, to a significant extent) to serve legitimate ends that its citizens have a civic responsibility to assist?[35] The quick answer is that there is no quick, general, or simple answer: everything will depend on the particularities of the case – on the character of the polity and of its criminal law, on the defendant's standing in the polity and her treatment by its institutions, on the details of the charges and the criminal process that face her. To the extent that she lives in a decent polity that treats her as a citizen; that she faces a warranted charge of criminal conduct that can reasonably be taken to constitute a public wrong; that the process (the trial and the investigative processes that led up to it) treats her with appropriate respect as a responsible agent who is called to answer the charge; that conviction would lead to a punishment, and further collateral consequences, that are just and non-destructive: we could say that she should plead guilty if and only if she knows that she is guilty – that she has good reason so to plead because this is what she owes her fellow citizens. But the strength, or the exclusionary force,[36] of that reason depends on the extent to which such conditions are satisfied. If they are fully or nearly fully satisfied, she ought so to plead; although she might be tempted to plead not guilty despite her knowledge of her guilt, in the hope of avoiding the burdens of conviction and punishment, it is a

depend on the specifics of the case: those will determine whether in going to trial and pleading guilty I can be said to be answering for my wrongdoing to the whole polity – to *all* my fellow citizens.

[34] See text following n 15.

[35] A complication: suppose those ends do not include calling wrongdoers to account (since that is, after all, not the only proper purpose of the criminal law)? We would then need to know more about those ends, and how the trial and the defendant's plea relates to them.

[36] That is, the extent to which it makes it improper for her even to attend to the self-interested reasons that might motivate a dishonest plea.

temptation that she ought to resist. However, the further they are from being satisfied, the more permissible, or normatively reasonable, it becomes to attend to such prudential reasons not as temptations that should be resisted, but as potentially guiding reasons; and also to attend to other, less prudential reasons – for instance to do with the likely effects of either plea on the defendant's family, or with whether and how far it matters that she display her respect, or contempt, for the law and this criminal process.

We could put the point in terms of deference to authority. In a well-functioning system of law, in our imagined *eutopia*, we can say that defendants (like all citizens) should defer to the law's authority – its authority not as the dictates of a sovereign in relation to whom they are merely subjects, but as the demands of a law that is their law. That authority does not demand unthinking obedience: citizens must think for themselves about how best to serve the law's legitimate aims, and exercise their discretion in their dealings with the law (*cf* Edmundson 2006); and they may, as we saw in previous sections, properly plead not guilty although they know that they are guilty in law, or even plead guilty when they know or suspect that the law would acquit them. But it does require honesty – such pleas must be openly explained and defended; and it does require deference to the final judgment of the court. However, insofar as the conditions that define our *eutopia* are not satisfied, that authority is undermined or weakened, even if it is not destroyed; it becomes more permissible for defendants to think strategically about which kind of plea would best serve their political, social or personal ends. Perhaps it is at least possible for a guilty plea to serve the proper ends of the criminal law, albeit imperfectly and at a cost to the defendant that we cannot expect or demand that citizens bear: in that case, a principled defendant could follow Socrates' (controversial) advice to behave *as if* he was in a *eutopia*;[37] we might see this either as a noble act or as a futile gesture. But as the imperfections become more serious, as the costs of pleading honestly increase, it becomes more rational, and more justifiable, to engage in the trial not as a serious enterprise of calling alleged wrongdoers to public account, but as a dangerous game in which the other side holds too many of the cards, and in which defendants must do what they can to minimise the harms (and injustices) they will suffer.

A final question: if a defendant who knows he is guilty has no civic duty to plead guilty, as seems plausible in our existing system, can we now see the guilty plea 'discount' not as an unjustified trial penalty,[38] but as a legitimate incentive to persuade the defendant to do what he has no duty to do? The weaker the ethical demand (of civic responsibility) to plead guilty, the more permissible it is to attend to prudential reasons for pleading not guilty: so is it now permissible for the polity to attempt to tilt the prudential balance of reasons by offering this incentive? One

[37] Plato, *Republic* Bk IX, 592b.

[38] See text at n 13; see also Chapter 5.

worry now would be that to offer such an incentive to plead guilty is to offer the defendant the wrong kind of reason: what should properly motivate a guilty plea, what it should express, is the defendant's recognition of his wrongdoing and his readiness to answer for it – not the prospect of a materially lighter sentence.[39] However, perhaps we could more plausibly say that a modest discount for pleading guilty could now be appropriate as a reward for those who plead guilty, serving the criminal law's aims, although they have no civic duty to do so.[40] (The reward would need to be modest, to avoid perverse incentives, although it is hard to say what should count as 'modest': 10 per cent does look like a reward, whereas 33 per cent, the current maximum 'discount' that English courts are to offer for an early guilty plea,[41] looks rather more like a potentially improper incentive.) Of course we know that what is offered as a reward for going beyond the call of duty is also likely to be treated as a prudential incentive by some (or perhaps many) of those to whom it is offered: but just as retributivists can see the predictable deterrent effects of punishment as beneficial side-effects, rather than as part of the aim of the penal system, so those who worry about seeking to induce guilty defendants to plead guilty by offering the wrong kind of (prudential) incentive might see that incentivising effect simply as a side-effect of offering the reward that those who plead guilty deserve.

V. Conclusion

My discussion in this chapter has been quite abstract: I have not even tried to describe the kinds of concrete context in which we could, or could not, say that defendants who know that they are guilty should plead guilty, while those who know that they are or suspect that they might be innocent should plead not guilty. Instead, my aim has been to show how, given the right kind of political and legal context (that of a relative *eutopia*), we could plausibly say that defendants have a civic responsibility to plead guilty if and only if they know that they are guilty; and how what we can say about defendants' responsibilities in this matter must be affected by the extent to which, and the ways in which, they live in a *dystopia* rather than in a *eutopia*. The task of describing the substantive contours of a *eutopia*, and of working out the implications of different kinds of *dystopia*, must be one for other occasions.

[39] Compare the objection to purely deterrent systems of criminal punishment, that they offer us the wrong kind of reason to refrain from crime: see Duff (2001: 84–85).

[40] See Chapter 5 (contrast the Sentencing Council's view, quoted in n 4, that 'the guilty plea reduction is in place to provide an incentive … and not a reward').

[41] See Sentencing Council Guidelines, www.sentencingcouncil.org.uk/overarching-guides/magistrates-court/item/reduction-in-sentence-for-a-guilty-plea-first-hearing-on-or-after-1-june-2017/; Ashworth and Kelly (2021: 173–76).

References

Ashworth, AJ and Kelly, R (2021) *Sentencing and Criminal Justice*, 7th edn (Oxford, Oxford University Press).

Austin, JL (1975) *How to Do Things with Words*, 2nd edn (Oxford, Oxford University Press).

Bibas, S (2003) 'Harmonizing Substantive-Criminal-Law Values and Criminal Procedure: The Case of *Alford* and Nolo Contendere Pleas' 88 *Cornell Law Review* 1361.

Bowers, J (2007) 'Punishing the Innocent' 156 *University of Pennsylvania Law Review* 1117.

Brockman, J (2010) 'An Offer You Can't Refuse: Pleading Guilty When Innocent' 56 *Criminal Law Quarterly* 116.

Duff, RA (2001) *Punishment, Communication, and Community* (New York, Oxford University Press).

—— (2013) 'Who Must Presume Whom to Be Innocent of What?' 42 *Netherlands Journal of Legal Philosophy* 170.

—— (2018) *The Realm of Criminal Law* (Oxford, Oxford University Press).

Duff, RA and Marshall, SE (2016) 'Civic Punishment' in A Dzur, I Loader and R Sparks (eds), *Democratic Theory and Mass Incarceration* (Oxford, Oxford University Press).

Duff, RA, Farmer, L, Marshall, SE and Tadros, V (2007) *The Trial on Trial III: Towards a Normative Theory of the Criminal Trial* (Oxford, Hart Publishing).

Dworkin, RM (1986) *A Matter of Principle* (Oxford, Oxford University Press).

Dzur, A (2012) *Punishment, Participatory Democracy, and the Jury* (New York, Oxford University Press).

Edmundson, W (2006) 'The Virtue of Law Abidance' 6 *Philosopher's Imprint* 1.

Helm, RK (2019) 'Conviction by Consent? Vulnerability, Autonomy and Conviction by Guilty Plea' 83 *Journal of Criminal Law* 161.

Johnson, T (2019) 'Fictional Pleas' 94 *Indiana Law Journal* 855.

Lippke, R (2011) *The Ethics of Plea Bargaining* (Oxford, Oxford University Press).

Longworth, G (2021) 'John Langshaw Austin' in E Zalta (ed), *Stanford Encyclopedia of Philosophy* (Fall edn) https://plato.stanford.edu/archives/fall2021/entries/austin-jl

Martin, GA (1993) *Report of the Attorney General's Advisory Committee on Charge Screening, Disclosure and Resolution Discussions* (Ontario, Ministry of the Attorney General).

Nance, D (1994) 'Civility and the Burden of Proof' 17 *Harvard Journal of Law & Public Policy* 647.

Nobles, R and Schiff, D (2019) 'Criminal Justice Unhinged: The Challenge of Guilty Pleas' 39 *Oxford Journal of Legal Studies* 100.

Peay, J and Player, E (2018) 'Pleading Guilty: Why Vulnerability Matters' 81 *Modern Law Review* 929.

Sentencing Council (2016) *Reduction in Sentence for a Guilty Plea Guideline – Consultation* (London, Sentencing Council).

Sentencing Council (2017) *Reduction in Sentence for a Guilty Plea Guideline. Definitive Guideline*, www.sentencingcouncil.org.uk/overarching-guides/magistrates-court/item/reduction-in-sentence-for-a-guilty-plea-first-hearing-on-or-after-1-june-2017/

Shipley, J (1987) 'The Alford Plea: A Necessary But Unpredictable Tool for the Criminal Defendant' 72 *Iowa Law Review* 1063.

Legislation

Bail Act 1976
Federal Rules on Criminal Procedure (US)

Cases

United Kingdom

R v Barton and Booth [2020] EWCA Crim 575
R v Newton [1982] 4 Cr App R (S) 388
R v R [1992] 1 AC 599
R v Turner [1970] 2 QB 321

United States

North Carolina v Alford 91 Cr App Ct 160 (1970)
Williams v Florida 399 US 78 (1970)

3

Guilty Plea Sentencing Discounts and Retributivism

JESPER RYBERG

I. Introduction

Should there be a sentence discount for defendants who plead guilty? There is no simple answer. Nor is it a question that attracts consensus among penal theorists. However, there is widespread agreement that providing sentence reductions for those who plead guilty has several pragmatic advantages.

First and foremost, a discount encourages guilty pleas and helps reduce the costs of the criminal justice system while also streamlining its operation. Pleas save costs that would otherwise have been expended on 'provision of judicial and court facilities, prosecutorial operations, the supply of legal aid to accused persons, witness fees, and the fees paid, and inconveniences caused, to jurors summoned to perform jury service' (Kirby in Bagaric and Brebner 2003). In fact, theorists have even argued that if all or almost all defendants were to plead not guilty – the likely result of abandoning discounts – and all elements of the offence had to be proven, courts in most countries would collapse (see, eg, Bagaric and Brebner 2003; Peay and Player 2018). Furthermore, guilty plea discounts may have other less practical advantages such as sparing witnesses from having to testify. Release from the duty to testify may be a significant benefit in cases that would have been humiliating for the witness (such as cases concerning sexual misconduct) or that might even involve danger (such as cases against organised violent gangs) (see, eg, Bradley 1999: 71; Chapter 9).

It has also been suggested that guilty pleas may reduce or eliminate the possibility of unethical behaviour, such as the temptation of witnesses to perjure themselves (Bradley 1999). Obviously, these consequential reasons still might not be sufficient to justify guilty plea discounts from a consequentialist point of view. For example, the consequentialist would have to engage in further considerations of whether such discounts would have benefits in terms of crime prevention or with regard to public opinion. The purpose here is not to examine all considerations that should be taken into account or to consider whether all the alleged benefits of a discount system rest on solid empirical ground. Rather, let us assume that, all things considered, there are strong consequentialist reasons for providing mitigations to defendants who plead guilty. The question is whether these benefits would suffice to justify such a system or whether other considerations block this conclusion.

More precisely, the question is whether there are justice-based considerations that would speak against such discounts. It only requires a cursory look to the literature to see that there are strong indications that this is the case. Several theorists have asserted that guilty plea discounts are at odds with a retributivist view of criminal justice. Such discounts are contested because they are 'unrelated to the critical retributive concepts of seriousness of the offense or the offender's level of culpability'; that 'it is clear why retributivists might view the practice with considerable unease'; or simply that 'from a purely retributive perspective, the practice of reducing a sentence … in exchange for a guilty plea … is unjustifiable'.[1] However, despite these contentions, remarkably little has been done to more thoroughly consider exactly why guilty plea discounts should be seen as inconsistent with retributivism.[2] Perhaps part of the explanation is that this so obviously seems to be the case that no further scrutiny is required. However, as we will see, this prima facie judgement is very much premature. In fact, as will be argued, the question is highly complex in terms of theory.

A. Overview

This chapter will proceed as follows: Section II concerns the first potential retributivist objection to plea-based discounts, namely that a discount practice implies that some factually guilty offenders will be sentenced too leniently. Section III deals with the common retributive critique, namely that guilty plea discounts imply that some factually innocent subjects will be sentenced. Section IV asks whether an overall assessment that combines the considerations of the previous two sections will support the conclusion that guilty plea discounts should be rejected on retributivist grounds. Finally, section V summarises and concludes. The purpose is to show that it is not justified to conclude that a retributivist approach to criminal justice implies that guilty plea discounts should be rejected. However, and importantly, this conclusion is not reached by arguing that retributivism is theoretically consistent with the practice of providing plea-based discounts, but rather by showing that it is basically unclear what retributivism implies. In other words, retributivism is theoretically incapable of delivering principled guidance for systems proving

[1] The three passages are quoted from Roberts and Bradford (2015: 188); Lippke (2006: 3); and Slobogin (2016: 1512), respectively.

[2] For a noteworthy exception, see Lippke (2006). However, Lippke's conclusions differ significantly from those drawn in this chapter.

such discounts. In short, it is suggested that the question of the justification of plea-based discounts reveals serious theoretical deficits of retributivism.

However, before embarking on these considerations, a few comments should be made concerning the scope of the discussion. First, retributivism covers a wide range of theories that differ significantly on many more detailed issues. Thus, in the following I will rely on some general features of retributivist theory that are shared across various versions of this approach to sentencing. Second, the discussion will not deal with the question (which would add even further to the theoretical complexity) of when consequence-based reasons are sufficiently strong to outweigh retributive justice; that is, whether one should favour a threshold version of retributivism and, if so, how such thresholds should be determined (see, eg, Ryberg 2021a). Third, systems that treat offenders who plead guilty more favourably can be implemented in many different ways. For instance, one possibility is to provide larger discounts for offenders who plead guilty earlier rather than later in the criminal process (see, eg, Ashworth 2005; Peay and Player 2018). However, in the following, I will not consider the possibility of variable discounts. The question as to whether there should be a discount for guilty pleas at all is sufficient to illustrate the theoretical challenges to which I wish to direct attention.

II. Guilty Plea Discounts and Sentencing Disparity

Suppose that two offenders – A and B – have committed crimes that are equally serious from a retributivist point of view. That is, suppose that the crimes are identical with regard to harm and culpability, or any other factors that a retributivist might regard as crucial in the determination of what an offender deserves. Suppose, further, that A pleads guilty at an early stage in the process, while B maintains his innocence, and that A consequently ends up being sentenced more leniently than B. Now, given the assumption that a guilty plea is not in itself included in the set of factors that determine an offender's desert, it seems to follow straightforwardly that the differential treatment of A and B is incompatible with the idea of retributive justice.[3] More precisely, the practice of providing guilty plea discounts seems

[3] It is widely accepted in the modern retributivist tradition that an offender's desert should be determined exclusively on the basis of features of the crime committed (and perhaps prior criminal record). The post-crime behaviour of the offender should not be taken into account in the determination of the sentence. Some theorists have suggested that other factors – such as remorse – should also be taken into account (see Chapter 5; Dagan and Roberts 2019). I cannot here enter into a discussion of the plausibility of a dynamic account of retributivism (but see Ryberg 2021b). However, two things should be noted. First, even if a dynamic theory is accepted this is not sufficient to undermine the considerations in this section. It would also have to be shown that a guilty plea in itself should be taken into account in the determination of desert (it is not sufficient to hold that remorse is a desert-relevant factor: an offender may plead guilty without being remorseful (see, eg, Ashworth 2005: 165)). Second, even if this is the case, the challenges concerning the punishment of innocents, to which we will turn in the following section, remain unaffected.

to violate ordinal proportionality; that more serious crimes should be sentenced more severely than less serious crimes, and that equally serious crime should be responded to with equally severe sentences.[4] Is this objection persuasive?[5]

The objection certainly has appeal. The differential punitive treatment of A and B clearly violates a requirement of ordinal proportionality. However, as we shall now see, this does not change the fact that the leap to concluding that the guilty plea discount should therefore be abandoned may well be premature. The problem facing the objection is that ordinal proportionality is not all that matters for the retributivist. No retributivist would hold that the observance of ordinal proportionality is all that is required for a sentencing system to be just. Such a view would imply that a system that punishes minor theft with 10 years behind bars, or one that gives two months of probation to a murderer, would both be retributively just, so long as ordinal proportionality is observed (ie as long as more serious crimes in the first case are punished more severely than 10 years of imprisonment and in the appropriate order, and that less serious crimes in the second case are punished more leniently and in the appropriate order). It is therefore generally agreed that the retributive view of justice also needs to incorporate considerations of how sentences non-relatively or cardinally relate to specific crimes. However, if this is the case, then the question of how A and B should be sentenced becomes much more complicated.

The concept of non-relative or cardinal proportionality is subject to somewhat different interpretations. Suppose, first, that it is the case that there is, for each individual crime of a certain degree of seriousness, a fitting sentence, such that any sentences that are more or less severe than this particular sentence would be cardinally disproportionate. In this interpretation it is obvious that the differential punitive treatment of A and B implies that not only ordinal, but also cardinal proportionality has been violated.[6] However, and importantly, it is not clear that this implies that the differential treatment should be abandoned. This is easily seen. If it is the case that the cardinally proportionate sentence for the crime A and B have committed is the one that B receives (or if the fitting sentence is even

[4] It might be questioned whether it is correct that retributivism is committed to ordinal proportionality (see, eg, Ryberg 2004; 2021d). However, in the following it will be assumed that this is the case – which is what retributivists usually believe.

[5] Slobogin has argued that guilty plea discounts are incompatible with a retributivist view of justice. He asserts that if one, within a system that offers discounts, compares the sentences of a defendant who either pleads guilty or does not plead guilty then, from a retributivist point of view, 'the important point is that, at best, only one of these sentences can reflect a defendant's true desert. While most retributivists are willing to contemplate a sentencing range for a given crime, those sentencing variations are meant to recognize that different offenders charged with the same crime might warrant different punishments, not that the same offender can receive divergent sentences' (2016: 1510).

[6] Some theorists – such as von Hirsch – have suggested that there are bounds of cardinal proportionality that should be regarded as shaded areas that grow progressively darker as a deviation becomes more drastic (von Hirsch 1993: 37). It is not absolutely clear how this view translates into the deontic question as to whether or not one should impose a particular sentence on an offender. However, be that as it may, this view does not change the reasoning presented here.

more severe) then it follows that the reduced sentence imposed on A would violate both ordinal and cardinal proportionality. However, if the opposite is the case, that is, if the cardinally proportionate sentence is the one that A receives (or if it is even more lenient than the one imposed on A), then it is no longer clear that A's sentence is at odds with retributive justice.[7] On the one hand, this sentence violates ordinal proportionality. However, on the other, the sentence seems preferable from the perspective of cardinal proportionality.[8] Therefore, the conclusion that the sentence imposed on A is retributively unacceptable does not seem justified.[9]

Suppose, alternatively, that it is not the case that there is for each individual crime a sentence of a certain degree of severity that is cardinally proportionate, but rather that there are sentences of varying severity that would all satisfy the requirement of being cardinally proportionate. That is, for each individual crime there will be a zone of cardinally acceptable sentences. In this case, the picture is the following. If the sentence imposed on B is cardinally proportionate, then either the sentence imposed on A will be disproportionately lenient (if it lies below the zone of cardinally proportionate sentences for this crime), or it will be cardinally proportionate (because it lies within this zone), in which case the sentence will only violate ordinal proportionality, but not cardinal proportionality. However, it might also be the case that the sentence imposed on A is cardinally proportionate, in which case the picture is the opposite: either the sentence imposed on B is disproportionate (because it lies above the zone of proportionate sentences) or it will be proportionate because it lies within the zone. Thus, there will be some cases in which it is no longer clear that the fact that A, due to the discount, is sentenced more leniently than B implies that this sentence – even though it involves a violation of ordinal proportionality – would be retributively worse when cardinal proportionality considerations are also factored into the assessment.

Thus, the crux of the matter is that there may be – independently of whether there is, for each individual crime, a particular sentence that is cardinally proportionate, or whether there are zones of cardinal proportionate sentences – cases in which there will be a conflict between ordinal and cardinal proportionality. In

[7] It might perhaps be argued that even if A receives the sentence that he deserves for the crime, this would nevertheless be objectionable if this sentence is imposed as a result of a guilty plea discount. That is, the sentence would be imposed for the wrong reasons. However, in the discussion of whether or not it would be desirable to provide a discount to A, it seems hard to believe that the retributivist would prefer A to be sentenced more severely than he deserves, rather than receiving the deserved sentence for the wrong reasons.

[8] If the cardinally proportionate sentence is even more lenient than the sentence imposed on A, then it seems reasonable to conclude, from a retributivist view, that the more lenient sentence imposed as a plea-based discount would be retributively preferable to the one imposed on B. However, the objection might be raised that both sentences would then violate a proportionality constraint and be morally wrong *simpliciter*. However, if this is what the retributivist holds, then he or she will have to give up the possibility of providing genuine action guidance under non-ideal circumstances; that is, in situations where the comparison is between scenarios that are both retributively non-ideal.

[9] It might, of course, also be the case that neither A nor B gets a cardinally proportionate sentence. The proportionate sentence could be located in between the sentences imposed on A and B. We will return to this possibility in Section IV.

these cases it will therefore be unclear what a retributivist view of justice implies. But how should such a conflict be resolved? From an overall point of view, there are three possible answers (see Duus-Otterström 2020; Ryberg 2021c).

The first possibility is to hold that ordinal proportionality always has primacy over considerations of cardinal proportionality. That is, there is a lexical ordering between the two types of proportionality and as a result ordinal proportionality always trumps cardinal proportionality. If this is the case, then the objection we are considering in this section would remain intact; that is, it would be unaffected by the previous considerations of cardinal proportionality. However, this view faces serious challenges. For instance, it implies that if an offender has been sentenced very harshly for a minor offence, say 10 years in prison for theft, and if another offender subsequently commits the same crime, then he or she should also be locked up behind bars for 10 years. Such an implication seems hard to accept.

The second possibility is to adopt the opposite view, namely that even though both ordinal and cardinal proportionality should count morally, it is always the case that cardinal proportionality has primacy over ordinal proportionality. This view also has dubious implications. For instance, suppose that penal levels for all crimes were reduced drastically, except for a single type of crime, but that crimes in this category were punished in a cardinally proportionate manner. In this case, any attempt to punish such crimes even marginally more leniently in order to get closer to levels for all the crimes (some of which would be more serious) would be wrong. As Duus-Otterström has noted, this implication seems 'far too drastic' (2020: 41). Moreover, it should be noted that if this view actually were correct, then the objection we are considering here – that guilty plea discounts violate ordinal proportionality – would be blocked by the considerations presented above; that is, in a system involving over-punishment it may be the case that the reduced sentence imposed on A is retributively preferable even though it involves a violation of ordinal proportionality.

The final possibility is to hold that the idea that one type of proportionality lexically dominates the other should be rejected and to instead hold that the two types of proportionality should be weighed against each other. Though surprisingly few modern retributivists have considered these theoretical questions of the relative weight of cardinal and ordinal proportionality, the small number of theorists who have in fact addressed the issue seem to believe that this constitutes the most plausible answer (see Duus-Otterström 2020; Kagan 2012). However, this leaves the question as to how the two types of proportionality should then be balanced against each other. At this point it is fair to say that no one has even tentatively outlined the contours of an answer. As Duus-Otterström rightly observes, 'weighing relative and absolute proportionality should be added to an already long list of fascinating and vexing problems facing retributivist thought' (2020: 48).

Then where do all these considerations leave us? The objection that guilty plea discounts violate ordinal proportionality seems convincing. However, on closer inspection we have seen that matters are much more complicated. Since cardinal proportionality considerations cannot be taken out of the equation, the appeal of the objection fades. There may be cases, such as in a context of over-punishment, where the reduced sentence imposed on A would be cardinally preferable. The retributivists' assessment therefore requires a theory of how ordinal and cardinal proportionality considerations should be weighed. This theoretical challenge remains unsolved. Thus, as a whole, the general objection that guilty plea discounts violate ordinal proportionality and that such discounts should therefore be rejected must be regarded as inconclusive. A proportionality-based objection would only seem warranted in the particular cases in which considerations of ordinal and cardinal proportionality coincide (that is, where the discount provided to A violates both ordinal and cardinal proportionality). But as we shall return to shortly, such cases may be rare in real-life criminal justice practice, and even in these rare cases there are other reasons to question the objection (because other retributivist considerations may also affect the assessment).

III. Guilty Plea Discounts and the Punishment of Innocents

The second retributivist objection against guilty plea discount has played an even more dominant role in the academic discussion. The claim is that guilty plea discounts will induce some defendants to plead guilty even though they are in fact innocent. There are two points worth emphasising in relation to this concern.

First, even though it might at first glance seem hard to believe that anyone would confess to a crime if they were in fact innocent, it is well documented that there are circumstances under which some people confess to crimes even when this is not encouraged by the prospect of a sentence reduction (see, eg, Kassin 2008; Scherr et al 2020). Furthermore, if there is the possibility of getting a sentence discount, this may be what some factually innocent but risk-averse defendants will choose. It has even been emphasised that the possibility of a guilty plea discount turns the criminal process into a kind of gamble where it may sometimes be rational for a factually innocent defendant to plead guilty.[10] Moreover, there is evidence that some innocent defendants are incentivised into 'cutting their losses' by pleading guilty (see Ashworth 2005: 179).[11] Thus, empirically the objection is on solid ground.

Second, if this is the case, then it constitutes a serious concern for the retributivist. Punishment of the innocent means punishment of the non-deserving. And while some negative retributivists would not object to cases where offenders are

[10] For a discussion of guilty plea discounts and plea bargaining from a game theoretical perspective, see, eg, Caldwell (2011).

[11] Rakoff conservatively estimates that of the 2.2 million Americans who are in prison, 'we are talking about an estimated 20,000 persons, or more, who are in prison for crimes to which they pleaded guilty but did not in fact commit' (2014: 5).

punished less severely than they deserve, it is clear that all retributivists would usually regard over-punishment, and indeed the special case of punishment of innocents, as a serious problem. But does this mean that the 'punishment of the innocent' objection provides sufficient grounds for rejecting guilty plea discounts if one believes in retributive justice? As will be argued, this conclusion is premature. However, first we need a clearer view of how precisely the retributivist objection should be interpreted.

At first glance the objection appears quite simple. In the classical modern discussion between consequentialists and retributivists, adherents of the latter position have repeatedly emphasised that the consequentialist approach is unacceptable because it implies that there are circumstances under which it would have the best consequences to punish an innocent.[12] This has been held to be counter-intuitive and to violate a retributivist constraint against punishment of innocents (or against disproportionate punishment).[13] However, if a system that provides guilty plea discounts is regarded as objectionable because this will violate a constraint against punishing innocents, this will have very significant implications. The problem is that false confessions are also made and innocents can be punished within a framework that does not provide sentence reductions for guilty pleas. Therefore, if the objection is interpreted as the contention that guilty plea discounts should be rejected because this will involve a violation of a constraint against punishment of innocents, then the very same objection can be raised against a system that does not allow for guilty plea discounts. In other words, the objection seems to rule out the entire punishment practice. This is precisely the reason why retributivists have usually held – in accordance with the standard view of moral constraints in deontological thinking – that the constraint against punishment of innocents is violated only in cases that involve *intentional* punishment of innocents (see, eg, Duff 1986; or Moore 1993). The inadvertent punishment of innocents does not constitute a constraint violation. But if a guilty plea discount, therefore, cannot just be interpreted as an instance of the traditional 'punishment of innocents' problem – that is, as involving constraint violations – then how should it be interpreted in order for it to be objectionable from a retributivist point of view?

On closer inspection it turns out not to be a simple matter to formulate the objection in a way that does not have unintended and unacceptable consequences. For instance, if one suggests that it is wrong to implement or maintain a practice that implies that more innocents are punished, then once again this will undermine the entire punishment system. Obviously, more innocents will be sentenced

[12] For a recent discussion of the 'punishment of the innocent' objection against a consequentialist view of punishment, see, eg, Ryberg (2023).

[13] In the present discussion it is not important whether one holds that there is a particular constraint against punishments of innocents or whether such punishments are considered a special instance of a violation of a broader constraint against disproportionately severe punishments. For a recent discussion of this, see Smilansky (2021).

if one upholds a punishment system than if the entire system is abandoned. Another possibility might be to suggest that a punishment system is unacceptable if one exceeds a certain ratio of factually innocent defendants who are punished. However, if this is the case then this ratio might of course be reached even within a system that does not provide guilty plea discounts, or it could be the case that the ratio would not be reached even if a system allows for such discounts. Therefore, in order for this suggestion to function as an objection against such discounts one would first have to identify the appropriate ratio and subsequently show that this ratio is exceeded precisely if one introduces a practice that allows for plea-based discounts. It is obvious that this will be very difficult to justify theoretically. Then how can the objection possibly be formulated?[14]

Perhaps the most appealing interpretation would be something like the following. If we have a punishment system which is justified, then it will be wrong to introduce, within this system, a practice that will increase the number of innocents that are punished. Plea-based discounts constitute a practice that will increase the number of innocents who are sentenced. Therefore, it will be wrong to introduce this practice within the punishment system. However, even if this interpretation circumvents the challenge that the justification of the entire punishment system will be undermined, it nevertheless faces several problems. One obvious challenge is that it is difficult to believe that the number of innocents who are inadvertently punished is all that matters in an overall retributivist assessment.[15] We will return to this shortly. But even if the focus is narrowly on the punishment of innocents, the objection is still hard to accept. This is easily seen. Suppose we either have a system that provides guilty plea discounts or one that does not. In that case, it is, as noted, reasonable to expect that more factually innocent defendants will be sentenced within the former system, because some defendants will plead guilty despite their innocence. However, this is not the only way innocents are affected. Within a system that does not provide discounts, there will be some factually innocent defendants who will be inadvertently sentenced and who would have pleaded guilty within a system that provided guilty plea discounts. Presumably, this group of innocents will be quite small. However, those who are inadvertently sentenced within this framework will get harsher sentences than if they had pleaded guilty within a system with discounts. But this means that we are comparing two scenarios: one in which a larger number of innocents are sentenced and

[14] Hoskins (Chapter 4) has suggested a new and interesting interpretation of the retributivist view of punishment of innocents. According to this view, the State should actively demonstrate its intention not to punish innocents. I cannot discuss this interpretation here except by mentioning that it is not clear to me what precisely this obligation implies.

[15] Obviously, the focus on the sentencing of innocents cannot be all that counts in the overall assessment of the entire punishment system. If this were the case, then – as we have seen – the system should be abolished. But if this is the case, then it becomes very difficult to explain that the focus should be placed solely on the sentencing of innocents when the practice of providing plea-based discounts is assessed from a retributivist point of view.

another in which a subset of these innocents are sentenced more severely.[16] Which scenario is preferable? Intuitively, the answer must depend on the differences in the number of innocents who are sentenced and in the severity of the sentences they receive under the two scenarios. However, it is fair to say that retributivists have not yet provided anything close to a principled answer to how this sort of weighing should be made; which means that, even if focus is placed solely on the inadvertent sentencing of innocents, the objection against a system that provides plea-based discounts will not be justified.

To summarise, the fact that guilty plea discounts will encourage some innocents to plead guilty constitutes a major concern from a retributivist point of view. However, once it is clear that this consequence of a discount system does not constitute an instance of the sort of constraint violation that has been at the centre of the traditional controversy between retributivist and consequentialist views, but should rather be seen as a question of how one should deal with the problem of inadvertent punishment of innocents, it becomes much more difficult to formulate the objection convincingly. The retributivist view of justice simply does not yet possess the theoretical resources to reject plea-based discounts exclusively by reference to the fact that some innocents will be inadvertently sentenced.

IV. The Overall Retributivist Assessment of Discounts

What we have seen so far is that the contention that guilty plea discounts constitute an obvious problem from a retributivist point of view was not – despite immediate appeal – easy to uphold on closer scrutiny. Neither the claim that discounts violate ordinal proportionality, nor that they will lead to sentencing of innocents, was sufficient to justify rejecting such discounts. However, obviously this is not the same as saying that violations of ordinal proportionality or the inadvertent punishment of innocents is not something that plays an important role in a retributivist assessment. Therefore, could it be held that none of these considerations, when viewed in isolation, provides a sufficient reason for rejecting guilty plea discounts, but rather it is the overall assessment, where such considerations are all taken into account, that would justify the rejection of plea-based discounts?

In order to consider this possibility, let us assume that we are comparing two punishment systems that are identical in all respects except for the fact that the first system provides discounts for guilty pleas, while the latter does not. For reasons of

[16] It seems plausible to believe that a subset of those innocents who would have pleaded guilty within a system that provides discounts would be sentenced even within a system that does not provide discounts. It is well documented that miscarriages of justice happen. But if it is correct that some of the factually innocents who have a bad case are those who will plead guilty if they get a discount, then it is also more plausible to believe that some of these defendants will end up being sentenced even if they plead not guilty within a system that does not provide discounts.

ease of exposition let us refer to the former as the 'discount system' and the latter as the 'no-discount system'. How should these two systems be assessed in terms of retributive justice?

Given the fact that sentencing of innocents is punishment of the non-deserving, this is obviously something that the retributivist would take into account. What this means, as we have just seen, is that the comparison would amount to the following: in the discount system there will be some factual innocents who are sentenced because they plead guilty; in the no-discount system there will be some of these innocents who will not be sentenced because they are found not guilty, but there will also be some (probably a few) who will be sentenced more harshly than in the discount system. However, this is only one aspect that would be ethically relevant for the retributivist. As we have also seen, another aspect concerns the fact that some factually guilty offenders (those who plead guilty) will receive more lenient sentences in the discount system, which is not the case in the no-discount system. As argued, though, the question as to whether this disparity in sentence between offenders who have committed equally serious crimes would constitute a justice problem was contingent on considerations of cardinal proportionality; that is, whether we are considering discounts within a system that punishes in a just manner, or whether offenders are being under- or over-punished from a retributivist point of view. But this means that if we combine the two different aspects into an overall assessment then we will have to distinguish between three possible scenarios.

The first possibility is that sentencing levels under the no-discount system are retributively just (or too low). In this case, the assessment that combines the two aspects will involve a comparison between a discount system, where more factually innocents (those who plead guilty) are sentenced, and a no-discount system, where some of these innocents receive even harsher sentences. It is also the case that a number of factually guilty offenders in the discount system are sentenced too leniently (or less disproportionately) than in the no-discount system, but that the former system, in contrast to the latter, also involves a violation of ordinal proportionality. In other words, the retributivist will have to consider how one should balance, on the one hand, more innocents who are sentenced and more guilty offenders who are under-punished and, on the other, guilty offenders who get what they deserve and a few innocents who are sentenced more harshly.

The second possibility is that sentence levels under the no-discount system are too harsh, but that these levels are also too low for those who plead guilty under the discount system (ie, the cardinally proportionate sentences lie somewhere between the sentences that are imposed with and without guilty plea discounts). In this case, the retributivist will again have to compare a discount system, where more factually innocents (those who plead guilty) are sentenced, and a no-discount system, where some of these innocents receive even harsher sentences. But this time one will also have to compare a no-discount system that over-punishes offenders with a discount system that under-punishes some offenders (those who plead guilty) and that also involves a violation of ordinal proportionality. In other words, one will have to compare a system that imposes sentences on more innocents and under-punishes some offenders, and a system that over-punishes the same offenders and gives harsher sentences to a smaller group of innocents.

The final possibility is that the sentencing levels for those offenders who plead guilty under the discount system are retributively appropriate (or too harsh) – that is, these offenders get what they deserve for the crimes committed (or they are sentenced less disproportionately) – while the sentences imposed under the no-discount system are too severe. In this case the retributivist will once again have to compare a discount system, where more factually innocents (those who plead guilty) are sentenced, and a no-discount system, where some of these innocents receive even harsher sentences. Furthermore, there will in the discount system be more factually guilty offenders who get the sentence they deserve (namely, those who plead guilty), whereas these offenders under the no-discount system will be over-punished. But the discount system will also involve a violation of ordinal proportionality, and this is not the case in the no-discount system. In short, one will have to compare, on the one hand, more innocents who are sentenced but also more guilty who get what they deserve and, on the other, guilty offenders who will not get what they deserve, because they are over-punished, but where there is no problem in terms of ordinal proportionality, and a few innocents who are sentenced more harshly than in the alternative system.

Where, then, do these comparisons ultimately leave us?[17] The point is simply to show that no matter whether we are considering systems where those offenders who do not get discounts are appropriately sentenced, where these offenders are over-punished but where those who get discounts get what they deserve, or where the deserved sentences lie between the sentences imposed with and without discounts, the retributivist assessment requires a weighing of factors that are all retributively relevant but that point in opposite directions. This challenge is less significant in the first case, where sentencing levels without discounts are retributively appropriate (or too lenient). In this case, there are several factors that point in favour of discounts, but only one that points in the opposite direction (ie, that some factually innocents will receive comparatively harsher sentences). However, it is worth bearing in mind that if we turn to real-life sentencing systems, it seems that this scenario is also the least likely. Modern retributivists have repeatedly emphasised that sentencing levels in many Western countries are much too high; offenders are over-punished.[18] Turning to the other two (and more realistic) scenarios, the assessments of a discount system and a no-discount system involved

[17] In practice, the picture may be even more complicated. That is, it need not be sufficient to distinguish between systems where the just sentences are either imposed in the no-discount system, in the discount system, or where the appropriate sentences lie in between the sentence levels in the two systems. It may well be the case that some offenders get what they deserve in the no-discount system while this is not the case for other offenders. It may also be the case that ordinal proportionality is not fully respected in this system. Under such circumstances it becomes even more theoretically demanding for the retributivist to tell whether guilty plea discounts would be justifiable.

[18] For instance, Singer has held that confinement should be reserved only for the most serious crimes and that it is a misconception of retributive theory to think of it as a derivative of a 'throw-away-the-key'

comparisons of several factors of retributivist significance pointing in the opposite directions. Briefly summarised, these comparisons would require answers to the following questions:

- How severely should individual crimes be sentenced?
- How should ordinal and cardinal proportionality be balanced?
- How should upward deviations and downward deviations from a fitting sentence be balanced?
- How should a larger number of innocents who are sentenced be balanced against a smaller number of innocents who are sentenced comparatively more severely?
- How should the punishment of innocents be balanced against violations of ordinal proportionality?
- How should the punishment of innocents be balanced against violations of cardinal proportionality in the sentencing of offenders?

When it comes to the first question, several so-called 'anchor theories' have been suggested that attempt to provide guidelines for how scales of crimes and punishments should be linked (see, eg, Davis 1992; Kleinig 1973; Lippke 2012; Scheid 1997; von Hirsch 1993; 2017). However, the theories have not been developed sufficiently to provide recommendations with regard to what constitutes appropriate penal levels. And the step from what constitutes the appropriate sentence levels for types of crime to the determination of sentences in individual criminal cases has often been theoretically obscure. Moreover, these theories have also been the subject of serious moral criticism.[19] Thus, with regard to the first question, current retributivist theory cannot yet be said to be on firm ground. Turning to the remaining questions it is clear that answers, to an even greater extent, are absent in the modern theoretical discussion. Retributivist theory, to my knowledge, has not even offered the first contours of what principled answers to these questions would look like. The theoretical resources that would be required to answer these questions are simply non-existent. Furthermore, it is hardly an overstatement to say that these questions do not allow for any simple answers.

In short, to contend that a criminal justice system that provides discounts for defendants who plead guilty is objectionable from an overall point of view that combines the various factors that should be included in a retributivist assessment is premature. However, the reason is not that it can be shown that plea-based discounts are consistent with retributivist theory – that is, that this practice agrees with retributivist recommendations – but rather that in this regard it is totally obscure what ultimately follows from a retributivist approach to criminal justice.

approach to punishment (1979). Murphy has suggested that, if retributive theory were to be followed consistently, one would punish less and in more decent ways than one actually does (1979). Von Hirsch has held that terms of imprisonment, even for the most serious crimes, should seldom exceed five years (von Hirsch 1993; von Hirsch and Ashworth 2005). See also Husak (2019) or Ryberg (2021e).

[19] For a critical discussion of the plausibility of various anchor theories, see Ryberg (2004).

V. Conclusion

The ethics of punishment as an academic field is often concerned with theorising, which is ideal in the sense that it provides answers as to how a criminal justice system should function and be designed if it were possible to rebuild it from scratch. However, real-life ethical challenges pertaining to State punishment usually have a very different character. They concern questions such as whether a particular procedure or practice should be implemented, abandoned or modified. That is, they usually concern potential changes within a penal system that is not in itself about to be fundamentally reformed and that may well function in various ways that do not live up to what would be ideally desirable. This means that ideal considerations of whether a particular practice would be justified if it were to be implemented may not be readily applicable. On the contrary, insofar as the purpose of the ethics of punishment is to deliver genuine guidance on action, one will have to engage in considerations of whether the practice in question is justifiable within a system which may diverge significantly from what is ideally desirable. Since all penal theorists agree that the ethics of punishment do not merely provide a justification of the existing penal order, but rather that there is often a significant discrepancy between what is ideally desirable and actual penal practice, it is also clear that the capacity to deliver answers within a non-ideal framework constitutes one of the very important features by which an ethical theory should be measured (see, eg, Murphy 2014; Ryberg 2004; 2023). However, it is precisely at this point I believe that modern retributivist theory faces serious challenges. The question of whether there should be sentence reductions for defendants who plead guilty serves as an illustration of this more general problem.

At first glance, a guilty plea discount appears at odds with a retributivist view of sentencing. If a guilty plea is not in itself a desert-relevant factor, then it seems that differential treatment of offenders who plead guilty and those who plead not guilty would violate proportionality. Furthermore, if a guilty plea induces some factually innocents to plead guilty, then this seems highly objectionable from a retributivist point of view. However, on closer scrutiny, these questions turned out to be much more complicated. What I have argued in the previous sections is that neither references to the fact the guilty plea discounts violate proportionality, nor that they lead to sentencing of innocents are sufficient reasons to abandon such discounts. Furthermore, it was argued that an approach that attempts to combine the different justice-relevant factors into an overall assessment did not succeed in establishing that guilty plea discounts should be abandoned. Therefore, contrary to what several theorists believe, the practice of providing guilty plea discounts is not in itself something that is a concern for the retributivist in the sense that such discounts should be rejected. However, this is only because there is a greater concern hidden in the debate; namely, the inability of retributivist theory to provide the requisite principled guidance for courts.

References

Ashworth, A (2005) *Sentencing and Criminal Justice* (Cambridge, Cambridge University Press).
Bagaric, M and Brebner, J (2003) 'The Solution to the Dilemma Presented by the Guilty Plea Discount: The Qualified Guilty Plea – I'm Pleading Guilty Only Because of the Discount' 30 *International Journal of the Sociology of Law* 51.
Bradley, GV (1999) 'Plea Bargaining and the Criminal Defendant's Obligation to Plead Guilty' 40 *Texas Law Review* 65.
Caldwell, HM (2011) 'Coercive Plea Bargaining: The Unrecognized Scourge of the Justice System' 61 *Catholic University Law Review* 63.
Dagan, N and Roberts, J (2019) 'Retributivism, Penal Censure, and Life Imprisonment without Parole' 39 *Criminal Justice Ethics* 1.
Davis, M (1992) *To Make the Punishment Fit the Crime* (New York, Westview Press).
Duff, A (1986) *Trials and Punishment* (Cambridge, Cambridge University Press).
Duus-Otterström, G (2020) 'Weighing Relative and Absolute Proportionality in Punishment' in M Tonry (ed), *On One-eyed and Toothless Miscreants: Making the Punishment Fit the Crime?* (New York, Oxford University Press).
Husak, D (2019) 'Why Philosophers (Including Retributivists) Should be Less Resistant to Risk-Based Sentencing' in J de Keijser, J Robert and J Ryberg (eds), *Predictive Sentencing* (Oxford, Hart Publishing).
Kagan, S (2012) *The Geometry of Desert* (Oxford, Oxford University Press).
Kassin SM (2008) 'False Confession: Causes, Consequences, and Implications for Reform' 17 *Current Directions in Psychological Science* 249.
Kleinig, J (1973) *Punishment and Desert* (The Hague, Martinus Nijhoff).
Lippke, R (2006) 'Retributivism and Plea Bargaining' *Criminal Justice Ethics*, summer/fall, 3.
—— (2012) 'Anchoring the Sentencing Scale: A Modest Proposal' 16 *Theoretical Criminology* 463.
Moore, M (1993) 'Justifying Retributivism' 27 *Israel Law Review* 15.
Murphy, JG (1979) *Retribution, Justice, and Therapy* (Dordrecht, Kluwer Academic Publishers).
—— (2014) 'Marxism and Retribution' in T Brooks (ed), *Retribution* (London, Routledge).
Peay, J and Player, E (2018) 'Pleading Guilty: Why Vulnerability Matters' 81 *Modern Law Review* 929.
Rakoff, JS (2014) 'Why Innocent People Plead Guilty', *The New York Review of Books*, November, 20.
Roberts, J and Bradford, B (2015) 'Sentence Reductions for the Guilty Plea in England and Wales: Exploring New Empirical Trends' 12 *Journal of Empirical Legal Studies* 187.
Ryberg, J (2004) *The Ethics of Proportionate Punishment* (Dordrecht, Kluwer Academic Publishers).
—— (2021a) 'Retributivism and the Proportionality Dilemma' 34 *Ratio* 158.
—— (2021b) 'Retributivism and the Dynamic Desert Model: Three Challenges to Dagan and Roberts' 40 *Criminal Justice Ethics* 56.
—— (2021c) 'Sentencing Disparity and Artificial Intelligence', *Journal of Value Inquiry* (online first).

—— (2021d) 'Retributivism and the (Lack of) Justification of Proportionality' 15 *Criminal Law and Philosophy* 447.
—— (2021e) 'The Ethics of Punishment and the Impact Assumption: Reconsidering the Role of Penal Ethicists' 40 *Criminal Justice Ethics* 235.
—— (2023, forthcoming) 'Consequentialism' in J Ryberg (ed), *The Oxford Handbook of the Philosophy of Punishment* (New York, Oxford University Press).
Scheid, DE (1997) 'Constructing a Theory of Punishment, Desert, and the Distribution of Punishment? 10 *The Canadian Journal of Law and Jurisprudence* 441.
Scherr, KC, Redlich AD and Kassin SM, (2020) 'Cumulative Disadvantage: A Psychological Framework for Understanding How Innocence Can Lead to Confession, Wrongful Conviction, and Beyond' 15 *Perspectives on Psychological Science* 353.
Singer, M (1979) *Just Deserts* (New York, Ballenger Publishing Company).
Slobogin, C (2016) 'Plea Bargaining and the Substantive and Procedural Goals of Criminal Justice: From Retribution and Adversarialism to Preventive Justice and Hybrid-inquisitorialism' 57 *William and Mary Law Review* 1505.
Smilansky, S (2021) 'Overpunishment and the Punishment of the Innocent' online first, *Analytic Philosophy* 1.
von Hirsch, A (1993) *Censure and Sanctions* (Oxford, Clarendon Press).
—— (2017) *Deserved Criminal Sentences* (Oxford, Hart Publishing).
von Hirsch, A and Ashworth, A (2005) *Proportionate Sentencing* (Oxford, Oxford University Press).

4

Guilty Pleas, Sentence Reductions, and Non-punishment of the Innocent

ZACHARY HOSKINS*

I. Introduction

It is standard practice in the United Kingdom, the United States and other common law countries to reduce criminal sentences in response to guilty pleas. Sentence reductions are intended as incentives to guilty defendants to plead guilty as early in the process as possible (see, eg, Sentencing Council 2017). Guilty pleas are thought to be beneficial in various ways: they may help to reduce victims' suffering, they can save victims and witnesses from having to testify, but the most often cited benefit is that they save time and money that would otherwise be spent on investigations and trials. As US Supreme Court Justice Anthony Kennedy wrote, 'criminal justice today is for the most part a system of pleas, not a system of trials' (*Lafler v Cooper* 2012), with more than 90 per cent of convictions in both the United Kingdom and the United States obtained via guilty pleas (see Nobles and Schiff 2019: 102). Some have suggested that were all those defendants to carry their cases to trial rather than pleading guilty, the criminal justice system would be in danger of collapse (see, eg, *R v Caley and others* 2012: 6, per Lord Justice Hughes).

Despite its widespread use, the practice of reducing sentences for guilty pleas raises a number of concerns. Some of these concerns are epistemic: the existence of these incentives to plead guilty may undermine our confidence that a guilty plea constitutes sufficiently reliable evidence of a defendant's guilt (especially evidence of guilt beyond a reasonable doubt). Other concerns relate to principles commonly endorsed as constraints on sentencing. For example, giving those who plead guilty a reduced sentence may seem to violate cardinal proportionality insofar as their sentence is less severe than they deserve given the seriousness of their crime and their culpability for it. Also, these sentence reductions may seem to violate ordinal

* I presented a previous draft of this paper at a workshop at Worcester College, Oxford, in March 2022. I am grateful for feedback from the participants at that event, and in particular to Antony Duff and Jesper Ryberg for helpful discussion at that event and afterward.

proportionality insofar as equally culpable offenders guilty of similarly serious crimes may receive sentences of different severity when one but not the other pleads guilty (but see Chapter 3).

This chapter focuses on another worry about sentence reductions for guilty pleas, namely that these reductions violate the commonly accepted prohibition on punishment of the innocent. It is well documented that innocent defendants sometimes plead guilty. Rebecca Helm reports, for example, that in England and Wales from 2012 to 2019, 'of the 128 cases referred to the Court of Appeal by the Criminal Cases Review Commission as potential miscarriages of justice (for review of conviction or conviction and sentence) … approximately 50 cases involved defendants who initially pleaded guilty' (Helm 2019: 425). In the United States, of 129 exonerations in 2020, 29 involved convictions resulting from guilty pleas (National Registry of Exonerations 2020). Innocence Canada has secured 24 exonerations since 1993, and at least five of these cases involved guilty pleas.[1]

Innocent defendants may be motivated to plead guilty for a variety of reasons. They may not be able to afford the costs of going to trial. They may want to avoid staying in prison on remand until the trial begins. They may mistakenly believe they committed the act(s) with which they are charged. They may be seeking to protect the actual culprit from prosecution and punishment (see Sherrin 2011: 7–13). Arguably the most significant incentive for innocent defendants to plead guilty, however, is the desire to minimise their sentences. As noted before, the explicit aim of sentence reductions is to induce *guilty* defendants to plead guilty. But insofar as there is a prudential incentive not to risk the significantly more severe sentence that might follow a trial, this is an incentive to innocent defendants as well as guilty ones. Whether innocent or guilty, if a defendant believes it likely that he would be convicted if he took his case to trial anyway, then it will be tempting to secure a less severe sentence by pleading guilty. Even if the defendant believes it fairly likely that he can win if he takes his case to trial, the range of sentences he would face if convicted at trial might be so unacceptable to him that he might choose to plead guilty and secure the lesser sentence rather than even to risk the more severe sentence. Empirical research generally supports the claim that the prospect of a reduced sentence sometimes motivates innocent people to plead guilty (see, eg, Redlich et al 2017: esp. 349).[2]

This chapter examines whether the practice of offering sentence reductions for guilty pleas violates the prohibition on punishment of the innocent. First, in

[1] See the Innocence Canada website at http://innocencecanada.com/exonerations. For two of the 24 cases, the website did not include details of whether the original conviction resulted from a guilty plea or a trial.

[2] Some studies have found that innocent defendants are less likely to plead guilty than guilty defendants. (See, eg, Gazal-Ayal and Tor 2012). We can acknowledge this discrepancy in the prevalence of guilty pleas while still recognising that innocent defendants are often motivated to plead guilty by the prospect of sentence reductions.

Section II, I consider various interpretations of what this prohibition requires of a system of punishment. Next, in Section III, I contend that insofar as sentence reductions often provide significant prudential incentives to innocent people to plead guilty, these reductions run afoul of the most plausible construal of the prohibition on punishment of the innocent. In Section IV, I consider and respond to some potential objections.

II. The Prohibition on Punishment of the Innocent

The prohibition on punishment of the innocent, as standardly articulated, is essentially a retributivist constraint: it holds that it is inherently wrong to punish the innocent – even if such punishment would contribute to some valuable social end(s) – because this treatment would be *undeserved* by virtue of their prior conduct. To punish an innocent person is thus to wrong that person, to violate her rights. Although the principle is itself retributivist insofar as it is grounded in considerations of desert, one could endorse the constraint without endorsing a uniformly retributivist theory of punishment. Indeed, hybrid accounts of punishment typically adopt it as a constraining principle, along with the prohibition of disproportionate punishment of the guilty. In fact, it is often thought to be a decisive strike against pure consequentialist accounts that they cannot provide principled grounding for these constraints; at best, such theories can endorse the constraints contingently, insofar as the constraints promote the best consequences overall (see, eg, McCloskey 1957; Boonin 2008: 41–46).

Although the prohibition on punishment of the innocent is widely endorsed by punishment theorists, it is often insufficiently clear what precisely the constraint requires. We might construe it as a necessary condition of the justification of particular impositions of punishment: thus, a specific instance of punishment is not justified if the person punished is innocent. This seems plausible enough. (We might, of course, think the State could be excused, albeit not justified, in punishing an innocent person, if it did so mistakenly and having followed the appropriate procedures and observing the relevant safeguards.) But what if we focus instead on the institution of punishment rather than individual instances? What does the prohibition on punishment of the innocent tell us about the institution? Here I consider several possible interpretations of the prohibition.

First, we might interpret it as holding that for the institution of punishment to be justified, innocent people must never be punished. Richard Lempert endorses this sort of construal as the basis for his objection to capital punishment. He writes, 'We know as a statistical matter that if a state executes often enough some innocent lives will be lost. … Nothing about retributivism allows us to sacrifice the lives of unknown innocents in the interest of just vengeance' (Lempert 1981: 1183). Although Lempert focuses on capital punishment, his argument has implications for punishment more generally. He contends essentially that any criminal justice system will inevitably make mistakes, and thus it will subject at least some innocent people to burdensome treatment that they do not deserve.[3] The retributivist constraint, as he interprets it, does not permit the imposition of undeserved burdens on the innocent even in rare cases, and so actual systems of punishment cannot be justified on retributivist terms.

But this seems too strict a construal. Even with robust safeguards in place to avoid conviction and punishment of innocent people, it is foreseeable that at least some innocent people will be mistakenly convicted and punished. To claim that the institution of punishment can only be justified if no innocent person is ever punished is, essentially, to claim that the institution of punishment cannot be justified. But those who endorse the prohibition on punishment of the innocent as a constraint are not typically abolitionists about punishment. This is not because they are unaware that even carefully designed systems for determining criminal guilt will inevitably result in the punishment of at least some innocent people. More plausibly, it is because they believe there is a compelling rationale for the institution of punishment (be it crime reduction, the communication of deserved censure, or something else), and they regard this rationale as sufficiently weighty that an institution that serves this function can be justified even if it foreseeably results in the inadvertent punishment of some innocent people. My own view is that the compelling rationale for punishment is to help protect public safety and well-being, and that this function is sufficiently important that the institution is not made illegitimate by the mistaken punishment of some innocent person(s). Thus, I suggest we should reject this strict interpretation of the prohibition on punishment of the innocent.

A second possible interpretation of this constraint is that it prohibits *deliberately* punishing the innocent (see, eg, Moore 1997: 158). Setting aside definitional questions of whether deliberately inflicting such treatment on those we know to be innocent constitutes punishment at all, it is clear at least that this construal of the prohibition does not imply that a system of punishment is unjustified if innocent people are ever mistakenly punished. If the first interpretation of the constraint was too strong, however, this second interpretation is too weak. It would fail to rule out a system in which, although innocent people were never deliberately punished, the risks of mistaken punishment of the innocent were widely recognised and entirely disregarded. That this weaker interpretation of the constraint cannot rule out a system of punishment that makes no effort to avoid inadvertent punishment of the innocent is, I suggest, good reason to reject it.

A third possible interpretation of the constraint is that it prohibits punishing the innocent except insofar as doing so facilitates punishment of the guilty to an

[3] Lempert suggests that his conclusion about capital punishment does not generalise to other forms of punishment, specifically to life imprisonment, because many who are sentenced to life in prison 'will prove their blamelessness after conviction, be released early from prison, and in all probability be compensated to some extent' (Lempert 1981: 1183 n 16). For a persuasive rebuttal of Lempert on this point, see Alexander (1983: 235).

extent that the justice of the latter outweighs the injustice of the former. Larry Alexander describes this view as 'strong retributivism', and he contends that it offers a plausible way of resisting objections to retributivism grounded in concerns about punishment of the innocent. Alexander writes:

> [Strong retributivism] deems as equally unjust failing to punish the guilty and punishing the innocent. Justice requires that we give everyone what he deserves, positively or negatively. A system of punishment will result in some innocent persons not getting what they deserve (freedom from punishment). Lack of a system of punishment will result in some guilty persons not getting what they deserve (punishment). Both results are equally unjust. But if unjust results are inevitable whether we punish or not, our preference is for fewer unjust results. A system of punishment, if well-designed, will produce fewer instances of injustice .... (1983: 238)

On this interpretation, a legal system that resulted in the punishment of some innocent people would be justifiable as long as such impositions of punishment made possible (or were an unavoidable side-effect of) the punishment of a greater number of guilty people who would not otherwise have been punished. A key problem with this interpretation, however, is that it equates the wrongness of failing to punish one offender with the wrongness of punishing one non-offender. Thus it leads to counterintuitive results. For example, if we have four suspects in custody for some crime, and we know that two of them are guilty and two are innocent, but we have no way of knowing which two are guilty, then according to 'strong retributivism' as Alexander characterises it, we would be as justified in punishing all four people as in letting all four go free. After all, letting all four go free would result in two cases of guilty people not getting what they deserve (punishment) whereas punishing all four would result in two cases of innocent people not getting what they deserve (freedom from punishment). Essentially, we could justifiably decide whether to punish none or all four with a coin flip. This will strike many of us as deeply unjust, though, because we think it is morally worse to subject an innocent person to intentionally burdensome, intentionally condemnatory treatment than to fail to subject a guilty person to such treatment.

This asymmetry in our intuitions about punishing the innocent and failing to punish the guilty is evident in William Blackstone's commonly endorsed principle that 'it is better that ten guilty persons escape than that one innocent suffer' (Blackstone 1893: ch 27). It is reflected in the common endorsement, by theorists who defend hybrid theories of punishment, of the constraint on punishment of the innocent but not a constraint on failure to punish the guilty (see, eg, Hart 1960; Corlett 2001, 78; Flanders 2017). It is also reflected in commonly held views about proportionality in sentencing: many argue that punishing offenders less severely than they deserve could in some cases be justified (for example, when mercy is warranted), but that punishing more severely than is warranted is never justified (see, eg, Duff 2001: 140–41; Corlett 2001: 78). The underlying intuition reflected in this asymmetry regarding deviations from proportionality in sentence severity is essentially the same as the intuition underlying the asymmetrical views about punishment of the innocent and non-punishment of the guilty: it is worse to impose onerous, condemnatory treatment when it is not deserved than it is to fail to impose such treatment when it is deserved. Thus we should reject this interpretation, grounded in Alexander's 'strong retributivism', of the prohibition on punishment of the innocent.

It seems, then, that a requirement that a system of punishment, to be legitimate, must never mistakenly punish anyone is too strict. But also, to require only that the system not intentionally punish the innocent could permit a system in which large numbers of innocent people are inadvertently punished. Similarly, a prohibition on mistaken punishment of the innocent except insofar as this contributes to more instances of punishment of the guilty could be consistent with a substantial number of mistaken punishments of the innocent.

A fourth option, then, would be to interpret the prohibition on punishment of the innocent as holding that a system of punishment is unjustified if it results in significant numbers of innocent people being punished. One challenge presented by this interpretation of the constraint would be in determining how many instances of punishment of the innocent would rise to the level of constituting *significant numbers* and thus would render the system illegitimate. There seems no obvious, non-arbitrary basis for settling this issue. This is complicated by the fact that we do not know how many innocent people have been mistakenly punished. Estimates of rates of mistaken conviction vary significantly: in the US context, for example, estimates range from as low as 0.5 per cent to as high as 15 per cent (see, eg, Zalman 2012; Gross et al 2014; Walsh et al 2017; McCloskey 1989; Poveda 2001). So as a practical matter, interpreting the prohibition on punishment of the innocent as a requirement that mistaken punishment of the innocent remains below some given level will create challenges. More fundamentally, this construal of the prohibition would permit a penal system in which the State made no real effort to avoid punishment of the innocent but, by sheer luck, did not in fact punish many innocent people. Many of us would object to such a system, and rightly so, as it fails to take the risk of mistaken punishment of the innocent sufficiently seriously.

A more plausible account, I suggest, will accept that punishment of the innocent, even if inadvertent, represents a serious challenge to the legitimacy of a penal system, and that it is not something that can be legitimated merely by corresponding gains in punishment of the guilty. But it also will acknowledge that the State has a compelling interest in protecting public safety and well-being, and that insofar as the institution of punishment plays a key role in this regard, the institution will not be rendered unjustified by the mistaken conviction and punishment of a comparatively small number of innocent people.

My suggestion for such a principle draws from another context, namely philosophical debates about the ethics of war. A central question in these debates is when, if ever, causing inadvertent civilian casualties can be morally permissible in the pursuit of some valuable goal in times of war. One prominent answer to this question is to invoke the Doctrine of Double Effect, which holds, basically, that if the casualties are an unintended side-effect of an action, rather than the means by which the action achieves its end, and if the good outcomes promoted by the action sufficiently outweigh the costs, then the action can be justified (see, eg, McIntyre 2018). The Doctrine of Double Effect has proved controversial (see Bennett 1981; see also Fitzpatrick 2012) and my aim here is not to defend it. Rather, I want to focus on one prominent objection to this doctrine, namely that it is too permissive. It is not enough that combatants do not intend to harm civilians; rather, what is required is that combatants *intend not to harm them*. Michael Walzer thus proposed that military actors must aim to avoid the foreseeable harm by making a positive commitment to save innocent lives, and indeed that they must be willing to accept additional risks or sacrifice some benefits in order to avoid harm to innocents (Walzer 1977: 151–59; see also Lee 2004).

In my view, these considerations are relevant to State punishment as well. For State impositions of punishment to be legitimate, it is not enough that the State not intend to punish innocent people; it should make a serious commitment not to punish the innocent. Institutions can reflect this intention by taking significant steps – even accepting some additional risks or sacrificing some benefits – to avoid punishment of the innocent. This is what the prohibition on punishment of the innocent requires of legitimate systems of punishment. It does not require that no innocent person ever be punished, but it requires more than merely the avoidance of deliberate punishment of the innocent. And it does not treat punishment of the innocent as a wrong that can easily be traded off against the supposedly equal wrong of non-punishment of the guilty. Rather, punishment of the innocent is a significantly more serious wrong than non-punishment of the guilty, and although the compelling interest in maintaining an institution of State punishment to help protect public safety and well-being is sufficiently significant that the institution's legitimacy is not cancelled by some instances of inadvertent punishment of the innocent, the institution's legitimacy does require that the State demonstrate its commitment not to punish the innocent by taking substantial steps to avoid this. In the next section, I consider whether this requirement is met in current legal practice.

III. Criminal Trials, Guilty Pleas and Not Punishing the Innocent

Do our criminal justice practices reflect a serious commitment not to punish the innocent? In this section, I contrast criminal trials with the plea process. In criminal trials, the State calls on defendants to answer to charges of wrongdoing, and it seeks to determine whether they are guilty because there is a compelling public interest in holding accountable those who have committed crimes. But also, a host of protections are in place to help guard against the conviction of innocent defendants. The presumption is that defendants are innocent and the burden falls on the prosecution to prove their guilt, rather than requiring defendants to prove their innocence. The prosecution must prove guilt to a very high standard, beyond reasonable doubt (rather than, say, the lower standards of 'balance of probabilities' or 'preponderance of evidence' used in civil cases). Defendants typically have a right to face, and have their defence counsel cross-examine, their accusers. They also have a right to access any exculpatory evidence possessed by the prosecution. Double jeopardy protections prevent those who are found not guilty from being prosecuted repeatedly for the same crime. What is more, defendants who are found guilty at trial have a right to appeal their convictions. Thus, while criminal trials reflect the State's interest in determining whether individuals are guilty of the crimes of which they are accused, so that the guilty can be held accountable, the various protections afforded to defendants also reflect a serious commitment to protect against conviction and punishment of innocent people.

As discussed earlier, however, the lion's share of convictions in the United Kingdom, the United States and many other countries come as a result of guilty pleas, typically incentivised by sentence reductions (see Fair Trials 2022). Criminal justice today is, as Justice Kennedy pointed out (*Lafler v Cooper* 2012), more a system of pleas than of trials. We should focus, then, on the plea system and whether it reflects a serious commitment to avoid punishment of innocent people.

Most importantly, as I have discussed, a system in which sentence reductions attach to guilty pleas creates a prudential incentive for defendants, innocent as well as guilty, to plead guilty. Arguably, a system that creates such incentives cannot be said to reflect a serious commitment to avoid punishment of the innocent. But several further features of existing plea systems exacerbate the issue. For example, the prospect of innocent defendants being induced to plead guilty is that much greater in jurisdictions where prosecutors intentionally offer the largest sentence reductions when their cases are the weakest. A Chicago defence attorney describes it this way:

> When a prosecutor has a dead-bang case, he is likely to come up with an impossible offer like thirty to fifty years. When the case has a hole in it, however, the prosecutor may scale the offer all the way down to probation. The prosecutors' goal is to get something from every defendant, and the correctional treatment the defendant may require is the last thing on their minds. (Quoted in Alschuler 1968: 60; see also, eg, Scott and Stuntz 1992: 1946)

Weakness of a case is not always a symptom of a defendant's innocence, but often it is. Thus, as Albert Alschuler writes, 'the greatest pressures to plead guilty are brought to bear on defendants who may be innocent' (1968).

Another feature of many plea systems is that the right of access to exculpatory evidence does not apply at the pre-plea stage. The prosecution is only required to disclose evidence that might indicate a defendant's innocence once the defendant has pleaded not guilty.[4] Thus whereas a defendant who takes his case to trial has a legal right to see exculpatory evidence police investigators may have found, it is often the case that defendants considering whether to plead guilty and receive a sentence reduction or go to trial and lose the reduction are not afforded access to this information.

The plea process also differs from the trial process with respect to the likelihood of appeals. In England and Wales, the Court of Appeal treats convictions based on guilty pleas as presumptively safe. As the court explained in *Asiedu*,

> ordinarily, once he has admitted such facts by an unambiguous and deliberately intended plea of guilty, there cannot then be an appeal against his conviction, for the simple reason that there is nothing unsafe about a conviction based on the defendant's own voluntary confession in open court. (*R v Asiedu* 2015: 19)

The right to appeal a conviction is therefore much more limited for those who plead guilty than for those found guilty at trial, and successful guilty plea appeals are rare. As Richard Nobles and David Schiff write:

> A plea will be treated as a nullity if it can be shown to be either equivocal or involuntary. Where it is not, it will be treated by the Court of Appeal as an acknowledgement of guilt by the defendant, giving rise to a definite presumption that the conviction is safe. That presumption operates in a manner close to a bar on appeals, given the difficulties of rebutting it. (2019: 105; see also Campbell et al 2019: 315–16)

So whereas an innocent defendant who loses his case at trial still has a reasonable chance to appeal his conviction – grounds for appeal might include fresh evidence, failure to disclose exculpatory evidence, and jury irregularities – an innocent defendant who pleads guilty has comparatively little prospect of a successful appeal.

Thus with the plea process we have a system in which defendants are offered significant incentives in the form of sentence reductions to plead guilty (in some cases, larger incentives the weaker the case against them), in which they are not afforded access to exculpatory information, and in which they have relatively little chance to appeal their conviction later. In my view, such a process does not reflect a serious commitment to avoid conviction and punishment of the innocent. I contend, then, that the plea process as it currently operates is inconsistent with the most plausible construal of the prohibition on punishment of the innocent.

Could current plea practices be reformed so as to be consistent with the prohibition on punishment of the innocent? Defendants could be given access to exculpatory evidence prior to making their plea decisions. Also, those who plead

[4] In the United Kingdom, the duty to disclose exculpatory evidence commences once the defendant (in the Magistrates' Court) has pleaded not guilty and the case goes to trial, or (for cases going to the Crown Court) once the case has been sent to trial (see Ministry of Justice 2020: 16). In the United States, federal courts have split about whether prosecutors have a duty to disclose prior to a guilty plea or not until the case goes to trial (see Petegorsky 2013; Clarke 2019).

guilty could be afforded more opportunity to appeal their convictions, in line with those who are found guilty at trial. And in those legal systems where prosecutors have discretion to offer the largest sentence reductions when their cases are the weakest, this discretion could be eliminated. Still, as long as a system offers innocent defendants a prudential incentive, in the form of a significant sentence reduction, to plead guilty, it is difficult to see the system as reflecting a serious commitment to avoid punishment of the innocent.

Rather than eliminating sentence reductions, of course, we might endorse reducing them to a level at which they would not provide innocent defendants with a significant incentive to plead guilty. Liz Campbell, Andrew Ashworth and Mike Redmayne, despite scepticism about the legitimacy of offering sentence reductions at all, suggest that sentence reductions of no more than 10 per cent would reduce the incentive to plead guilty to a tolerable level and ensure that the innocent defendant's freedom of choice is maintained (Campbell et al 2019: 341).[5] The worry with such a proposal, however, is that it either will not address the injustice it aims to address, or it will undermine the central rationale for offering sentence reductions for guilty pleas. That is, it seems that either the prospect of a sentence reduction will provide a compelling prudential reason to plead guilty for a defendant worried about the prospect of losing at trial and facing a stiffer sentence, or it will not. If this prospect does provide such a prudential reason for guilty defendants, then it will, by the same token, be a reason for many innocent defendants too. If it does not provide such a reason for innocent defendants (because we have reduced the maximum discount to a level that would not be a significant incentive for them), then it will not provide such a reason for guilty defendants either, and thus we would lose the central rationale for the discounts: to persuade guilty defendants to plead guilty and thus forego a trial.

It is possible, however, despite the worry just discussed, that some modest level of sentence discount exists that would entice a significant number of guilty defendants to plead guilty without similarly persuading a significant number of innocent defendants to plead guilty. Perhaps innocent defendants are, on balance, somewhat less receptive to the prudential incentives of a sentence discount, as they are also motivated (whereas guilty defendants are not) by the knowledge that they are innocent and a desire not to confess to a crime they did not commit (see, eg, Gazal-Ayal et al 2012). It is an empirical question, beyond the scope of this chapter, whether some modest level of sentence discount could serve to motivate guilty pleas from a significant number of guilty defendants while not also motivating guilty pleas from a significant number of innocent defendants. For present purposes, however, two things are worth noting. First, if such a modest level of sentence reduction could be found, it would be significantly lower than the sentence discounts currently on offer in many legal systems.

[5] See also Gormley et al (2020: 14) for the suggestion that current levels of discounts, at least in England and Wales, may often be sufficiently modest in this respect.

Second, even if some modest level of sentence discount could be said not to incentivise guilty pleas from a significant number of innocent defendants, reducing existing guilty plea sentence reductions to such a level would not in itself be sufficient to render the plea process consistent with the prohibition on punishment of the innocent. I have contended that the most plausible interpretation of this constraint is that the State should demonstrate a serious commitment to avoid punishment of the innocent. I have further argued that a system that creates incentives for innocent people to plead guilty violates this constraint. But even if the State does not actively create such incentives, this in itself is not enough to demonstrate its commitment to avoid punishment of the innocent. Analogously, it is not sufficient to demonstrate my commitment to minimising vandalism of university property that I stop offering cash prizes to my students to see who can hit the vice chancellor's window with the most tomatoes in under a minute. More generally, not incentivising X is not sufficient to demonstrate a commitment to minimising X. Thus, in addition to eliminating sentence reductions, or at least reducing them to a level that does not provide a significant incentive for innocent defenders to plead guilty, the State would also need to incorporate measures into the plea process to help ensure that innocent defendants do not plead guilty. As noted earlier, such measures should include, at least, a requirement to disclose to defendants exculpatory evidence prior to their plea decision, and more robust opportunities to appeal convictions resulting from guilty pleas. In the next section, I consider potential objections to my account.

IV. Objections and Responses

I have argued that a commitment to avoid punishment of the innocent prohibits creating incentives to plead guilty, in the form of sentence discounts, because, even if these discounts are expressly intended to motivate guilty defendants to plead guilty, we know they also serve to motivate innocent defendants to plead guilty. One might object, however, that we create analogous incentive structures in other contexts without apparently doing anything impermissible. Consider, for example, the sale of alcohol and assume for argument's sake that whereas it is permissible to sell alcohol to adults, we should not sell to minors. Suppose, too, that sellers not only should not deliberately sell to minors but, further, should demonstrate a commitment not to sell to them. Now suppose that a store manager launches a promotional campaign to boost sales, including the offer of some incentive (eg, entry into a prize draw with each purchase). The aim is to motivate adults to buy, but the store manager knows the new incentive will also motivate at least some minors to attempt to purchase alcohol. Despite introducing some additional safeguards (more stringent ID checks, etc), the manager is reasonably sure that at least some clever minors, motivated by the new incentive, will manage to buy alcohol. The objection, then, is that in such a case it is nevertheless permissible to offer the incentive, and as this case is analogous in relevant respects to the offering of guilty plea sentence discounts, it is similarly permissible to offer such discounts.[6]

There is an important respect, however, in which we can distinguish the offer of guilty plea sentence discounts from cases such as the example of incentivising the purchase of alcohol. Although we think it is undesirable for various reasons for minors to purchase and drink alcohol, the minor who buys and drinks alcohol is not thereby wronged. Thus, when the store manager mistakenly sells alcohol to the minor, he does not wrong the minor (or contribute to the minor's being wronged).[7] By contrast, the State does wrong the innocent person when it punishes her. I mentioned earlier that the State may be excused for punishing the innocent person if, say, it took appropriate steps to determine her guilt and afforded her proper safeguards, etc. But the innocent person subjected to intentionally burdensome, condemnatory treatment is wronged nonetheless. I have argued above that the mere fact that the State inadvertently wrongs some individuals does not in itself demonstrate that the institution of punishment is unjustified. But for the institution to be justified, it must be structured in a way that demonstrates a serious commitment to avoid punishing the innocent. This means, among other things, that the State should not create incentives for innocent people to plead guilty.

Does a commitment to avoid punishment of the innocent also prohibit the State from making defendants aware of existing reasons to plead guilty? A prosecutor, acting as the agent of the State, might explain to a defendant the strength of the case against her, and on the basis of this information the defendant might decide to plead guilty (even if there were no guilty plea sentence reductions, the defendant might simply not want to go to trial if an acquittal seemed highly unlikely). Such information might serve to motivate innocent defendants as well as guilty ones. In this sort of case, however, the prosecutor does not create incentives to plead guilty; he merely makes defendants aware of existing considerations that may be relevant to their choice of plea. The likelihood of losing at trial may be an incentive to some defendants to plead guilty and avoid the hassle, but the prosecutor does not create this incentive. In my view, making defendants aware of the strength of the case against them is consistent with demonstrating a commitment to avoid punishment of the innocent.

A different sort of objection to my critique of guilty plea sentence reductions might focus on the benefits of the practice. As mentioned before, guilty pleas may relieve victims and witnesses of the stress of having to testify, and they may help reduce the impact of the crime on victims. If sentence reductions facilitate these benefits, then this seems to count in their favour. What is more, insofar as sentence reductions result in a higher proportion of guilty defendants being convicted and

[6] Thanks to Antony Duff for suggesting this example.

[7] One might argue, I suppose, that the State does wrong minors when it (even inadvertently) sells them alcohol. I am sceptical that such an argument would succeed. But if it were successful, then it would follow on my account that creating incentives to purchase alcohol, which will inevitably motivate minors as well as adults, would be impermissible.

punished than would otherwise be the case, they would seem, at least in this regard, to further the ends of maintaining a system of punishment. This is true whether the appropriate rationale for punishment is to help reduce crime (through deterrence, incapacitation or reform) or to convey deserved censure or mete out deserved suffering. One might worry, then, that my critique of sentence reductions does not take seriously enough the benefits that guilty pleas promote, and thus the importance of sentence reductions in achieving these valuable ends.

I accept that there are benefits to allowing defendants the option of pleading guilty rather than taking their case to trial. It is inappropriate, however, for the State to pursue these benefits at the expense of innocent defendants. This does not mean that offering the option of guilty pleas is unjustified if it ever results in innocent defendants pleading guilty and facing punishment. But I have argued that the State must demonstrate a serious concern to avoid punishment of the innocent. Demonstrating such a concern need not commit the State to removing the option of guilty pleas, and thus requiring that every case be tried in court. But it does require, among other things, that the State not create significant prudential incentives to innocent defendants to plead guilty. If not creating such incentives means also that more guilty defendants take their cases to trial, and this leads to additional stress for some victims or witnesses, or if it means that guilty defendants are acquitted who would otherwise have pleaded guilty and faced punishment, then I acknowledge that these are genuine costs. But in my view, they are outweighed by the wrong done when innocent defendants are incentivised to plead guilty.

A different possible objection focuses on the value of guilty plea sentence reductions to innocent defendants themselves. According to this objection, if our concern is to protect against punishment of the innocent, then this could count in favour of guilty plea sentence discounts as well as against them. First, we know that some number of innocent defendants will plead guilty even without the incentive of sentence reductions. If sentence reductions are eliminated, then these innocent people will be punished more severely than they will be if the reductions are offered (see Chapter 3). Similarly, some number of innocent defendants may, without the incentive of a guilty plea sentence reduction, choose to take their case to court, and some of these defendants will be convicted. These defendants might have chosen to plead guilty to get the sentence reduction had it been offered; thus here again, the availability of the sentence reduction might contribute to less punishment of the innocent.

I have contended that the best construal of the prohibition on punishment of the innocent is that the State is required to demonstrate a serious commitment to avoid such punishment. Suppose, then, a system in which guilty plea sentence reductions are not offered; suppose, too, that the State knows that in this system some number of innocent defendants plead guilty and are subject to punishment, and also that some number of innocent people take their cases to court and are convicted. The question is what the State might do to demonstrate a serious commitment to avoid punishing the innocent. Specifically, could the State demonstrate such a commitment by introducing a practice of offering sentence discounts as prudential incentives to plead guilty, knowing that this will persuade some innocent defendants to plead guilty who would not otherwise have done so but also will lessen the punishment of those people who were going to plead guilty regardless or who would otherwise take their cases to court and lose?

It strikes me as counterintuitive that introducing such a practice would demonstrate a commitment to avoid punishing the innocent. To see why, consider again the prohibition on punishment of the innocent. Earlier, I wrote that this constraint is essentially a retributivist principle (though it may be an element of hybrid accounts as well as pure retributivist accounts); it holds that punishment of the innocent is inherently wrong because it is undeserved. Although retributivism is typically contrasted with consequentialism, some theorists have pointed out that one might endorse a consequentialist version of retributivism, according to which just desert, which has inherent value, is to be promoted or maximised (see, eg, Moore 1997: 156–58; but see Dolinko 1997). On a consequentialist view, whatever it is that we take to have value, the appropriate response is to promote it (see Pettit 1991: 19). Importantly, if violating or undermining the value in some instances leads to more of it overall, then this is what consequentialism tells us to do.[8] If we interpret the retributivist prohibition on punishment of the innocent in this consequentialist sense, then it might make sense to institute a practice that incentivises some innocent defendants to plead guilty and face undeserved punishment if doing so contributed to less undeserved punishment more generally.

The problem with interpreting the constraint as a consequentialist-retributivist principle is that it opens the constraint up to just the sort of objection that retributivists have often levelled against consequentialist theories of punishment more generally: this is the Kantian objection that consequentialist punishment uses the offender as a mere means to promote some ostensibly valuable social end (see, eg, Murphy 1973: 219). To attempt to justify a practice that incentivises some innocent defendants to plead guilty and face punishment (which thereby wrongs them) on grounds that this practice promotes less punishment of the innocent overall appears similarly to use these innocent defendants as mere means, or tools, to the end of minimising punishment of the innocent. It is true that in some cases innocent defendants who are persuaded to plead guilty to secure the reduced sentence would otherwise have been convicted at trial; it might seem that these defendants are not used as *mere* means in the service of reducing punishment of the innocent, as they themselves benefit from such a reduction. But there will be some number of innocent defendants who will be persuaded to plead guilty by the prudential

[8] This is the case not only for direct forms of consequentialism such as act consequentialism, but also for indirect forms of consequentialism such as rule consequentialism or motive consequentialism. On any of these accounts, the rightness or wrongness of our action, rules for action, motives for action, etc, will be a matter of their consequences. And if occasionally acting in violation of what we value (or acting on a rule that tells us sometimes to violate what we value, or acting from a motive to violate what we value) thereby promotes more of the value overall, then consequentialism tells us to do that.

incentive of a sentence discount who would have been acquitted had they taken their case to trial.[9] These people, it seems, are treated as mere means in the service of reducing punishment of the guilty overall. But again, retributivists often critique consequentialist accounts specifically for implying that it can be permissible to use some people as mere means to securing some valuable social end.

I contend that the prohibition on punishment of the innocent is best interpreted instead as a deontological-retributivist principle rather than a consequentialist-retributivist principle. A deontological account holds that the right response to whatever we value may sometimes be to respect it, or honour it, rather than to promote it (see Pettit 1991: 19). For a deontologist, respecting some value will sometimes mean not violating it even if doing so would result in an overall net gain of that value. (A deontologist who values honesty, for example, may hold that lying is wrong even if by telling a few lies a person could promote more honesty overall.) A deontological interpretation of the prohibition on punishment of the innocent holds that such punishment is unjustified insofar as it is undeserved, and the State should demonstrate a serious commitment to avoid such punishment; this is so even if a practice that incentivises some innocent people to plead guilty contributes to less punishment of the innocent overall.

This same sort of reasoning can also help to make clear why it would not be appropriate to impose a sentence *premium* for guilty pleas. One might think, given the account I have defended here, with its emphasis on demonstrating a commitment not to punish the innocent, that the State should therefore impose a premium for guilty pleas to disincentivise them. Such a suggestion will likely strike many as implausible, but one might wonder whether an endorsement of not offering guilty plea sentence discounts must also commit us to this further measure.[10]

Demonstrating a commitment to avoid punishment of the innocent need not commit us to take every step that might serve this end, however; we can acknowledge that there are appropriate and inappropriate ways to demonstrate this commitment. One key problem with imposing guilty plea sentence premiums is that guilty defendants who want to accept responsibility for what they have done by pleading guilty will be punished more severely for doing so. In effect, this would be to subject such defendants to a greater degree of intentionally burdensome, censuring treatment simply because they chose to be honest, to take responsibility for what they did. The additional punishment represented by the sentence premium would thus be undeserved, and just as punishing innocent people wrongs them insofar as the punishment is undeserved, punishing guilty people more severely than they deserve wrongs them, too. If, as I have argued, the concern motivating the prohibition on punishment of the innocent is the deontological-retributivist concern not to subject people to harsh treatment they do not deserve, then we cannot justify a policy that leads to the imposition of undeserved degrees

[9] We should expect such cases to be especially common in jurisdictions where, as discussed earlier, prosecutors offer the largest discounts when their cases are the weakest.

[10] Thanks to Jesper Ryberg for raising this concern.

of punishment on guilty defendants simply for their choice to own up to what they did, even if such a policy also serves to reduce undeserved punishment of some innocent defendants by dissuading them from pleading guilty. Subjecting honest guilty defendants to this undeserved punishment (thus wronging them) merely in the service of reducing undeserved punishment of other, innocent defendants would be to use the guilty defendants as mere means to this further end.

There are other ways to demonstrate a commitment to avoid punishment of the innocent, however, that do not require using some defendants as mere means. For those innocent people who plead guilty regardless of the sentence reduction, we should ask why this happens and if there are any steps that we can take to minimise this. Some innocent defendants plead guilty to avoid long periods of pre-trial detention. We should thus work to shorten the time between arrest and the trial so that this becomes less of an incentive for innocent people to plead guilty. Other defendants plead guilty because they cannot afford the financial costs of a trial. A concern to avoid punishment of the innocent should spur us to look for ways to alleviate the financial burdens of taking one's case to trial. For those innocent defendants who do take their cases to trial, there are numerous measures in place (some of which I mentioned earlier) to protect against conviction and punishment of the innocent. Although, foreseeably, some innocent people are mistakenly convicted anyway, it is nonetheless the case that the State demonstrates a commitment to avoid such outcomes. If, however, we begin to discover that large numbers of people convicted at trial are in fact innocent, then a commitment to avoid punishment of the innocent should spur us to consider whether additional safeguards are warranted.

V. Conclusion

I have contended that the practice of offering significant sentence discounts as prudential incentives to defendants to plead guilty violates the prohibition on punishment of the innocent. In this concluding section, I want to return to the claim, mentioned at the start of this chapter, that were most defendants who now plead guilty to take their cases to trial instead, the criminal justice system would be in danger of collapse. Insofar as sentence discounts incentivise guilty pleas, one might worry that any proposal to eliminate or greatly restrict the use of such discounts would threaten to bring the system to a halt. To make matters worse, I have also suggested that a commitment to avoid punishing innocent people should lead us to require disclosure of exculpatory evidence to defendants at the pre-plea stage; to offer defendants convicted based on guilty pleas more opportunity to appeal their convictions; to reduce the time spent in pre-trial detention; and to reduce or eliminate the financial burdens of trials for defendants. These measures would all require additional resources. Thus it may seem that these proposals, albeit well intended, are ultimately unrealistic.

If the criminal justice system would creak under the weight of what I take to be reasonable proposals on their merits, then I suggest we would do better to ask why the system itself has got to this point. It has not always been the case that more than 90 per cent of convictions came from pleas rather than trials (see, eg, Langbein 2003, 18–20; Rakoff 2014; Chapter 12). Why is the current system such that without a practice that incentivises high levels of guilty pleas, it cannot function? One plausible contributing factor is that too much conduct is criminalised. In England and Wales, for example, the Law Commission reported that more than 3,000 crimes were added to the statute book between 1997 and 2010 (Criminal Liability in Regulatory Contexts 2010: 5; on over-criminalisation in the American context, see Husak 2008). Lower levels of criminalisation would lead to fewer people being brought into the criminal justice process, which would reduce the strain on the system's resources. Conversely, if the public or our lawmakers are unwilling to accept a smaller criminal justice system, then we should be prepared to pay the additional costs required to ensure that the system operates in a justifiable way. In particular, if demonstrating a serious commitment to avoid punishing the innocent means the criminal justice system becomes less efficient or more expensive, then that is the price we should pay. To borrow a quote from detective Kima Griggs in *The Wire*, 'sometimes things just got to play hard'.

References

Alexander, L (1983) 'Retributivism and the Inadvertent Punishment of the Innocent' 2 *Law and Philosophy* 233.

Alschuler, AW (1968) 'The Prosecutor's Role in Plea Bargaining' 36 *University of Chicago Law Review* 50.

Bennett, J (1981) 'Morality and Consequences' in S McMurrin (ed), *The Tanner Lectures on Human Values* II (Salt Lake City, UT, University of Utah Press).

Blackstone, W (1893) *Commentaries on the Laws of England in Four Books*, vol 2 (Philadelphia, PA: J.B. Lippincott Co) https://oll.libertyfund.org/title/sharswood-commentaries-on-the-laws-of-england-in-four-books-vol-2

Boonin, D (2008) *The Problem of Punishment* (Cambridge, Cambridge University Press).

Campbell, L, Ashworth, A and Redmayne, M (2019) *The Criminal Process*, 5th edn (Oxford, Oxford University Press).

Clarke, E (2019) 'Entitling the Accused to Exculpatory Evidence: Why Prosecutors Should Have to Disclose During Plea Bargaining' 56 *American Criminal Law Review* 65.

Corlett, JA (2001) 'Making Sense of Retributivism' 76 *Philosophy* 77.

Criminal Liability in Regulatory Contexts (2010) *The Law Commission, Consultation Paper No. 195*, www.lawcom.gov.uk/app/uploads/2015/06/cp195_Criminal_Liability_consultation.pdf

Dolinko, D (1997) 'Retributivism, Consequentialism, and the Intrinsic Goodness of Punishment' 16 *Law and Philosophy* 507.

Duff, RA (2001) *Punishment, Communication, and Community* (Oxford, Oxford University Press).

Fair Trials (2022) *The Disappearing Trial*, www.fairtrials.org/app/uploads/2022/01/The-Disappearing-Trial-report.pdf
Fitzpatrick, WJ (2012) 'The Doctrine of Double Effect: Intention and Permissibility' 7 *Philosophy Compass* 183.
Flanders, C (2017) 'Punishment, Liberalism, and Public Reason' 36 *Criminal Justice Ethics* 61.
Gazal-Ayal, O and Tor, A (2012) 'The Innocence Effect' 62 *Duke Law Journal* 339.
Gormley, J, Roberts, JV, Bild, J and Harris, L (2020) 'Sentence Reductions for Guilty Pleas: A Review of Policy, Practice, and Research', *Sentencing Academy*, https://sentencingacademy.org.uk/wp-content/uploads/2020/12/Sentence-Reductions-for-Guilty-Pleas-3.pdf
Gross, SR, O'Brien, B, Hu, C and Kennedy, EH (2014) 'Rate of False Conviction of Criminal Defendants Who Are Sentenced to Death' 111 *Proceedings of the National Academy of Sciences* 7230.
Hart, HLA (1960) 'Prolegomenon to the Principles of Punishment' 60 *Proceedings of the Aristotelian Society* 1.
Helm, RK (2019) 'Constrained Waiver of Trial Rights? Incentives to Plead Guilty and the Right to a Fair Trial' 46 *Journal of Law and Society* 423.
Husak, D (2008) *Overcriminalization: The Limits of the Criminal Law* (Oxford, Oxford University Press).
Kelly, W, Hussemann, J, Flynn, A, Yahner, J and Golian, L (2017) 'Estimating the Prevalence of Wrongful Conviction', www.ncjrs.gov/pdffiles1/nij/grants/251115.pdf
Langbein, JH (2003) *The Origins of Adversary Criminal Trial* (Oxford, Oxford University Press).
Lee, S (2004) 'Double Effect, Double Intention, and Asymmetric Warfare' 3 *Journal of Military Ethics* 233.
Lempert, RO (1981) 'Desert and Deterrence: An Assessment of the Moral Bases of the Case for Capital Punishment' 79 *Michigan Law Review* 1177.
McCloskey, HJ (1957) 'An Examination of Restricted Utilitarianism' 66 *The Philosophical Review* 466.
McCloskey, J (1989) 'Commentary: Convicting the Innocent' 8 *Criminal Justice Ethics* 2.
McIntyre, A (2018) 'Doctrine of Double Effect' in EN Zalta (ed), *Stanford Encyclopedia of Philosophy*, https://plato.stanford.edu/archives/spr2019/entries/double-effect/
Ministry of Justice (2020) *Criminal Procedure and Investigations Act 1996 (sec 23(1)) Code of Practice* (September), https://assets.publishing.service.gov.uk/government/uploads/system/uploads/attachment_data/file/931173/Criminal-procedure-and-investigations-act-1996.pdf
Moore, M (1997) *Placing Blame* (Oxford, Oxford University Press).
Murphy, JG (1973) 'Marxism and Retribution' 2 *Philosophy & Public Affairs* 217.
National Registry of Exonerations (2020) 'Annual Report', www.law.umich.edu/special/exoneration/Documents/2021AnnualReport.pdf
Nobles, R and Schiff, D (2019) 'Criminal Justice Unhinged: The Challenge of Guilty Pleas' 39 *Oxford Journal of Legal Studies* 100.
Petegorsky, M (2013) 'Plea Bargaining in the Dark: The Duty to Disclose Exculpatory *Brady* Evidence During Plea Bargaining' 81 *Fordham Law Review* 3599.
Pettit, P (1991) 'Consequentialism' in P Singer (ed), *A Companion to Ethics* (Oxford, Blackwell Publishers Ltd).
Poveda, TG (2001) 'Estimating Wrongful Convictions' 18 *Justice Quarterly* 689.

Rakoff, JS (2014) 'Why Innocent People Plead Guilty', *The New York Review of Books*, www.nybooks.com/articles/2014/11/20/why-innocent-people-plead-guilty/
Redlich, AD, Bibas, S, Edkins, VA and Madon, S (2017) 'The Psychology of Defendant Plea Decision Making' 72 *American Psychologist* 339.
Scott, RE and Stuntz, WJ (1992) 'Plea Bargaining as a Contract' 101 *Yale Law Journal* 1909.
Sentencing Council (2017) *Reduction in Sentence for Guilty Plea: Definitive Guideline*, www.sentencingcouncil.org.uk/wp-content/uploads/Reduction-in-Sentence-for-Guilty-Plea-definitive-guideline-SC-Web.pdf
Sherrin, C (2011) 'Guilty Pleas from the Innocent' 30 *Windsor Review of Legal and Social Issues* 1.
Walsh, K, Hussemann, J, Flynn, A, Yahner, J and Golian, L (2017) 'Estimating the Prevalence of Wrongful Conviction', US Department of Justice, www.ncjrs.gov/pdffiles1/nij/grants/251115.pdf.
Walzer, M (1977) *Just and Unjust Wars* (New York, Basic Books).
Zalman, M (2012) 'Qualitatively Estimating the Incidence of Wrongful Convictions' 48 *Criminal Law Bulletin* 221.

Cases

United Kingdom

R v Asiedu [2015] EWCA Crim 714
R v David Caley and others [2012] EWCA Crim 2821

United States

Lafler v Cooper 566 US 156 (2012)

5

Rewarding Virtue: An Ethical Defence of Plea-based Sentence Reductions

JULIAN V ROBERTS AND NETANEL DAGAN*

I. Introduction

Should the State mitigate punishment for defendants who plead guilty? If the answer is yes, should these reductions be stipulated publicly, in advance of the defendant's decision, and if so, by whom? And how generous should the sentence reductions be, very significant or modest? This chapter addresses these and related questions.

Guilty plea mitigation (GPM) has biblical origins grounded in the concept of mercy[1] although the justifications for contemporary practice are principally utilitarian. The policy that courts should treat self-convicting offenders more leniently has existed for decades in common law systems (Beard 2017).[2] Sentence reductions for a guilty plea and acceptance of responsibility also operate at the level of international criminal law and ad hoc international tribunals. While the Rome Statute of the International Criminal Court (ICC) is silent on the issue, Rule 145(2)(ii) of the ICC's Rules of Procedure and Evidence include 'The convicted person's conduct after the act, including any efforts by the person to compensate the victims and any cooperation with the Court' as a mitigating circumstance (see Ambos 2014; D'Ascoli 2011).

The ubiquity of the practice – over time, across jurisdictions and legal regimes – suggests it has a sound foundation (Langer 2021; Gillieron 2019; Russell and Hollander 2017; Turner and Weigend 2020). Yet this near-universal[3] feature

* Our thanks to the seminar participants for feedback on the chapter, and in particular Andrew Ashworth for comments on an earlier draft.

[1] Proverbs 28:13: 'He that covereth his sins shall not prosper: but whosoever confesseth and forsaketh them shall have mercy'.

[2] Criminal Justice Act 2003, s 144; House of Commons 2017: 4.

[3] There are few universal features of sentencing. The criminal history sentencing premium is another ubiquitous practice found in both adversarial and inquisitorial systems. But while some jurisdictions prohibit consideration of prior convictions at sentencing, to our knowledge no modern system ignores the defendant's plea. Even civil law systems with mandatory prosecution policies extend sentence mitigation for the defendants who accept responsibility for the offence (Heinze and Fyfe 2020).

of sentencing has long been controversial. Researchers have identified several adverse, unintended consequences. As a result, some scholars have called for GPM to be abolished or at least greatly restricted.

This chapter explores the ethical dimension of awarding mitigated punishments to defendants who plead guilty. In brief, our core argument is that abolishing (or greatly curtailing) plea-based sentence reductions would result in the loss of an ethically defensible element of sentencing. The difficulties created by plea-based sentence reductions are largely problems of practice not principle (see Chapter 1).

The chapter does not discuss the complex issue of plea bargaining wherein the parties engage in potentially protracted (and often one-sided) discussions regarding plea (Chapter 12; Lippke 2011; Flynn and Freiberg 2018). GPM is the engine that drives these adversarial negotiations (Baldwin and McConville 1977). However, the nature and role of plea bargaining varies considerably across jurisdictions, making it hard to draw general conclusions. Plea negotiations play a very important role in determining sentencing outcomes in the United States, but are less central in England and Wales. Plea bargaining raises issues which go beyond the concept of plea-based sentencing reductions. Here we are concerned only with the ethicality and consequences of a sentence reduction for defendants who accept their guilt and relinquish their right to trial. Is plea-based mitigation ethically sound? If not, the rewards should be discontinued regardless of any practical disadvantages. On the other hand, if plea-based reductions are ethically sound, we then need to weigh their benefits against any adverse consequences.

A. Overview of Chapter

Section II defends GPM from an ethical perspective. For the purposes of discussion, we imagine a sentencing regime which offers no rewards for pleading guilty. In this imaginary jurisdiction, defendants are encouraged to plead guilty, but mitigation is neither promised nor awarded. The remorsefully repentant and the rebarbatively defiant are sentenced alike. This section explores the ethical duties upon the State and the defendant. Section III reviews the principal reforms proposed in the literature. Section IV suggests some key elements of an appropriate plea regime which retains the ethical benefits while minimising unintended consequences.

II. An Ethical Defence of Plea-based Sentence Reductions

Before describing an acceptable sentence reduction regime, we defend plea-based reductions as an ethical sentencing practice. One way of doing this is to consider a sentencing regime *without* plea-based mitigation. Critics of GPM seldom discuss the ethical value in rewarding a defendant who, accepting responsibility for the crime alleged, pleads guilty. Their focus is almost exclusively on the potential effects on wrongful convictions, or offence-based proportionality. Indeed, the ethical benefits are overlooked or almost disregarded. Leverick, for example, concludes that 'the *only* plausible justification for sentencing discounting is that of efficiency' (2004: 384, emphasis added), while Baldwin and McConville argue that discounting sentences for a guilty plea can 'scarcely be squared with justice and … exists because of administrative efficiency' (1979b: 300).

A. A World without Plea-based Sentence Reductions

Imagine a court system without GPM, without formal pleas; all defendants proceed to trial for adjudication. Now consider two contrasting offenders charged with the same crime. One defendant promptly accepts responsibility for the crime, and acknowledges guilt. Her advocate highlights any inculpatory admissions made as early as the first police interview. This defendant concedes key facts, or accepts incriminating claims in a way that spares the prosecution from having to call additional witnesses. Finally, either personally or through her advocate, this defendant accepts responsibility and acknowledges guilt in open court (at the sentencing hearing). Contrast this individual with an accused who actively disavows any wrongdoing throughout the criminal process, even after conviction. Despite their differences, the court imposes exactly the same penalty on both offenders. Does this make sense? These two individuals have normatively different profiles, yet the moral distinctions between these two defendants would be completely obscured if they both received the same sentence.[4]

A court could simply thank the defendant, acknowledging his acceptance of guilt, and leave it at that. The court's expression of approval would be the offender's only reward. We see two difficulties here. First, there is a parallel with von Hirsch's justification for the hard treatment element of desert-based sentence (1992: 12). He argues that in a celestial judicial system, where the defendants are angels, oral reproof would suffice to achieve the moral transformation sought by the court through its sentence. Mortals, however, require more; a prudential disincentive in the form of the sentence's hard treatment. In the context of the guilty plea, there is a need for a tangible reward to encourage and recognise the defendant's virtuous decision to plead guilty. In everyday life we reward people for all kinds of ethical behaviour. These rewards serve a dual purpose; they reinforce the norm the individual is upholding, and they offer a prudential incentive for others to act in a similar fashion.

[4] There is a parallel with previous convictions. A sentencing regime which sentenced multiple recidivists and first offenders in the same way would also fail to make an important distinction between morally distinguishable offenders. As with GPM, sentencing to reflect these different offenders triggers a number of adverse consequences (Frase and Roberts 2019).

This issue relates to the instrumental function of GPM, but there is also an ethical objection to merely acknowledging the defendant's plea without offering any reward. The State has conveyed a paradoxical message to the defendant: 'You should plead guilty once you accept, and only if you accept, that you are criminally responsible in the way charged on the indictment. But don't expect the court to acknowledge such admissions or reward them in any way.' The second difficulty is that words alone are insufficient reward for the offender's very significant concessions. The State should offer more than merely passive acknowledgement of the defendant's acceptance of responsibility; it should actively *reward* such conduct. And since the State's communication with the defendant is penological, the reward should employ the currency of penal sanctions. We do not support proposals to reward the offender in other ways, such as by monetary rewards[5] (see Lippke 2008: 195–96).

B. Diminished Culpability Claims[6]

An additional justification for awarding sentence reductions for a guilty plea relates to one of the twin pillars of a proportional sentence: the offender's level of culpability. Consider the repentant and the rebarbative[7] offenders through the lens of culpability. Traditionally, retributive scholars have placed strict temporal limits on the determination of an offender's culpability. Actions taken *after* the crime are seen as irrelevant to the offender's blameworthiness for the offence. On this view, once the crime is committed, the offender's level of culpability sets like concrete. Nothing they can do changes this reality. The offender who spontaneously assists the victim, or offers voluntary compensation may be deemed more virtuous, but not less culpable. This narrow approach to blameworthiness is too restrictive and dooms the offender to carry the maximal liability for his offence. Censure-based accounts of sentencing should be sensitive, within limits, to the offender's conduct after the crime. Why?

[5] In our view, monetary rewards are inappropriate and insufficient 'currency' to reflect the magnitude of the 'sacrifice' made by the pleading offender.

[6] We focus here on the defendant's decision to plead guilty. However, the offender may finally accept responsibility after being convicted at trial. Here too, the State should recognise and reward this post-plea acceptance of guilt. And so it does: offenders who accept their conviction are more likely to be granted privileges in prison or early release on parole. Again, we can contrast the prisoner who accepts responsibility early in their prison term and the one who rejects all imputations of guilt until the expiry of their sentence.

[7] There is a third category – offenders who have been caught 'red-handed'. They are pleading guilty, so it is claimed, only because they have no choice. They could be rebarbative or repentant. Or they may initially be one and then the other. The term is an over-simplification as it is based on an early sighting of the evidence in the case. Nevertheless, these so-called 'caught red-handed' defendants are still deserving of plea-based mitigation as they are taking a step which spares the State from unnecessary investigation and prosecution, and victims from having to testify at trial.

First, a more temporally dynamic approach argues that the State should be attentive to the defendant's moral deliberation after the crime as this affects the level of deserved censure. The censuring process should reach beyond the crime, and positive post-offence actions may affect the degree of the defendant's deserved censure (see discussion in Roberts and Maslen 2014; Smith 2014; Roberts and Dagan 2019).[8] Sentencing should not be deaf to the defendant's plea: accepting responsibility for the crime, possibly showing remorse and sparing the victim further harm, are acts related to the crime that merit reduced censure. In contrast, ignoring the defendant conveys a message of indifference. No matter what she does after the crime, it is all irrelevant to the State. In everyday life, people blame (and punish) others less when the wrongdoer accepts responsibility for misconduct.[9] The existence of discounted blame in social contexts alone does not justify the importation of the concept into the realm of legal punishment. Nevertheless, it creates a disjuncture between legal and public censure, one which may have adverse consequences for the sentencing process.

Second, pleading guilty may better reflect the defendant's true character. Crimes are often committed in the heat of the moment when the offender was under the influence of external forces or in a heightened (or drug-induced) state of arousal. The decision to plead guilty can be taken after considerable reflection and with the benefit of legal advice. As such, the defendant's real (or reformed) character may emerge – one that is less culpable than at the time of the crime. This approach provides an additional culpability-based justification for GPM. Guilty pleas can derive from purely instrumental reasons and not from a genuine character change or censure-related responsiveness. However, if we disregard the possibility of moral improvement, then we have lost the baby with the bathwater. Our conclusion here is that offenders who plead guilty are less culpable and as such worthy of less censure than offenders convicted following trial.

C. Ethical Duties on Defendants and the State

When confronted with a criminal charge, the defendant's ethical duty is to enter the plea which reflects his understanding of his legal status with respect to that charge – assuming he has a sufficient level of knowledge.[10]

[8] Nick Smith describes this approach as 'dialectical retributivism' and concludes that 'Post-offence behaviour should influence our judgments regarding appropriate punishments' (2014: 153).

[9] Acknowledgement of fault is a deep and abiding virtue, valued by many cultures. The joyous reception accorded the prodigal son reflected more than merely his return to the family home; it also recognised his acknowledgment of fault (Luke 15:11–32). The drug treatment, restorative justice and desistance literature is replete with rituals and ceremonies which recognise re-entry, and the offender's acceptance of responsibility is a key element, indeed even a prerequisite.

[10] See Chapter 2 for discussion of whether citizens aware of their guilt have a civic responsibility to plead guilty.

Wrongful pleas may take one of two forms: defendants who plead guilty knowing they are innocent, and offenders aware of their guilt who nevertheless demand a trial.[11] Both cases constitute miscarriages of justice, and both carry costs for the community. A wrongful *guilty* plea triggers unjustified legal punishment and stigma which affects the defendant as well as any family members and dependents. A wrongful guilty plea (particularly if entered soon after the charge is laid) also curtails further investigation by police and prosecutors and contributes to an additional injustice, namely protecting the unprosecuted offender (Nobles and Schiff 2019). A wrongful *not guilty* plea wastes CJS (criminal justice system) resources and inconveniences and often distresses victims and witnesses.[12] In the event that it succeeds, a wrongful not guilty plea confirms a miscarriage of justice, namely a wrongful acquittal.

In most cases,[13] assuming full Crown disclosure (and legal advice to interpret that disclosure) defendants will know whether they are guilty or innocent. They will infer this from the fit between their actions (of which they are well aware) and their understanding of the criminal nature of that conduct (for which the assistance of counsel may be necessary). In reality, many defendants will understand their legal status much earlier, and without the benefit of any Crown disclosure or legal advice. They know what they knew when they received the stolen goods; they can recall their actions and state of mind when they threw the punch. The legal meaning may be unclear, but not the offender's actions.

The State has a duty to encourage and reward, not dismiss or disregard, ethical decisions by the defendant. Indeed, the CJS does exactly that throughout the criminal process. Suspects are encouraged to compensate their alleged victims, and in return are rewarded with a caution. Some alleged perpetrators are diverted from further State action if they accept responsibility for an offence. Accused persons agreeing to meet the victim within a restorative justice context receive a more lenient sentence. Drug-addicted defendants who cooperate with the State in their own drug rehabilitation are rewarded with very significant mitigation in drug treatment courts. In fact, in most drug treatment courts a plea is a necessary condition for entry and this underlines the importance of the plea. And in discretionary release regimes, prisoners who undertake virtuous acts or take steps towards self-reformation are released sooner from prison. We could go on.

[11] We do not have the space to explore the source of the defendant's moral obligation to accurately plead guilty but it derives from a general duty to act honestly as well as respecting the autonomy of other citizens to make informed choices.

[12] It also raises community concerns about the police and the prosecution branches of the CJS.

[13] There will also be some cases where there is genuine legal doubt about the legal classification relevant to the defendant's case – not whether he is guilty of some offence, but rather which crime. Some of these doubts can only be resolved at trial through a jury's verdict. The existence of these cases underlines the need to ensure timely disclosure, legal advice and a reward system which permits sufficient discretion for a court to recognise this ambiguity in the reduction it ultimately awards.

D. Rewards for Offenders who Assist the Administration of Justice

A telling parallel exists with offenders who assist the State in prosecuting other offenders. Again, all jurisdictions reward such assistance by mitigating sentence. In England and Wales section 74 of the Sentencing Act 2020 permits a court to reduce the sentence of an offender who has assisted, or merely *offered* to assist, the prosecution. The magnitude of sentence reductions for State assistance are less predictable than plea-based reductions as the guideline does not provide specific levels of reduction for state assistance. The level of reduction normally tracks the utility of the information provided (Thomas 2008) and generally exceeds plea-based reductions by a significant margin. Thomas provides the example of an offender sentenced for murder who has pleaded guilty and entered into a written agreement to provide assistance to the police. Thomas suggests the assistance to the CJS would attract a 50 per cent reduction and the plea only one-third. In addition, under the guidelines' methodology, assistance is deducted before plea is considered, thereby enhancing their effect still further.[14] Generously rewarded for assisting in the conviction of these other individuals, defendants are now denied significant mitigation for convicting *themselves*?[15] Does that make sense?

In its response to crime and its dealings with suspects, defendants and offenders, the State should encourage acceptance of responsibility in the same way that in everyday life we encourage transgressors to acknowledge their misconduct and discourage impenitence. This is true of a wide range of contexts, from university disciplinary hearings through to national Truth and Reconciliation Commissions. Acceptance of responsibility is arguably the most common and powerful source of mitigation in everyday life. A system blind to the voluntary acceptance of guilt would depart markedly from all other formal and informal disciplinary regimes, including those found in religious codes. Upon hearing a confession of wrongdoing, what kind of priest queries the penitent? Who, in everyday life, censures and sanctions a transgressor with the same level of punitiveness, regardless of whether that individual accepts responsibility?

We conclude that it is ethically sound practice to extend leniency when the offender acknowledges guilt. This being the case, denying plea-based reductions is unethical. Disregarding a guilty plea also fails to respect the offender's publicly expressed confession. The State should not remain indifferent, or worse, totally deaf, to the defendant's communications. This is particularly true when

[14] Under the English sentencing guidelines, assisting the police or prosecution and the guilty plea occupy separate steps (3 and then 4) under the guidelines' methodology. Research demonstrates that cooperation with authorities regularly appears as a common mitigating factor (Sentencing Council 2012: 28).

[15] Plea-mitigation abolitionists may call for the abolition of state cooperation mitigation too, in which case in addition to jamming the court system, investigative policing will also be irredeemably compromised.

the defendant's message runs so clearly against her own self-interest. The laying of a criminal charge creates an opportunity for the defendant to reflect on past behaviour. If convinced of her responsibility for the crime, the plea hearing offers a chance to accept liability.[16] Denying the individual this opportunity is a moral failure by the State. This is one reason why, notwithstanding a robust critique of the practice, all jurisdictions, civil and common law, distinguish between defendants on the basis of their public response to the criminal charge. A sentencing regime which offers guilty plea reductions conveys different messages to the guilty and the innocent. Defendants aware of their guilt learn of a reward for expressing that acceptance of responsibility. If the defendant is secure in the knowledge of her innocence (following Crown disclosure and adequate legal advice) she should disregard the reduced sentence; it has no relevance for her.

E. Respecting the Offender's Agency

A number of scholars have underlined the importance of respect in the CJS (eg Watson 2020). Suspects, defendants, offenders, prisoners and parolees all deserve respect from criminal justice agencies and actors, for ethical and instrumental reasons. If defendants are denied respect, they are less likely to recognise the legitimacy of the prosecuting or punishing agent. Offenders who feel disrespected may also be less likely to comply with judicial orders or exhortations. The conditions attached to probation or parole orders may be seen to be imposed without legitimate authority. This is why offenders are encouraged to participate in the sentencing hearing and speak to sentence, either directly or through their legal adviser. One key element of respect in criminal justice is hearing the defendant's voice (Watson 2020: 65). When the defendant raises his voice to accept responsibility for the crime, the State should both attend to this communication and respond in an appropriate way. If the pleading offender receives no or only derisory mitigation, this suggests the State is not actually listening to his communication.

Offender agency is a related but distinct concept. Contemporary criminal justice attempts to encourage litigants to take responsibility for their lives and to act as autonomous agents. Scholars have long recognised that rehabilitation cannot be imposed or coerced (eg von Hirsch 2017). Reformation involves a partnership with the offender, one that recognises his sense of autonomous agency. One of the tasks of the defence advocate is to help the court understand the offender's individual circumstances. Drug treatment courts represent the apotheosis of this trend: the agency of the offender plays a key role, and the rituals of the court lay great emphasis on respect, agency and rewards for compliance. A guilty plea sentence

[16] The defendant is not a disinterested third party coolly observing the criminal process unfold and waiting to see whether the state can prove the criminal charge. She has unique information relevant to the proceedings. The State should not compel defendants to share their knowledge of the offence, but it can (and should) reward those who freely choose to do so.

regime thus engages the concepts of respect and agency. By accepting the defendant's plea and discontinuing the trial process the State recognises the offender's autonomy and agency.

F. The Victim's Interest

Finally, we note the State's duty to the crime victim (and see Chapter 9). Critics of GPM generally overlook this issue. There is literature on the role of the victim during plea discussions (eg Verdun-Jones and Tijerino 2004), but victims' reactions to plea-based mitigation per se have attracted little attention. Disregarding the victim's interests carries instrumental as well as ethical costs. With regard to the former, disenchanted victims may be less likely to participate in the current or future prosecutions. They may become reluctant to report crimes, testify at trial, submit victim impact statements or appear at sentencing.

For many victims, a criminal trial is a potentially arduous and stressful experience, particularly for victims of violence or sexual aggression. At the very least, if the case proceeds to trial, the victim will have to wait for months before a verdict is reached and then additional weeks before a separate hearing for sentencing. A guilty plea eliminates these potentially protracted delays.[17] Many victims will prefer the certainty and celerity of a plea-based conviction to an uncertain and dilatory criminal trial, even if the offender then benefits from a mitigated sentence. Of course, some victims may hope that a trial takes place. They may seek their time in court in order to participate in the process and possibly to communicate a message to the offender (eg Dawes et al 2011). Yet a criminal trial is unnecessary for this to occur. Victim participation and communication can be achieved through the use of a victim impact statement, which can be delivered at the sentencing hearing. The victim is likely to have a greater interest in a hearing focused on the punishment of the person responsible for his victimisation, and where his victim statement will assume a more central role than his witness statement at trial. Even for victims anticipating a trial, this may well be an acceptable alternative.

Moreover, for many victims, hearing the defendant accept responsibility for the crime by entering a guilty plea is a most welcome development. The victim is vindicated in her claims by the perpetrator and this can carry more significance than a merely State-determined conviction. The offender accepting guilt will likely be more important than the State ascribing guilt in the face of the offender's denial. It is the equivalent of an offender who apologises spontaneously compared to one who apologises only after being called to account by a court. In this way, offenders who plead guilty may contribute to victim healing. The plea contributes to mitigating the harmful consequences of the crime, which may linger for some

[17] Flynn and Freiberg note the emotional distress caused to victims when the case remains unresolved (2018: 11).

time after victimisation. The plea replaces the adversarial relationship because the offender accepts the legitimacy of the victim's allegation: they agree on guilt. In cases where the victim and offender had a prior relationship, a guilty plea is likely to contribute to restoring that relationship. Restorative justice is unlikely to emerge if the defendant contests the allegation through the course of a trial. These arguments justify the use of sentence reductions in return for a guilty plea. To disregard them would be to act unethically with respect to the crime victim, to whom the State owes a duty of care.

G. Summary

Let us summarise the argument so far in two simple propositions. First, mitigating punishment for the self-convicting offender is an ethical State response, albeit one which may carry risks (such as increasing the likelihood of a wrongful self-conviction). A system which relied exclusively on trials would, in Lippke's words, be of 'doubtful normative defensibility' (2016: 54). Second, there are instrumental and ethical reasons why abolishing plea-based mitigation is both impractical and undesirable. If GPM is an ethically sound element of sentencing, what remedies may address the potential dangers of the practice identified in Chapter 1 of this volume?

III. Evaluating Reform Proposals

Critics of plea-based discounts offer little in the way of plausible remedies for the problems they identify.[18] Abolitionists, in particular, offer no solutions for the inevitable increase in courts' caseload. Three[19] principal reform options emerge from the literature: (1) abolish plea-based reductions, imposing the same sentences on offenders regardless of whether they were convicted following a plea or a trial; (2) greatly reduce the magnitude of plea-based reductions; (3) retain sentence reductions at present levels, but withhold information about their impact from defendants.

A number of scholars and policy makers[20] have called for the abolition of plea-based discounts. Such scholars have referred to plea bargaining as 'a disaster'

[18] McConville and Marsh (2014) provide the most trenchant critique of the guilty plea reduction (and in particular the role of the judiciary). Curiously, their critique contains no remedy, although it seems reasonable to infer that they favour abolition of the practice.

[19] Bagaric and Brebner (2002) proposed a system in which innocent defendants would plead guilty but later make submissions consistent with claims of innocence. Punishing defendants who claim to be innocent seems even less likely than abolishing all plea-based discounts, so we do not explore their proposal here.

[20] During the 1970s–80s, several US policy makers (attorney generals, prosecutors or legislators) in Alaska, New York, Texas, Arizona and California abolished plea bargains. These reforms were unsuccessful due to caseload burdens on court systems (Weninger 1987).

(Schulhofer 1991;: 2009) that 'should be abolished' based on both instrumental and retributive reasons (Tonry, 2020: 193). This claim is usually made in the context of plea bargaining in the United States[21] (eg Bibas 2004). But sentence reductions are the engine which drive negotiations, so abolition of GPM is a natural consequence of this view. This reform is the least likely to be implemented, for instrumental reasons.

The second option – curbing the power of a plea to reduce sentence – is more practical. The principal determinant of whether, and to what extent, these concerns arise is the magnitude of the plea-based sentence reduction. Very generous reductions generate the most problems; modest reductions will have few adverse effects. Campbell, Ashworth and Redmayne (2019) and Lippke (2008), for example, propose a 10 per cent *maximum* reduction. This level of reduction will likely prove insufficient incentive for defendants inclined to plead guilty (see Chapter 4). Nor, in our view, does such a small reduction adequately reflect the full ethical significance of surrendering the right to trial. The only constituency likely to support such a proposal would be penal populists who see GPM as yet another manifestation of an offender-friendly CJS.

Scholars who favour minimal discounts are caught in a trap. On the one hand, they stress the sanctity of the presumption of innocence, the need for strict protections for that presumption, and the importance of the defendant's right to trial. On the other hand, they advocate a regime which offers only minimal reductions to defendants who plead guilty. We have argued that citizens have a duty to plead guilty if accept, following disclosure and legal advice, that they are guilty. But this does not relieve the State of an obligation to prove the case in the event that the defendant pleads not guilty. And if the defendant waives this fundamental right, she should receive a substantial sentence reduction. If the right to trial is so sacrosanct, then the defendant who relinquishes this right should receive a substantial concession from the State. In England and Wales at least, she will not get it. On a six-month custodial sentence (half of which is served in prison) the guilty plea offender will serve a few weeks less than his co-accused who was convicted after trial. Is this adequate recompense for the ethical decision to plead guilty? In practice, is it enough to encourage the defendant to even consider pleading guilty? Would anyone – even the two prisoners – notice the difference between the two sentences?

When a citizen waives the right to trial, she relinquishes the most valued constitutional individual protection. That is worth rather more than a couple of weeks in prison. When the offender self-convicts she also waives a raft of other constitutionally protected rights – for example to remain silent in response to interrogation, to cross-examine witnesses and other trial-based rights. Awarding very modest reductions in return for a guilty plea diminishes the stature of these

[21] Writing with reference to England and Wales, Welsh, Skinns and Sanders propose abolishing the guilty plea altogether (2021: 387).

key protections. Very modest sentence reductions convey the message that accepting responsibility carries the same weight as a minor mitigating factor.

Views will naturally differ on whether a 10 per cent reduction is trivial, modest or significant. Similarly, what appears to be a reasonable incentive to some will be characterised by others as constituting an unacceptably coercive inducement. The question may be hard to resolve. One strategy is to view the reductions from the perspective of the defendant. Would a few weeks off a 12-month prison sentence be regarded by defendants as generous or trivial? On the basis of the limited research, we suspect the latter. A second yardstick is to compare the plea-based reduction with other reductions, such as for assisting the State (see Section IID). Here too, the English maximum of one-third seems well aligned with rewards for State assistance. That being the case, again the reduction does not seem excessive. Ten per cent may not be trivial per se, but it will readily be seen as such if other sources of mitigation carry more weight. The same may be said in aggravation. A 10 per cent increase in sentence length to reflect multiple victims will seem trivial if premeditation or some mental state factor attracts a higher increase. It is all relative.

Feinberg proposed two conditions which would establish whether sentence reductions should be considered coercive. First, the difference between two alternatives must be significant enough for one to be deemed unacceptable. Second, the State must have engineered the choice independent of any actions by the person required to make the choice. Modest discounts such as those found in England and Wales cannot fulfil the first condition, and as Holman (2023) notes, the second prerequisite is absent since the criminal proceeding has been triggered by the defendant himself.[22]

Under the third option, sentence reductions would be decoupled from the plea, and largely hidden from the defendant. Campbell, Ashworth and Redmayne note that 'insofar as the discount is known to the defendant it is likely to exert considerable pressure' (2019: 327). Following this approach, defendants would be encouraged to plead guilty if they genuinely accepted their guilt and wished for whatever reason to expedite the criminal process. They would be told that this decision would be considered at sentencing – along with all other mitigating factors. But at no point prior to conviction would there be any information about the effect of the plea on the sentence – and certainly not from a judge. No awareness, no pressure. In this way, innocent defendants will not be tempted by a clearly signalled reduction. In fact, many common law jurisdictions conform to this description. Across Australia, the Sentencing Advisory Council of Tasmania noted that 'There has traditionally been uncertainty in relation to the extent to which a sentence is reduced, or the nature of the sentence is changed' (2018: 32).

Courts in Canada have no sentencing guideline regulating plea-based sentence reductions to guide their decisions. Neither the provincial/territorial courts of

[22] Assuming good faith on the part of police and prosecutors, although in practice this may not exist, particularly in the United States.

appeal nor the apex court have issued guidance regarding the appropriate level of reduction. This determination is left entirely to trial court discretion. Nor is there any less formal guidance – the equivalent of the *Crown Court Compendium* in England and Wales. This explains why sentencing texts and practitioner manuals offer no insight into the likely effect of a plea on sentence (eg Manson 2001). Finally, since plea is not recorded in the official court statistics, even the most determined researcher will be unable to document or estimate the impact of plea on sentences imposed. Under these conditions, defence counsel can offer very little in the way of advice regarding the effect of a guilty plea beyond a vague 'your sentence will be lighter if you plead guilty' (see Cole and Roberts 2019). Is it fair to expect defendants to enter a plea under such conditions?

One alleged benefit of a reward system which is unclear and decoupled from the adjudicator is that defendants will not feel intimidated into pleading. If the goal of this 'veil of ignorance' approach is to conceal the reward from defendants – to avoid wrongly incentivising the innocent – defence counsel should also be discouraged or prohibited from discussing the issue beyond a vague statement to the effect that a guilty plea is a mitigating factor at sentencing. Under this arrangement, defendants would have little or no clear incentive to plead – but that is the point. Such a proposal flies in the face of common sense, rule of law considerations and crime reduction aims. There is a clear duty on the Crown to provide full disclosure of the case against the defendant. This is necessary for her to form an informed opinion regarding the State's case. The defendant also needs to be educated about the consequences of the guilty plea. Other stakeholders, including the crime victim, also need clarity about the impact of a plea.

Greater clarity regarding the consequences of a guilty plea can be achieved by means of a sentencing guideline. A guideline may also help resolve the age-old conundrum: does the difference between the guilty plea sentence and the sentence following trial constitute a benefit for pleading guilty or a penalty for requiring the State to run a trial? The English sentencing guidelines specify a starting point sentence and a range of sentence for each crime. For example, a street robbery of low seriousness committed by an offender of medium-level culpability carries a starting point sentence of 24 months.[23] A court will use this starting point and add or subtract months to reflect additional mitigating and aggravating factors. The sentence ultimately imposed will then reflect the essential components of harm and culpability, and all other circumstances deemed relevant. This provisional sentence reflects the assumption that the offender is convicted following a trial. The defendant may elect to plead guilty and thereby reduce the sentence by no more than one-third.

Constructed in this way, the regime is clearly consistent with Nozick's (1969) description of an offer, rather than a threat. As Nozick argued, when distinguishing between offers and threats, 'offers of inducements, incentives, rewards … do not

[23] 'Robbery – street and less sophisticated commercial', www.sentencingcouncil.org.uk/offences/crown-court/item/robbery-street-and-less-sophisticated-commercial/.

normally constitute threats, and the person who accepts them is not normally coerced' (1969: 447). It is a derogation rather than an uplift from the norm; it makes the offender's status better rather than worse.[24] The important point here is that the guideline establishes a standard. Or as von Hirsch states, speaking of the first offender – recidivist sentencing differential, 'one cannot say whether we are speaking of a discount or a premium unless we introduce a reference point – namely how a crime would be punished in the absence of a prior record' (1985: 88). The reference point for the plea regime is the proportionate sentence for a conviction following trial as stipulated in a statutorily binding guideline. Under the prosecution-dominated plea bargaining in the United States, this may not be true. Hence the need to avoid generalising across very disparate sentencing regimes.

To conclude, none of these reform proposals recognises the value of a genuine guilty plea. Yet if the practice of plea-based reductions is to be retained, the problems that researchers have identified need a remedy. In the next section we sketch the essential features of a model plea reduction regime.

IV. Criteria for Self-conviction: A Model Regime

The existence of GPM does not mean the State loses its monopoly on ascribing criminal liability for the purposes of legal punishment. The accused's affirmation of guilt alone is insufficient grounds for the imposition of legal punishment, and in some cases, the State will need to reject a defendant's guilty plea. Cases will arise where individuals plead guilty to crimes for which they are not responsible. More commonly, defendants will enter wrongful guilty pleas. No guilty plea should be accepted unless a number of conditions are met.

A. Components of an Ethical Plea-based Sentence Reduction Regime

First, there must be a prima facie case, supported by evidence, that the self-convicting individual is guilty. The State should not accept the word of a person who simply walks into a police station claiming to have committed a crime. The police need to investigate and supply any relevant evidence for the prosecutor to decide whether the evidential sufficiency criterion for a charge has been met. The threshold prosecution for the laying of a criminal charge largely fulfils this requirement. A number of scholars have suggested it may also be necessary for the court to scrutinise the evidence prior to accepting the defendant's guilty

[24] As Nozick put it, 'If it makes the consequences of Q's action worse than they would have been in the normal and expected course of events, it is a threat; if it makes the consequences better, it is an offer' (1969: 447).

plea (Newman 2021; Kim 2018), and many jurisdictions follow the model of the US Federal Rules of Criminal Procedure, which impose a duty on a court to be satisfied that 'there is a factual basis for the plea before entering judgement' (Rule 11(b)(3)).

Second, prior to formal acceptance of a guilty plea the State must ensure that the defendant has been made aware of the case against him. Full (and timely) Crown disclosure is necessary, and a plea entered without this information would be unacceptable.

Third, the defendant must have received, or waived his right to receive, adequate legal advice to understand the extent and nature of the case against him, as well as the consequences of pleading guilty. The defendant must have a clear and accurate idea of the penalty likely following conviction after trial *and* conviction by plea. Vague advice is insufficient. The difference between the plea-based and trial sentencing outcome needs to be crystal clear to the defendant. This in turn requires a public-facing and clear regime which specifies the levels of sentence reductions according to different categories of plea – in short, a sentencing guideline to regulate plea-based sentence reductions.

Sentence reductions for a guilty plea should be stated in advance. The rationale for reducing sentence should be clarified and communicated to all stakeholders.[25] As noted earlier, sentence reductions for a guilty plea in many jurisdictions have traditionally been inscrutable. Sentencing regimes fail to identify the likely impact of a plea in advance, and courts have failed to specify the reductions they award. In Australian courts, for example, the Tasmania Advisory Council noted that

> the traditional approach of the court has been not to specify the sentencing reduction for a guilty plea in a particular case that there has been no general indication from the Court of Appeal of the range of the discount for guilty pleas that may be appropriate (2018: 78).

GPM should be neither be a matter of judicial mercy nor fully discretionary. Transparency is also important from the perspective of the crime victim and the general public. Unprepared for a substantial reduction, some crime victims may be dismayed to learn that the offender benefited from a discretionary decision to reduce the sentence by a substantial degree.

Some scholars oppose sentence indications given by the judge (Campbell, Ashworth and Redmayne 2019: 341). In England and Wales, defendants may ask for an indication of the likely sentence the court will impose in the event of a guilty plea. This indication then restricts the court's power at sentencing. Plea-based sentence reductions should be transparent, not opaque, and predictable, not uncertain. Expecting defendants to enter a plea without full awareness of the consequences is as unethical as requiring a plea without full disclosure of the prosecution's case.

[25] Cheng notes that the courts are 'essentially communicating the sentence discount for the courts; repeat clientele, the audience in the courtroom, including other defendants present and the general public' (2022: 60).

Fourth, the defendant needs sufficient time in which to consider her plea, to evaluate the evidence to be adduced by the prosecution in light of legal advice. Plea regimes should not require very early indications of guilt or collapse the mitigation to a trivial level as soon as the defendant declines the first opportunity to plead guilty. As with all the elements of the regime, a balance must be struck. Allowing the defendant to receive the same reduction right up to closing arguments at trial would make no sense from an ethical or instrumental perspective.

Fifth, and most importantly, at the plea hearing, the court should conduct an inquiry to ensure that the criteria just enumerated have been fulfilled. If the court is not satisfied – for example because the defendant reveals a lack of understanding of the evidence or consequences of conviction, including its collateral consequences – then the plea should be rejected and the case adjourned. The adjournment provides an opportunity to address the court's concern, and failing that, the case should proceed to trial. A judicial plea inquiry would prevent all but a small minority of wrongful convictions. Racial disparity at sentencing arising from differential plea rates may be a harder nut to crack. Reducing the level of reduction would minimise the problem. Frase and Roberts (2019) advocate reducing current criminal history enhancements in order to address the problem of racial disproportionality in imprisonment. Applying the same approach to plea-based reductions would have a similarly salutary effect. However, eliminating plea reductions simply because one profile of offender is less likely to plead really would be a case of throwing the baby out with the bathwater. A judicial inquiry would shed light on the defendant's motivation for pleading guilty and whether she felt her plea had been coerced. Plea inquiries, or indeed any enhanced judicial role regarding plea, will take more time, but any additional resources need to be set against the costs arising from wrongful convictions.[26]

The judicial inquiry could be preceded by a more rigorous attempt to determine whether the defendant understands the consequences of the plea.[27] Well before any judicial inquiry, at the time the plea is entered, the defendant could be required to read and consider information about the plea and its consequences. Perhaps she and her counsel could be required to sign a form acknowledging she has read this penal 'health warning' with regard to her plea.[28]

There is also a need for special protocols to guide practitioners in the case of particularly vulnerable defendants – those most likely to enter a wrongful guilty plea. The court may also need to review the basis of plea – the factual account accepted by the offender – to ensure that it is consistent with the prosecution's disclosure. Finally, the plea regime needs to be alive to the possibility that defendants denied bail and detained pre trial may be more likely to plead guilty, simply to secure release from prison (see discussion in Peterson 2019; Chapter 10).

[26] Under the US Federal Rules of Criminal Procedure (s 11(b)(1)) the defendant should be under oath when entering her plea and must be directly informed in open court of the right to trial.

[27] *Padilla v Kentucky* 559 US 356 (2010).

[28] This is current practice in Israeli courts, although it is not required in law.

Reducing the number of pre-trial detainees is beyond the scope of the plea discount regime but is an important priority to ensure its integrity.

Courts should always be alive to the possibility of a miscarriage of justice.[29] Even within the adversarial model judges retain the discretion to intervene – for example during cross-examination. In some countries courts are required to make inquiries of the prosecution and the defence in order to ensure compliance with rule of law requirements or to otherwise achieve an appropriate outcome.[30] Judicial inquiries of the defendant's plea are particularly important if the outcome of the guilty plea is a change in sanction (see earlier sections of this chapter).

Sixth, the appellate courts should not blindly accept the truth of the guilty plea. Some mechanism is needed to afford post-conviction relief even for defendants who have pleaded guilty. Post-conviction relief statutes exist in a number of US jurisdictions and represent a remedy to the problem of defendants who seek to overturn a false guilty plea (see Joy and McMunigal 2020).[31]

A number of these prerequisites carry policy options. We conclude with a commentary on the single most important decision confronting an appellate authority or Council issuing guidance (as well as a trial court determining the reduction in individual cases): to what degree (and how) should a guilty plea mitigate sentence?

B. How Great a Reduction Is Ethical?

The magnitude of plea-based sentence reductions varies. Most systems (eg Maryland,[32] Canada[33] and Israel[34]) place no limit on GPM, reflecting the view that such mitigation 'cannot be reduced to any formula'.[35] Some jurisdictions restrict the reduction: up to 40 per cent (South Australia) or one-third (England and Wales). Elsewhere the reduction is even higher: for example 50 per cent in Singapore. The federal US guidelines operate two levels of reduction in the guidelines grid,[36] while

[29] Limitations on space prevent us from discussing the effect a guilty plea may have on any subsequent conviction appeal.

[30] For example, in Canada judges are directed to inquire of the prosecutor whether the victim has been informed of the right to submit a victim impact statement.

[31] The CJS should address factors external to the sentencing process but which affect whether defendants plead guilty. Two obvious factors are the accessibility of legal aid, and pre-trial detention. Defendants without sufficient legal advice are more likely to enter a wrongful guilty plea, as are those who are detained pre trial (eg Peterson 2019).

[32] See Maryland Penal Code, p 364.

[33] *R v Daya* (2007) 227 CCC (3d) 367 (Ont CA) holding that GPM 'will vary with the circumstances of each case'.

[34] The Israeli penal law, as amended in 2012, allows mitigation within the 'proportionate sentencing range whether 'the offender took responsibility for his actions, and the degree to which he has become, or is making an effort to become, law-abiding' (s 40k(4)) and the 'offender's cooperation with law enforcement agencies' (s 40k(6)).

[35] *R v Faulds* (1994) 20 OR (3d) 13 (CA), para 14.

[36] Section §3E1.1 states: 'If the defendant clearly demonstrates acceptance of responsibility for his offense, decrease the offense level by 2 levels'.

some Australian systems restrict the reduction to one-quarter of the sentence. The most common reduction is one-third.[37] Are these levels of reduction appropriate, excessive or insufficient?

Determining the appropriate level of reduction is far from straightforward, and judgements of current levels vary greatly. As Newman notes, 'it is practically impossible to determine when an inducement exceeds the legitimate threshold' (2021: 387). Yet many scholars see the relatively modest English levels of reduction as excessive. For example, Campbell, Ashworth and Redmayne consider the size of the reduction in England and Wales 'too great' (2019: 343) but without explaining the basis for this conclusion. Jacobson, Hunter and Kirby state that a guilty plea 'can have an enormous impact on sentencing' (2015: 60). McConville and Marsh describe a state of affairs where all defendants 'were likely to be placed under such pressure that a guilty plea could no longer be a product of a free choice' (2014: 73).

Others take a different view. In opposing the use of plea to make a difference between a custodial and a community-based sentence, Helm suggests that a one-third reduction 'may appear reasonable and modest' (2019: 171). We concur. In all likelihood, the question of whether an incentive is also coercive will depend upon a range of factors, including the magnitude of the reduction, the personal characteristics of defendants and the quality of legal advice, to name just a few. Some sentence reductions may seem coercive to certain defendants and not at all to others. There is no obvious test which would establish whether the magnitude of reductions is excessive although a number of indicators may assist. From an instrumental perspective, evidence of significant numbers of wrongful convictions would suggest the reductions are excessive. But from an ethical perspective the question is harder to answer.

The outcome for common prison sentences offers some insight. Offenders pleading guilty in England and Wales receive on average four months off the average prison sentence. Since normally half the sentence is served in prison, half in the community, the plea reduces time in prison by two months, which seems small reward for relinquishing the right to trial. Further research is clearly necessary to establish the extent to which the discount affects defendants' decision to plead guilty. Research by the Sentencing Council (Dawes et al 2011) suggested that the magnitude of the reduction was a minor consideration in the decision to plead guilty. The most important consideration was the strength of the prosecution's case. This finding is consistent with research involving defendants at a much earlier period when the discount was greater than today. Bottoms and McClean report that the response 'To get a lighter sentence' was the reason for pleading guilty in only 5 per cent of defendants (1976: Table 5.7).

[37] This has long been the level awarded in England and Wales, even before it was formalised in the current sentencing guidelines (*R v De Haan* [1968] 2 QB 108). Most other common law jurisdictions operate a similar level, and one-third also operates at the level of the international tribunals and the ICC (see D'Ascoli 2011; Ambos 2014).

How much mitigation should be allowed? No magic number may be identified. Most common law jurisdictions operate a reduction of one-third (Cheng 2022; Roberts and Bradford 2015). The mitigation should be generous enough to reward the offender for self-convicting, but not so powerful as to elicit wrongful pleas. That is easier said than done. The best we can say is that there should be some limit placed upon the reduction. We agree with Lippke, who argues that defendants who plead guilty 'should be granted modest but fixed discounts' (2011: 2). The *maximum* one-third permitted under the English guideline seems a reasonable compromise.[38] A number of jurisdictions have legislated directions to courts to ensure the reductions do not result in disproportionate mitigation. In New South Wales, for example, s 22(1A) of the Crimes (Sentencing Procedure) Act 1999 states that 'A lesser penalty imposed under this section must not be unreasonably disproportionate to the nature of the offence'.[39] This well-intentioned provision is useful but vague; far better to provide a more prescriptive guideline for courts to follow.

C. Should the Plea Change the Nature of the Sanction?

More problematically from the perspective of the defendant, the power of plea could be restricted to a reduction in the quantum of punishment.[40] The prospect of receiving a suspended sentence or a community order rather than an immediate prison sentence will prove attractive and may cause wrongful self-convictions. Several authors have argued that a guilty plea should not be able to change the nature of the sanction – for example from imprisonment to a community punishment (Roberts and Harris 2017; Thomas 1979: 52; Helm, Dehaghani and Newman 2021; Helm and Reyna 2017). In one Australian study members of the public and jurors were more supportive of reducing the custodial sentence length than changing the nature of the sentence (eg Warner et al 2020: Table 2). Prohibiting a change in sanction protects proportionality and parity more effectively, but may fail to provide sufficient reward for the most meritorious defendants. One solution would be to

[38] The effect of plea is further restricted for murder in England and Wales. Allowing a one-third reduction off the minimum term for murder would mean that an offender facing, say, a 24-year minimum term would save eight years by pleading guilty. Eight years is the equivalent of 16 years of a standard determinate sentence with release at the 50% point. For this reason, the guideline caps the reduction for murder at one-sixth of the term, or no more than five years (Sentencing Council 2017).

[39] The Tasmania Sentencing Council advocated a similar 'proportionality' check by amending the Sentencing Act in that state such that the reduced sentence 'must not be unreasonably disproportionate to the nature and circumstances of the offence' (Sentencing Advisory Council 2018: 74).

[40] The English plea-based sentence reduction guideline permits a court to change the sentence from imprisonment to a community order (Sentencing Council 2017). Unfortunately, no statistics are available on the question of how often a plea changes the sanction, rather than simply reducing the quantum of imprisonment or fine, or the onerousness of a community order.

allow a change in the nature of the sanction only in exceptional circumstances and only when public safety would not be compromised. It would be unwise to remove the possibility altogether.

V. Conclusion

When a defendant admits criminal responsibility and enters a guilty plea, she relinquishes her most important legal right. Assuming the plea is entered in a state of sufficient awareness of the prosecution case and the consequences of conviction (and without undue pressure from legal agents), this is a virtuous act, one that should attract significant State recognition and reward. The offender has made an ethical decision and it would be unethical for the State to disregard this gesture. The State should offer a substantial, but limited, reduction, one that should be clear, transparent and grounded in a guideline.

References

Ambos, K (2014) *Treatise on International Criminal Law*. Volume II. The Crimes and Sentencing (Oxford, Oxford University Press).

Bagaric, M and Brebner, J (2002) 'The Solution to the Dilemma Presented by the Guilty Plea Discount: The Qualified Guilty Plea – I'm Pleading Guilty Only Because of the Discount' 30 *International Journal of the Sociology of Law* 51.

Baldwin, J and —— (1977) *Negotiated Justice. Pressures to Plead Guilty*. (London, Martin Robertson).

—— and McConville, M (1979a) *Jury Trials* (Oxford, Clarendon Press).

—— and —— (1979b) 'Plea Bargaining and Plea Negotiation in England' 13 *Law and Society Review* 287.

Beard, J (2017) *Reduction in Sentence for a Guilty Plea*. Briefing paper, 5974 (London, House of Commons Library).

Bibas, S (2004) 'Plea Bargaining Outside the Shadow of Trial' 117 *Harvard Law Review* 2463.

Bottoms, A and McLean, J (1976) *Defendants in the Criminal Process* (London, Routledge and Kegan Paul).

Campbell, L, Ashworth, A and Redmayne, M (2019) *The Criminal Process* (Oxford, Oxford University Press).

Cheng, K. (2022) *The Timing of Guilty Pleas: Lessons from Common Law Jurisdictions* (Cambridge, Cambridge University Press).

Cole, D and Roberts, JV (2019) 'What's the Point of Pleading Guilty?' 44 *Criminal Reports* 44.

D'Ascoli, S. (2011) *Sentencing in International Criminal Law: The UN Ad Hoc Tribunals and Future Perspectives for the ICC* (London, Bloomsbury).

Dawes, W, Harvey, P, McIntosh, B, Nunney, F and Phillips, A (2011) *Attitudes to Guilty Plea Reductions* (London, Sentencing Council).

Flynn, A and Freiberg, A (2018) *Plea Negotiations: Pragmatic Justice in an Imperfect World* (Cham, Palgrave Macmillan).

Frase, RS and Roberts, JV (2019) *Paying for the Past: The Case against Prior Record Sentence Enhancements* (Oxford, Oxford University Press).
Gillieron, G (2019) 'Comparing Plea Bargaining and Abbreviated Trial Procedures' in DK Brown, J Turner and B Weisser (eds), *The Oxford Handbook of Criminal Process* (Oxford, Oxford University Press).
Heinze, A and Fyfe, S (2020) 'The Role of the Prosecutor' in K Ambos, A Duff, J Roberts and T Weigend (eds), *Core Concepts in Criminal Law and Criminal Justice*, vol 1 (Oxford, Oxford University Press).
Helm, RK (2019) 'Conviction by Consent? Vulnerability, Autonomy and Conviction by Guilty Plea' 83 *The Journal of Criminal Law* 161.
Helm, RK and Reyna, V. (2017) 'Logical but Incompetent Plea Decisions: A New Approach to Plea Bargaining Grounded in Cognitive Theory' 213 *Psychology, Public Policy, and Law* 367.
Helm, RK, Dehaghani, R and Newman, D (2021) 'Guilty Plea Decisions: Moving Beyond the Autonomy Myth' 85 *Modern Law Review* 133.
Holmen, S (2023, in press) *Guilty Pleas* in J Ryberg (ed), *The Handbook of Legal Philosophy* (Oxford, Oxford University Press).
Jacobson, J, Hunter, G and Kirby, A (2015) *Inside Crown Court: Personal Experiences and Questions of Legitimacy* (Bristol, Policy Press).
Joy, P and McMunigal, K (2020) 'Post-conviction Relief After a Guilty Plea' 35 *Criminal Justice* 53.
Kim, M (2018) 'Conviction Beyond a Reasonable Suspicion: The Need for Strengthening the Factual Basis Requirement in Guilty Pleas' 3 *Concordia Law Review* 102.
Langer, M (2021) 'Plea Bargaining, Conviction without Trial, and the Global Administration of Criminal Convictions' 4 *Annual Review of Criminology* 377.
Leverick, F (2004) 'Tensions and Balances, Costs and Rewards: The Sentence Discount in Scotland' 8 *Edinburgh Law Review* 360.
Lippke, R. (2008) 'To Waive or Not to Waive: The Right to Trial and Plea Bargaining' 2 *Criminal Law and Philosophy* 181.
—— (2011) *The Ethics of Plea bargaining* (Oxford, Oxford University Press).
—— (2016) *Taming the Presumption of Innocence* (Oxford, Oxford University Press).
Manson, A (2001) *The Law of Sentencing in Canada* (Toronto, Irwin Law).
McConville, M and Marsh, L (2014) *Criminal Judges: Legitimacy, Courts and State-induced Guilty Pleas in Britain* (Cheltenham, Edward Elgar Publishing).
Newman, B (2021) 'Managerial Induced Guilty Pleas in England and Israel – Legitimacy and the Role of the Judiciary: Reclaiming Judicial Responsibility Through Managerial Means' 32 *Criminal Law Forum* 355.
Nobles, R and Schiff, D (2019) 'Criminal Justice Unhinged: The Challenge of Guilty Pleas' 39 *Oxford Journal of Legal Studies* 100.
Nozick, Robert (1969). 'Coercion' in S Morgenbesser, P Suppes and M White (eds), *Philosophy, Science, and Method: Essays in Honor of Ernest Nagel* (New York, St Martin's Press).
Peterson, N (2019) 'Do Detainees Plead Guilty Faster? A Survival Analysis of Pretrial Detention and the Timing of Guilty Pleas' 31 *Criminal Justice Policy Review* 1015.
Roberts, JV and Maslen, H (2014) 'After the Crime: Retributivism, Post-offence Conduct, and Penal Censure' in A Simester, U Neumann and A du Bois-Pedain (eds), *Liberal Criminal Theory: Essays for Andreas von Hirsch* (Oxford, Hart Publishing).

Roberts, JV and Bradford, B (2015) Sentence Reductions for a Guilty Plea: New Empirical Evidence from England and Wales 12 *Journal of Empirical Legal Studies* 187.
Roberts, JV and Harris, L (2017) 'Reconceptualizing the Custody Threshold in England and Wales' 28 *Criminal Law Forum* 477.
Roberts, JV and Dagan, N (2019) 'Just Deserts, Penal Censure, and Parole' in A Bottoms and A Pedain-Dubois (eds), *Penal Censure. Engagements Within and Beyond Desert Theory* (Oxford, Hart Publishing).
Russell, J and Hollander, N (2017) 'The Disappearing Trial: The Global Spread of Incentives to Encourage Suspects to Waive their Right to a Trial and Plead Guilty' 8 *New Journal of European Criminal Law* 309.
Schulhofer, SJ (1991) 'Plea Bargaining as Disaster' 101 *Yale Law Journal* 1979.
Sentencing Council (2012) *Crown Court Sentencing Survey. Annual Publication* (London, Sentencing Council).
—— (2017) *Reduction in Sentence for a Guilty Plea: Definitive Guideline* (London, Sentencing Council).
Smith, N (2014) *Justice Through Apologies* (Cambridge, Cambridge University Press).
Tasmania Sentencing Advisory Council (2018) *Statutory Sentencing Reductions for a Guilty Plea. Report No. 10* (Tasmania Sentencing Advisory Council)
Thomas, D (1979) *Principles of Sentencing*, 2nd edn (London, Heinemann).
—— (2008) 'Sentencing; Assistance to Prosecutor or Investigator' 2 *Criminal Law Review* 147.
Tonry, M (2020) *Doing Justice, Preventing Crime* (Oxford, Oxford University Press).
Turner, J and Weigend, T (2020) 'Negotiated Case Dispositions in Germany, England and the United States' in K Ambos, A Duff, JV Roberts, T Weigend and A Heinze (eds), *Core Concepts in Criminal Justice*. Volume 1 (Cambridge, Cambridge University Press).
Verdun-Jones, S and Tijerino, A (2004) 'Four Models of Victim Involvement During Plea Negotiations' 46 *Canadian Journal of Criminology and Criminal Justice* 471.
von Hirsch, A (1985) *Past or Future Crimes* (New Brunswick, Rutgers University Press).
—— (1992) *Censure and Sanction* (Oxford, Clarendon Press).
—— (2017) *Deserved Criminal Sentences* (Oxford, Hart Publishing).
Warner, K, Spiranovic, C, Bartels, B, Roberts, L and Gelb, K (2020) 'Juror and Community Views of the Guilty Plea Sentencing Discount: Findings from a National Australian Study' 22 *Criminology and Criminal Justice* 78.
Watson, G (2020) *Respect and Criminal Justice* (Oxford, Oxford University Press).
Welsh, L, Skinns, L and Sanders, A (2021) *Sanders and Young's Criminal Justice*, 5th edn (Oxford, Oxford University Press).
Weninger, R (1987) 'The Abolition of Plea Bargaining: A Case Study of El Paso County, Texas' 35 *UCLA Law Review* 265.

Cases

R v Daya (2007) 227 CCC (3d) 367 (Ont CA)
R v Faulds (1994) 20 OR (3d) 13 (CA)

6

The Limited Moral Relevance of Pleas and Verdicts

ADAM J KOLBER*

I. Introduction

Criminal convictions are sometimes seen as transformative, altering attitudes toward the accused in profound ways. Prior to conviction, we are cautious about stigmatisation. No matter how much incriminating evidence there may be, for example, the press speaks of *alleged* burglars or *alleged* murderers. After conviction, by contrast, defendants may be stigmatised in ways that exceed the evidence against them. For example, those convicted and formerly incarcerated for cocaine possession are likely considered non-starters as US presidential candidates, even though two presidents have admitted or strongly implied past cocaine use for which they were never convicted (Seelye 2006; Weisman 1999).

One hypothesis is that the presence or absence of a conviction has special weight in our moral appraisals that goes beyond the underlying evidence.[1] If so, I argue, we are mistaken. Aside from the bits of morally relevant information pleas and verdicts can convey, in most cases they should not substantially alter the ways that well-informed observers morally appraise defendants. Convictions are *legally* transformative because they determine whom we punish, but that does not mean pleas and verdicts should affect our *moral* assessments in ways that extend beyond the underlying evidence.

Consider an analogy: a student writes a year-long paper and receives a 'C' grade. Disappointed, she approaches an equally qualified instructor from a different university to honestly evaluate her work using comparable standards. The second instructor believes the paper deserves an 'A'. When rationally appraising the paper, we should give no special weight to the official instructor's grade simply because it holds the university's official imprimatur. The official grade may disadvantage

* For helpful comments on earlier drafts, I thank Antony Duff, Julian Roberts, Jesper Ryberg and the participants in 'The Ethics of Guilty Pleas' workshop hosted by Oxford University's Faculty of Law.

[1] I do not preclude other hypotheses: journalists worry about defamation, and views about fitness to hold office may reflect irrational class or other biases.

the student in the eyes of future employers who have limited resources to investigate. But the first instructor's evaluation is merely more official and not necessarily more accurate. It should have no special weight in our assessments of the student's performance simply because it is official.

Similarly, I argue, pleas and verdicts sometimes reveal bits of morally relevant information that clarify the truth. They may help us fine-tune promotion of traditional consequentialist goals such as deterrence, incapacitation and rehabilitation. They may also fine-tune retributivist assessments of moral desert. But just as the authoritative teacher's grade has no special impact on our epistemic appraisal of the student, authoritative legal acts have no special impact on moral appraisal beyond that of similar non-authoritative acts that convey comparable information. Nothing magical happens at plea allocutions or upon jury verdicts to substantially transform moral assessments of defendants.

Therefore, I claim, there are no special (non-instrumental) symbolic or communicative reasons for journalists to require the cautionary language of allegation until conviction.[2] And there are no special non-instrumental symbolic or communicative reasons why fitness for presidential office should turn on the absence of a conviction. In fact, for retributivists, when conviction is followed by punishment, offenders *are* morally transformed because punishment reduces or eliminates their desert debt. If anything, those who serve their sentences are, all else being equal, more deserving presidential candidates from a retributivist perspective.

A. Overview of Chapter

In Section II, I discuss the limited morally relevant information pleas and verdicts provide to traditional consequentialist and retributivist views (traditional in the sense that they are not directly concerned with the symbolic or communicative value of pleas and verdicts). I claim that the information pleas and verdicts provide may alter the moral assessments of well-informed traditional theorists but only modestly. In Section III, I address theories of punishment that purport to find non-instrumental symbolic or communicative value in pleas and verdicts. I raise doubts about their ability to do so, at least when they are understood according to a leading communicative account of punishment. In particular, I argue that the 'radical indeterminacy of punishment severity' undermines the ability of pleas and convictions to communicate amounts of condemnation.

[2] One might defend journalistic convention by claiming that labels like 'robber' are legal terms of art: you cannot be a robber prior to conviction because no legal determination has been made yet. But journalists are not using formal legal terms. If they were, their use of 'alleged robber' would be mysterious. Why would they allege someone just accused of a crime to have already been convicted? What journalists are actually alleging is that a suspect engaged in conduct that makes him a robber even absent formal conviction.

II. Traditional Consequentialist and Retributivist Perspectives

In this section, I note the limited extent to which pleas and verdicts inform decisions about whether alleged perpetrators are actual perpetrators and, hence, the limited extent to which pleas and verdicts should alter traditional consequentialist and retributivist assessments. While one can argue about the details, the main point is that accurate moral assessments should not outstrip our underlying information.

A. Jury Verdicts

Criminal *trials* undoubtedly reveal morally relevant information. They provide substantive evidence about a defendant's past behaviour. Perhaps an unexpected eyewitness will take the stand and confidently identify the defendant. Still, we do not need juries to tell us what happens at trial. In the United States and many other countries, trials are ordinarily open to the public. All that juries do is process information already available to us. No new underlying evidence about an alleged crime is revealed right after a verdict is announced relative to right before.

Provided we have carefully considered the evidence, verdicts should change little about our moral attitudes toward the accused. Jurors are not experts. They usually have no special training in science, statistics, causation, criminal law, criminology and so on. They not only lack special expertise but often lack motivation to serve except to satisfy a legal obligation. Potential jurors with the most helpful skill sets may also be the most adept at avoiding jury duty. When jurors do serve, they receive little, if any, meaningful feedback on their performance, and many will never serve again anyhow. Jury instructions are often complicated and confusing. Jurors are prohibited from conducting their own research to fill gaps in their knowledge and have limited opportunities to ask questions. Judges can prohibit jurors from taking notes (eg *State v Crawford* 2004: [127]), even in cases that stretch over many weeks or months.

Further complicating the jury's task, we deliberately restrict evidence jurors are permitted to hear. In the United States, we often exclude relevant evidence related to defendants' character, prior criminal history, privileged communications, decisions to exercise Fifth Amendment rights not to testify, and more. A defendant might have possessed 50 kilograms of cocaine, but if the drugs are confiscated in a search that violates the Fourth Amendment, the evidence will be excluded (*Mapp v Ohio* 1961), even when it is undoubtedly relevant to wrongdoing.

Juries do have an advantage over any one of us in that they have more brains – typically 12. If those brains deliberate together and agree on a verdict, should we not increase our confidence in whatever conclusion they reach? In recent years, epistemologists have hotly debated the topic of 'peer disagreement' – whether, and if so how, we should update confidence in our beliefs based on the views of epistemic peers (Frances and Matheson 2018). For example, suppose you believe we should promote solar power to best combat climate change but run into someone you consider roughly your epistemic peer who disagrees. Some say the mere fact that your epistemic peer disagrees should reduce your confidence in the proposition that we should promote solar power to best combat climate change. Others say it should not affect your assessment unless you are exposed to new substantive facts or arguments.

Similarly, some would say, because a jury verdict does not reveal new underlying information about an alleged crime, it should not alter the views of an ordinary observer who has at least as much evidence. Others would say the beliefs of epistemic peers *should* alter an observer's confidence in the pertinent propositions, at least to some degree. We need not resolve the matter, however. Either we should not alter our views based on the verdict, or we should give the verdict modest effect. The effect is particularly modest because jurors are not epistemic peers of a smart, well-financed investigator. Such a person can convene the best experts around the world to form a mock jury that is epistemically superior to any actual jury. So even if a jury's verdict should not be totally inert with respect to our confidence, its effect should be small, especially when we are well informed and well resourced.

B. Pleas

Guilty pleas are sometimes quite bare. A defendant might merely admit violating the elements of an offence and claim his plea is voluntary, informed and intelligent. Such pleas still convey some useful information. A defendant who pleads guilty probably believes doing so is his best available option. Since the defendant and his attorney often have the most information about an alleged crime, the pleas they accept or reject reveal how they perceive the evidence likely to come to light at trial.

But even guilty pleas give a little signal with a lot of noise because defendants face well-known pressures to plead guilty. About 95 per cent of cases in the United States that are not dismissed end in guilty pleas (Gramlich 2019). Prosecutors have tremendous leverage to pressure defendants to plead by threatening to bring additional charges, including charges with mandatory minimum sentences. Prosecutors can further incentivise pleas with promises to drop charges or to ask judges for light sentences. These pressures reduce our ability to trust the veracity of guilty pleas.

Guilty pleas may send unclear signals for other reasons. A defendant might plead guilty to divert law enforcement attention away from friends, loved ones, or co-conspirators. A defendant might plead guilty but be mistaken about his own involvement, due either to drug use, mental illness or confusion about the law. Since the vast majority of defendants plead guilty, learning that a defendant is pleading guilty is usually unsurprising (although plea details may be surprising). In cases of bare guilty pleas, the way we assess defendants before a plea is not likely to change much afterwards, absent a plea that gives substantial new, verifiable information.

During an extended plea allocution, an offender might describe his conduct in some depth. The admission might even provide key information, such as the location of stolen goods or a dead body, that can be independently verified to significantly revise assessments of guilt. When the information cannot be independently verified, we must discount it to some extent, especially if there is a threat of incarceration. Incarceration is a bit like state-authorised abduction. Just as we do not expect abductees to tell the truth in front of their abductors, we cannot expect those facing pseudo-abduction to prison to tell the truth when their freedom is at stake.

Importantly, there is nothing special about the information provided at a plea allocution relative to the same information provided through other means. If an apology during a plea allocution seems genuine, it may ease the victim's trauma and reduce our estimates of the likelihood of recidivism. The apology has no special force, however, simply because it was offered inside a courtroom. In fact, quite the opposite may be true: when defendants are highly incentivised to express remorse, we have less confidence that their remorse is genuine. By contrast, those speaking in unofficial contexts with no audience to impress may, all else being equal, give us greater confidence in their truthfulness.[3]

C. Consequentialist Perspectives

Consequentialists typically believe that the morally right action is the one that leads to the best consequences. Since pleas and verdicts provide only limited information bearing on traditional consequentialist considerations such as dangerousness, verdicts will typically have little impact on a well-informed consequentialist's understanding of defendants' attributes. Whatever basic dispositions a defendant has five minutes before a plea or verdict are likely to be the same five minutes after. Whatever impulsiveness, aggression and selfishness are attributable to a defendant that might incline him to behave badly in the future are determined by our best evidence, not whether he happens to receive a formal conviction.

There are two important caveats to the claim that pleas and verdicts have limited significance for traditional consequentialists. First, we are speaking to the significance of verdicts and pleas themselves. Conviction may set in motion events that do change offenders over time. They may be traumatised at sentencing, deprived of liberty in prison and stigmatised upon release in ways that gradually change offender attributes in ways quite relevant to consequentialists.

[3] I assume perjury constraints are inapplicable to expressions of apology, remorse and repentance.

Second, consequentialists might deliberately deviate from their interests in accuracy to promote other goals. They might believe that when confronted with tricky factual issues, it is very helpful to have a recognised mechanism to decide guilt. We make that mechanism authoritative not because it is cloaked in fine epistemic armour, but because it helps coordinate people around a particular solution.

If multiple juries decided how we treat defendants, we would need to determine which jury's decision is legally binding. Having one official jury coordinates behaviour and expectations at relatively low cost. Perhaps juries should be eliminated and replaced with something else entirely, but if we are going to have juries, consequentialists can recognise their usefulness without giving special epistemic significance to some particular group of semi-random jurors.

Similarly, consequentialists can recognise a useful role for guilty pleas, even if prosecutors tend to exert so much leverage over defendants that pleas reveal less information than they otherwise could. For consequentialists, pleas and verdicts sometimes provide new information, but their value can easily be accounted for in consequentialist terms without supposing them to have non-instrumental symbolic or communicative moral significance.

D. Retributivist Perspectives

Under a traditional retributivist view (that ignores non-instrumental symbolic or communicative value), offenders deserve to suffer or be deprived of liberty in proportion to their wrongdoing. While details vary, retributivists typically believe we are morally justified in imposing suffering or deprivation of liberty upon offenders so long as we never purposely or knowingly punish in excess of what is proportional.

For retributivists who hold such a view, a defendant's wrongdoing solely depends on facts about the crime at issue.[4] Nothing juries do alters facts about prior wrongdoing. Verdicts, as discussed, provide some information about the past, but it is filtered through biased and imperfect juries that are systematically denied relevant evidence. Some evidence is excluded to promote policies unrelated to the case at bar (for example, to encourage open communication with attorneys or obedience to the Fourth Amendment) and will leave jurors with incomplete pictures of desert. In any event, exclusion of at least some relevant evidence puts jurors in a poor epistemic position and limits the moral significance of their verdicts.

Just as they do for consequentialists, guilty pleas convey some information that is morally relevant to retributivists. Both kinds of theorist seek to understand the underlying facts, either because they concern prior wrongdoing (retributivists) or affect predictions (consequentialists). Importantly, though, morally relevant

[4] Ryberg (Chapter 3) identifies scholars who seem to understand retributivism in this fashion.

information from pleas and verdicts gets filtered through a legal lens. Jury questions are decided by fallible jurors, and defendants plead to laws crafted by fallible legislators. Moral questions, by contrast, are not resolved by vote. Schoolyard bullies may vote you the most evil child in the playground, but their votes do not make it so. Similarly, no matter the vote jurors settle on or the crimes to which one pleads guilty, associated moral condemnation is not morally authoritative.[5]

In this section, we have seen why traditional consequentialists and retributivists care about facts related to prior wrongdoing. Pleas and verdicts usually have limited bearing on our beliefs about the past, so they are not especially likely to alter traditional moral assessments. In the next section, we consider whether the symbolic or communicative meaning of pleas and verdicts should alter our moral assessments.

III. Communicative Perspectives

In recent decades, scholars have renewed focus on expressive and communicative aspects of criminal justice. According to Joel Feinberg,

> punishment is a conventional device for the expression of attitudes of resentment and indignation, and of judgments of disapproval and reprobation, on the part either of the punishing authority itself or those 'in whose name' the punishment is inflicted. Punishment, in short, has a *symbolic significance* largely missing from other kinds of penalties. (Feinberg 1970: 98)

Antony Duff has argued that punishment should be a communicative enterprise. On Duff's influential account, 'censure is expressed [among other ways] by the formal convictions that follow on proof of guilt at a criminal trial' (Duff 2000: 29). He writes:

> A criminal trial is also a communicative enterprise in which a citizen is called to answer a charge of wrongdoing and to take part in the process by which that charge is tested. If he is convicted, his conviction communicates to him (and to others) the censure that he has been proved to deserve for his crime. He is expected (but not compelled) to understand and accept the censure as justified: to understand and accept that he committed a wrong for which the community now properly censures him. ... [The law aims to persuade people] to accept not just that certain kinds of conduct are 'prohibited' by the law but that and why such conduct is wrong. (Duff 2000: 80–81, citation omitted)

Importantly for Duff, we should seek to persuade offenders with rational and moral considerations, not threats of harm:

> If I am to respect another as a rational moral agent, I need not refrain from trying to persuade her to modify her conduct: respect does not preclude attempted persuasion.

[5] Some may be more likely to consider jurors epistemic peers as to matters of fact about which there is less methodological disagreement than as to matters of value about which there is more methodological disagreement.

> Respect does, however, preclude manipulation or coercion …; that is, I should attempt to modify her conduct only by giving her *relevant* reasons to modify it herself. … [T]hreatening to inflict harm on her if she remains unpersuaded [would] cease to treat or respect her as a rational moral agent …. (Duff 1996: 14)

Let us consider a Duffian-style communicative account that makes the following two claims: (1) pleas and verdicts can be valuable methods of communicating condemnation as part of a dialogue with offenders, and their value need not arise from further good consequences; and (2) because the communicative process seeks to persuade rational agents, the persuasion must be based on information that is true (or at least sincerely believed). I will argue that pleas and verdicts do not satisfy both conditions simultaneously. If we need to communicate truthfully, legally authoritative pleas and verdicts will play no special role in that story because they have no morally authoritative claim to accuracy. We can engage in communicative dialogue with offenders about as well while their juries deliberate as we can afterwards.

A. What Do Verdicts and Pleas Communicate?

On the communicative account under discussion, the main party a jury verdict is supposed to persuade is the defendant himself. Juries, however, will not persuade many defendants about underlying (non-moral) facts. The jury's epistemic position is generally vastly inferior to the defendant's, considering that the defendant is usually an eyewitness to the key events of an alleged crime. There are certainly exceptions where, for example, a defendant was under the influence of drugs or suffered from memory problems, but as a general rule, the defendant will know more about underlying facts than jurors.

Juries often address mixed questions of law and fact, as when a jury must decide if a defendant was criminally negligent. Perhaps such verdicts reveal something important about how a defendant's peers morally evaluate his conduct. It will, however, be difficult or impossible to determine the extent to which a jury's decision relied on non-moral fact finding (about which jurors are epistemic inferiors) or on value assessments (about which jurors are arguably superior or non-inferior). It seems difficult to persuade a rational defendant that the jury has something to teach when we do not know whether its decision turned on something about which it is epistemically superior.

For Duff, offenders often know they did something wrong, and punishment is supposed to communicate at a more emotional, less cognitive level:

> [I]n many instances it would be wrong to suggest that offenders commit their crimes from moral ignorance or error. … The problem is not that they do not realize that what they are doing is wrong but that they do not care enough about it, or fail to attend to that aspect of their conduct, or give in to temptation. They do not need education to teach them what they already know. (Duff 2000: 91)

It is not obvious, however, that verdicts play a role in correcting these non-cognitive errors. Even if they do, one must be careful to adjust offender moral emotions in ways that honour the Duffian commitment to *rational* persuasion. For Duff, we need not actually succeed in persuading offenders to repent. He writes:

> The moral possibility of trials and punishments does not, of course, depend upon their actual success in bringing wrongdoers to engage in the communicative enterprise, or to answer for, to repent, or to make amends for their crimes: we must address the wrongdoer as someone who *could* respond appropriately. (Duff 2009: 91)

It is enough that we try to communicate with wrongdoers in ways that honour their rational agency. But presumably we cannot honour their rational agency unless we communicate in ways that *should* persuade rational agents.

Even if offenders should be open to learning from jurors about both moral and non-moral considerations, verdicts are extremely blunt tools of expression. They only reveal whether a defendant is liable for the smallest quantum of punishment – maybe a trivial fine or a suspended sentence.[6] To convey condemnation, one must communicate something about the magnitude of the condemnation – something that distinguishes a litterer from a murderer – if we are to communicate not just censure but 'the censure that criminals deserve' (Duff 2000: 86).

Jury verdicts, however, cannot convey magnitude or do so with only the broadest of brushstrokes.[7] Even when a conviction entails a mandatory minimum sentence, we cannot read the sentence as a jury communication since juries are almost always deprived of sentencing information (Kolber 2021: 111; Bellin 2010). (In the next two sections, we will consider whether verdicts combined with sentences adequately communicate condemnation. For now, we see that sentences imposed by judges do not reveal the magnitude of the *jury's* condemnation.)

It is even harder to persuade defendants of the wrongfulness of their conduct through the defendant's own guilty plea. We tell defendants that they are presumed innocent prior to conviction but then use prosecutorial leverage to induce them to plead guilty and waive their rights to a trial. Defendants themselves gain no new information from the fact of their own guilty pleas; at most we can try to rationally persuade them using emotional appeals and facts that go beyond the case itself. But again, to the extent a principal form of persuasion is emotional, it raises questions about whether we are persuading on rational grounds that recognise offenders as rational agents.

Guilty pleas do communicate confession (and maybe remorse, apology, repentance and so on) to crime victims, victims' families and society more generally. A bare guilty plea need not include remorse, apology and repentance, but certainly

[6] A small number of jurisdictions give juries greater say in sentencing.

[7] A jury might convey some magnitude information, as when it decides between manslaughter and murder or between assault and aggravated assault. But these offences still leave tremendous amounts of uncertainty as to the level of condemnation in the minds of jurors. For example, some manslaughter convictions may lead to longer sentences than some murder convictions.

some plea allocutions will include open-ended statements from defendants that make those expressions. To consequentialists, such communications can certainly have instrumental significance if they provide evidence that an offender is less likely to recidivate.

To retributivists, reactions may vary. Some will deny the relevance of remorse, apology and repentance to deserved punishment, while others may think they reduce a defendant's remaining negative desert or show that the defendant was never quite as deserving of retribution as we thought. Whatever their value to these retributivists, they are not made special because they arise during an authoritative plea allocution. If we hold constant other pertinent variables such as the audience and the level of sincerity (and assume perjury is mostly inapplicable to remorse, apology and repentance), it does not matter whether they are part of a plea or not. If we lived in an ancient society without a formal legal system, remorse, apology and repentance would arguably be no less significant for lack of formality. We may even have better markers of sincerity when these expressions are made informally and not induced by anticipated sentence reductions.[8]

Duff takes the perhaps surprising position that, in the courtroom, we should only expect offenders to engage in the formal ritual of confession (and, perhaps, formal rituals of remorse, apology and repentance):

> [A] liberal polity that respects its citizens' privacy and freedom should not inquire into the sincerity of their public performances; it should address them and require conduct of them as if they were sincere. The script is generic: the sentence leaves no room for offenders to communicate more nuanced messages. But that is because it is a formal public procedure, appropriate between citizens who are (relative) strangers: the language of punishment is a ritual, conventional language in which appropriate formal messages about the crime are communicated. An offender might want to find other ways of communicating some more personal message to the victim or to others (and the sentencing process could include a meeting with the victim at which each could speak more personally); but this is the way in which she must formally communicate, as an offender-citizen with her fellow citizens. (Duff 2011: 373–74; see also Brownlee 2011: 54)

But even if Duff is right that we ought not formally inquire into the sincerity of offender public performances, sincerity is still important no matter whether one cares principally about consequentialist or retributivist considerations. If Duff is right that we ought not inquire, that would further limit the moral relevance of courtroom performances in our moral assessments of offenders. Offenders would either make the public performance or not, but without an inquiry into sincerity, it is hard to know what is communicated. A confession could represent anything from the most genuine and sincere expression of remorse to the most emotionless, robotic recitation of lines in a script to the most convincing but deceptive hoax perpetrated on those already victimised.

[8] Some may agree that nothing special happens to remorse, apology and repentance simply by attachment to a formal plea. The point is worth emphasising, however, because the state sometimes promotes propagandistic faith in the criminal legal system. I worry that the journalistic convention of speaking only of *alleged* criminals until formal conviction and not afterwards portrays false accuracy and finality.

B. The 'Part of a Process' Objection

One might claim that I have misleadingly disconnected the pieces of the criminal legal system. Jury verdicts reveal little by themselves because they are part of a system with multiple actors in a communicative exchange. A verdict signals a judge to craft a sentence commensurate with the conviction. The sentence adds the judge's communicative content and reflects any mandatory maxima or minima that the legislature may have imposed as its communicative contribution to an offender's sentence.

But like the children's game of telephone, a meaningful condemnatory message would struggle to survive the process, at least if the message is meant to persuade rational agents. As noted, juries simply decide whether the defendant is liable to receive an iota of punishment. If the defendant has committed a serious offence, such as murder, the defendant will likely presume the jury communicated serious condemnation. That inference, however, comes from defendants' background assumptions rather than anything the jury's verdict has actually communicated.

Moreover, the inference of substantial condemnation will sometimes be incorrect. Suppose a defendant believed he was being attacked with deadly force and responded by killing his attacker. In fact, the defendant was mistaken; he was actually attacked with ordinary force. After much deliberation and a close judgement call, the jury decides the defendant's use of force was just shy of being reasonable. In most jurisdictions, the defendant would lose his self-defence claim entirely and be guilty of murder. Nevertheless, the offender's punishment should be quite modest from a retributivist perspective. He has little culpability if he just barely crossed the line into unreasonableness and might be only negligibly more dangerous than a reasonable person in the same situation.

There is so little substantive communication between judges and juries, however, that many judges presiding over a case like this would still impose a substantial sentence. They may never know that the jury considered a defence to be a close one, and they may fear raising eyebrows by giving a murderer a light sentence. Even if the judge also considered it a close call, many judges would give substantial sentences for fear that doing otherwise would be perceived as failing to honour the jury's verdict (even though it would actually be better honoured by a light sentence).[9]

This example may seem idiosyncratic, but it illustrates a deep feature of the criminal legal system: it is hard to be confident that jurors understand the law they apply. Consider a case in Colorado in which an experienced skier was charged

[9] In *Hines v State* (2002), for example, a sentencing judge refused to grant a downward departure, even though the defendant's self-defence claim was arguably close to the line. The trial judge refused to reduce the sentence because the jury, at least formally, rejected the defendant's self-defence claim. According to the appellate court, 'The trial court apparently believed that it was not allowed to consider the' partial self-defence evidence 'because the jury had rejected [the defendant's] self-defense argument' (*Hines v State* 2002: 965). While the appellate court reversed, in many such cases we would not know enough about why a judge refused to reduce the defendant's sentence to successfully appeal.

with unintentional homicide for colliding with another skier who subsequently died (*People v Hall* 2000). The defendant was convicted of negligent homicide, meaning that he caused death by taking a substantial and unjustifiable risk that grossly deviated from the care of a reasonable person. In a subsequent news report, the last hold-out juror told a reporter:

> [I]t became inescapable that the gross deviation was that a beginner skier who was where he needed to be should not be killed by being hit from behind by a better skier, particularly one who is employed on the mountain and therefore has a mandate in our community, more than anybody else, to protect the people on the mountain. (Lipsher 2000)

In my view, the key consideration that swayed this juror – that people employed on the mountain skiing at their leisure have greater than normal obligations to ski carefully – reflects an obligation that goes beyond the law itself. Either way, while the juror's message is condemnatory, it is hard to know whether it is morally or legally condemnatory and whether it aligned with that of other jurors.

Of course, courts try to help jurors apply the law, but we generally do not know when they are successful. Juries may convict for reasons quite different than those that later lead a judge to pick a particular sentence. This structural feature of our court system does not jibe well with Duff's aim to persuade 'only by a communicative process that seeks to bring citizens to recognize and to accept not just that certain kinds of conduct are "prohibited" by the law … but that and why such conduct is wrong' (Duff 2000: 81). For some crimes – blackmail and insider trading come to mind – there may not even be a consensus as to why conduct is wrong, even if there is consensus that it is wrong.

While we could make the criminal legal system more communicative by, say, having jurors state reasons for their decisions, communication is currently rather limited and has been for centuries. If the criminal legal system cannot send a clearly discernible message of condemnation with a recognisable condemnatory magnitude, it cannot live up to Igor Primoratz's urging that 'Society may legitimately express moral condemnation by punishment only when its conscience speaks strongly and unequivocally, with one voice' (Primoratz 1989: 205).

C. The 'Sentences Reveal Magnitude' Objection

Even if various parts of the criminal legal system could communicate, they have no common language in which to express condemnatory magnitude. A 20-year sentence for murder seems to express more condemnation than a two-year sentence for burglary, but even such an extreme example may be misconstrued due to what I call the 'radical indeterminacy of punishment severity'.

Punishment is almost universally viewed as an *intentional* infliction. As Duff puts it, 'punishment is, typically, something intended to be burdensome or painful, imposed on a (supposed) offender for a (supposed) offense by someone with (supposedly) the authority to do so' (Duff 2000: xiv–xv). Pleas and verdicts, however, eventually lead to formal announcement of a sentence not a punishment (at least not as punishment is traditionally understood by theorists). A sentence is a legal declaration of planned hard treatment, but it does not tell us which aspects of an offender's sentence involve intentional inflictions and which do not. Sentences describe planned hard treatment that may involve both intentional and non-intentional inflictions. By contrast, punishments, at least traditionally, are intentional inflictions. Radical indeterminacy arises when we seek to derive the severity of punishment from the way punishment is expressed as a sentence.

Suppose, for example, that a jurisdiction imposes a \$10,000 civil fine for releasing a certain chemical into groundwater entirely accidentally or a \$25,000 criminal fine for doing so negligently (but never imposes both). Assume that some particular defendant is convicted (by plea or jury verdict) of negligently releasing the chemical and is sentenced to pay the \$25,000 criminal fine.

One possibility is that the sentence equals the punishment: a full \$25,000 fine. That is hardly the only interpretation, however. Merely causing the harm leads to a \$10,000 civil fine. Assume that all civil fines and \$10,000 of criminal fines fund environmental remediation. Now one could argue that, of sentences to pay the \$25,000 criminal fine, only \$15,000 represents punishment and the other \$10,000 is compensation for environmental damage that would be paid even for entirely accidental spills. We probably should not view the full \$25,000 as intended to be burdensome or painful when we would expect \$10,000 of that to be paid anyway in a non-burdensome, non-painful fashion for entirely accidental spills.

There are still other interpretations. Maybe it is hard to tell what portion of criminal fines compensate remediation efforts. Suppose accounting experts give varying answers between \$5,000 and \$15,000. So a *sentence* of a \$25,000 fine could refer to a *punishment* of \$25,000 or of any punishment between \$10,000 and \$20,000 (depending on the amount we subtract as compensation). In fact, any portion of the \$25,000 fine could constitute punishment depending on how much is intended to be painful or burdensome.

We impose civil fines, in part, to deter bad behaviour, but we don't consider such fines to be punishment. Perhaps, then, the portion of criminal fines motivated by deterrence are non-punitive as well. A sentence of a \$25,000 criminal fine might constitute a punishment with severity of \$1 or of 25,000 times that amount depending on what portion of the fine is intended to achieve a non-punitive deterrent effect.

There are no obvious rules or conventions governing what our intentions are or are supposed to be when we impose criminal fines. A jurisdiction might distinguish punitive fines from restitution, but it might not. Even if it does, it is not obvious that a formal breakdown in a statute is authoritative (for example, the statute might inaccurately describe how funds are actually used or are believed to be used by sentencing judges).

Similarly, there are no clear conventions dictating whose punitive intentions ultimately matter: the legislature's? the sentencing judge's? the average person's?

Given the indeterminacy of the severity of criminal fines, I do not see how revealing sentences to offenders even roughly communicates an amount of condemnation. An offender sentenced to pay $25,000 for committing an environmental offence may have a friend sentenced to pay a criminal fine of $10,000 for some entirely different offence. Though their sentences appear the same, we do not know whose punishment expresses greater condemnation.

Other complications are possible: a judge could sentence someone to a $25,000 fine, intending $15,000 (in the judge's mind) as punishment. After issuing the sentence, she decides (again in her mind) that $20,000 actually represents the punishment. Has the friend's punishment become more severe post sentencing? Must the judge's change of heart (which might have occurred while showering two months after the sentence was imposed) be communicated to have an effect? If the offender already paid the fine, can her *punishment* increase retroactively? If the goal of criminal justice is to communicate condemnation to offenders and correct their misconceptions, we must communicate the right amount of condemnation (not too much, not too little), and so far, amounts of punishment have been too indeterminate to meaningfully relay.

The indeterminacy of punishment severity is not just a problem for criminal fines. Consider a fictitious imposition called 'truncation' (Kolber 2009: 188). Offenders who are truncated are forced against a wall while a sharp blade swings horizontally at exactly six feet in the air. Short people are entirely unharmed. Those around six feet tall receive a sloppy and sometimes bloody haircut. Those significantly above six feet tall are beheaded.

Truncation vividly illustrates key differences between sentences and punishments. Sentences, as noted, are legal declarations of expected hard treatment. Interpreted in a very objective fashion, we could say that all people sentenced to truncation receive the same sentence. But assuming punishers know offender heights, offenders are receiving very different punishments because they receive different intended inflictions (ranging, in essence, from nothing to death).

An offender sentenced to truncation might, based on the sentencing judge's intentions, be set to receive the punishment of an embarrassingly imprecise haircut. To everyone's surprise, however, the offender has a big growth spurt right after sentencing and his truncation two months later causes a bloody mess that precipitates his death. Even though the offender died (his hard treatment was quite severe), his punishment was still just the sloppy haircut the judge intended.

So merely knowing a person will be truncated vastly underdetermines the hard treatment he will experience. Absent detailed information about whose intentions are pertinent and what those intentions actually are, the severity of condemnation associated with truncation is indeterminate. It seems rather pointless to communicate condemnation to offenders and society with the punishment of truncation unless we provide additional information about intentions (assuming as I am, that condemnation, like punishment, is viewed as depending on intent).

Incarceration raises similar issues as truncation but in less exaggerated form. Assume Judge Purpose is sentencing Purp in one jurisdiction, and Judge Foresight is sentencing Fore in another.[10] The offenders are equally blameworthy and equally deserving of retributivist punishment. The key difference is that Judge Purpose *intends* most of the deprivations of liberty associated with prison to be painful. He thinks Purp should lose his rights to free expression, to association, to procreation, to personal privacy (and so on) as part of his punishment because Purp deserves severe liberty deprivations. Having determined the severity of each liberty deprivation he intends to impose, Judge Purpose sets a four-year sentence as the duration required to impose proportional punishment.

By contrast, Judge Foresight intends to deprive Fore of some liberty of movement – an essential feature of incarceration – but treats the loss or limitation of these other liberties as merely foreseen consequences of incarceration. (Assume, too, that in Judge Purpose's jurisdiction, the legislature, governor and prison administrators share Judge Purpose's approach to prison, while in Judge Foresight's jurisdiction, they share Judge Foresight's approach.) Though Judge Foresight may seem more humanitarian, he needs to deprive Fore of liberty with a 12-year sentence in order to intentionally deprive Fore of the *same amount* of liberty as Purp. Fore's sentence is longer because he is deprived of liberty more slowly than Purp. Punishing these equally blameworthy offenders equally could mean giving one a four-year sentence and the other a 12-year sentence.

Even if we knew the intentions of all relevant parties in the criminal legal system, it would still be difficult to communicate precisely which liberty deprivations associated with incarceration are intentional and how severe they are individually or collectively. Moreover, there are about a million questions related to intentionality that we would need to resolve: if punishment severity depends on the intentions of multiple people, do they all need to *intend* burdensome or painful inflictions? What if some intend an infliction to be burdensome and others do not? Do we average them? Is intentionality binary (see, eg, Tang 2014)? Can we not intend something in degrees or along multiple axes (such as wholeheartedness and confidence of success)? If intentionality comes in degrees or along multiple axes, would not the nature and quality of intentions affect the extent to which an associated infliction is punishment?

Judges Purpose and Foresight remind us of three key points: first, offenders are not primarily focused on punishment. They care primarily about how harshly they are treated, no matter whether the treatment is intentional or merely foreseen. Nevertheless, communicative accounts focus on intent because it is the intentional components of punishment that most clearly communicate condemnation. A communicative account cannot count all hard treatment because some hard treatment, say the death of the fast-growing truncated offender who was only supposed to receive a bad haircut, would not accurately reflect his condemnation; he just had the bad luck of an unexpected growth spurt.

To take a more realistic example, part of the hard treatment of incarceration might include an increased risk of physical or sexual assault. But most people

[10] The example in the text is based on Kolber (2012: 8–12).

do not consider such risk to be part of either the offender's condemnation or punishment. They consider it a mere unintended side-effect of something that was intended. So those who care about intrinsic communicative significance cannot simply swap in proportional hard treatment for proportional punishment.[11]

Second, the indeterminacy of punishment severity poses a particularly serious threat to retributivists. Retributivists generally promote proportional punishment and insist that we never purposely or knowingly punish in excess of what is proportional. Retributivists have long had a difficult time explaining punishment proportionality. But if Purp and Fore are punished equally when one has a four-year sentence and the other a 12-year sentence, proportionality is in muddier water than is generally recognised (Kolber 2013).[12]

Finally, our actual criminal legal system – as well as nearby cousins we could imagine – do not have the tools to adequately convey amounts of condemnatory punishment.[13] Punishment on Duff's communicative account is supposed to convey the seriousness of condemnation and draw the offender's attention to his wrongdoing in a manner that promotes repentance. This is difficult to do with the existing criminal justice tools of pleas, verdicts and sentences.

D. The 'Community of Peers' Objection

I have argued that a jury is just a group of laypeople whose verdict carries no greater moral significance than that of a similar mock jury. And a confession or apology given at a plea allocution has no greater moral significance than a comparable confession or apology given to the same audience outside the courtroom.

In response, one might argue that I have neglected to consider important political dimensions. After all, the jury deciding a case arose from, let us assume, a democratic process. The community voted on representatives who passed legislation structuring a court system with rules governing selection of judges and jurors

[11] By contrast, I do think we can profitably understand punishment severity in ways that focus on hard treatment. See Kolber (2023, in press). It is just that, to the extent we care about *condemnation*, theorists seem to focus on intentional rather than non-intentional inflictions.

[12] To the extent Duff and other theorists shy away from precise measures of proportionality, they have less risk of acting inconsistently. But there are still deep questions about whether condemnatory messages are sufficiently determinate to be meaningful and whether non-instrumental communicative accounts of punishment can be justified without relying on more determinate accounts of proportionality.

[13] Perhaps we must communicate not only condemnation, but also our confidence in that condemnation. But when and how do we convey it to defendants? Doubts about condemnation may extend beyond the question of whether a defendant violated all the statutory elements of an offence. What if I am only 80% confident that we have the kind of free will that generates retributive condemnation? Do we discount punishment by, say, 20% to more accurately reflect a community's confidence that condemnation is morally appropriate (see Kolber 2018)? If courts and legislatures in some jurisdictions are free will sceptics, do their sentences reflect any condemnation at all? Accurate communication of condemnation arguably requires measures of both magnitude and confidence, unless confidence is already factored into magnitude.

and rules governing plea allocutions and so on. A guilty verdict from *a defendant's* jury is morally significant, one could argue, because it arises from fair and reasonable conditions of political morality that give special significance to *the defendant's* jury as the mouthpiece of his community. Similarly, one might argue, a guilty plea in the defendant's courtroom has special significance because it is the courtroom assigned by his community through fair and reasonable processes to arrange for the public disposition of his case.

This response may blunt some legal or procedural complaints a defendant might raise. It may explain why, despite the good and bad luck that can inevitably arise during jury selection or plea bargaining, *the defendant's* jury (but not a mock jury) can lead to his imprisonment. And the defendant's official guilty plea can proximately cause his imprisonment in a way that the confession and apology he offers his victim directly cannot.

But I do not see how considerations of political community affect efforts to rationally persuade defendants to recognise and repent their wrongdoing. Nothing about a jury makes it generally epistemically superior to other possible juries. Nothing about a confession and apology made directly to a victim generally communicates less meaningfully than a comparable confession and apology during an official proceeding.

So long as the factors driving appropriate treatment of offenders consist of consequentialist considerations (such as deterrence, incapacitation and rehabilitation) or retributivist considerations (such as prior wrongdoing), then accurate moral assessment of an offender will depend on accurate assessment of those considerations. Given that a communicative account like Duff's requires truthful (or at least sincere) communication, the communication must be driven by our most accurate assessments. Granting non-instrumental symbolic or communicative moral significance to pleas and verdicts steers us away from the accuracy that must be central to the persuasion of rational agents.

IV. Conclusion

We have pragmatic reasons to treat pleas and verdicts as though they have special significance. Doing so promotes the impression that there is a single society-wide determination of a person's status as an offender, non-offender, former offender and so on. Such rituals of clarity and cleansing may be useful, but they are misleading: pleas and verdicts do not have special accuracy when it comes to morally assessing offenders.

The basic principle here is that moral attitudes towards offenders should depend on our best information and not formal legal events. If theorists believe censure should be conveyed and persuasive communicative arguments constructed based on authoritative mechanisms like verdicts or guilty pleas, then they would not be conveying our most accurate information. I recognise many instrumental reasons for focusing on these mechanisms but raise doubts about whether we can use them to persuade defendants as rational agents.

References

Bellin, J (2010) 'Is Punishment Relevant After All? A Prescription for Informing Juries of the Consequences of Conviction' 90 *Boston University Law Review* 2223.

Brownlee, K (2011) 'The Offender's Part in the Dialogue' in R Cruft, MH Kramer and MR Reiff (eds), *Crime, Punishment, and Responsibility: The Jurisprudence of Antony Duff* (New York, Oxford University Press).

Duff, RA (1996) 'Penal Communications: Recent Work in the Philosophy of Punishment' 20 *Crime and Justice* 1.

—— (2000) *Punishment, Communication, and Community* (New York, Oxford University Press).

—— (2009) 'Can We Punish the Perpetrators of Atrocities?' in T Brudholm and T Cushman (eds), *The Religious in Responses to Mass Atrocity: Interdisciplinary Perspectives* (New York, Cambridge University Press).

—— (2011) 'In Response' in R Cruft, MH Kramer and MR Reiff (eds), *Crime, Punishment, and Responsibility: The Jurisprudence of Antony Duff* (New York, Oxford University Press).

Feinberg, J (1970) *Doing and Deserving: Essays in the Theory of Responsibility* (Princeton, NJ, Princeton University Press).

Frances, B and Matheson, J (2018) 'Disagreement' in *Stanford Encyclopedia of Philosophy*, https://plato.stanford.edu/entries/disagreement/.

Gramlich, J (2019) 'Only 2% of federal criminal defendants go to trial, and most who do are found guilty' (Pew Research Center).

Kolber, AJ (2009) 'The Subjective Experience of Punishment' 109 *Columbia Law Review* 182.

—— (2012) 'Unintentional Punishment' 18 *Legal Theory* 29.

—— (2013) 'Against Proportional Punishment' 66 *Vanderbilt Law Review* 1141.

—— (2018) 'Punishment and Moral Risk' 2018 *University of Illinois Law Review* 487.

—— (2021) 'Line Drawing in the Dark' 22 *Theoretical Inquiries in Law* 111.

—— (2023, in press) 'Measuring Punishment Severity' in J Ryberg (ed), *The Oxford Handbook of Punishment Theory and Philosophy* (New York, Oxford University Press).

Lipsher, S (2000) 'Ski Verdict Tough, Juror Says', *Denver Post*, 20 November.

Primoratz, I (1989) 'Punishment as Language' 64 *Philosophy* 187.

Seelye, KQ (2006) 'Barack Obama, asked about drug history, admits he inhaled', *New York Times*, 24 October.

Tang, WH (2014) 'Intentionality and Partial Belief' 191 *Synthese* 1433.

Weisman, J (1999) 'Bush says he's been drug-free 25 years; Pressed, he declines to offer more details', *Baltimore Sun*, 20 August.

Cases

Hines v State 817 So 2d 964 (Fla Dist Ct App 2002)
Mapp v Ohio 367 US 643 (1961)
People v Hall 999 P2d 207 (CO 2000)
State v Crawford 163 NC App 122 (2004)

7

The Guilty Plea and Self-respect

GABRIELLE WATSON*

I. Introduction

The guilty plea can both affirm and erode a defendant's self-respect. For this reason alone, it has a strong claim to our attention. On one view, the entering of a guilty plea can be a gesture of contrition, a form of atonement, and a public acceptance of legal responsibility. On another view, the guilty plea is an incentivisation tool employed by the State, designed to appeal not only to the factually guilty, but also to the factually innocent, who routinely waive their right to trial and plead 'guilty' in exchange for a sentence reduction.[1] The guilty plea, then, has the capacity to generate quite conflicting sentiments, where we might at once morally approve and morally object to its existence.

The chapter proceeds as follows. It begins by introducing the statutory framework and the role of the guilty plea in the sentencing process of England and Wales. It then proposes the concept of self-respect as a new conceptual tool for sentencing scholarship and a means by which to deepen our understanding of the guilty plea from an ethical perspective. In principle, the guilty plea allows a defendant to take responsibility for his wrongdoing and emerge from the criminal process with his self-respect intact. Yet, there is good reason to be sceptical that the guilty plea regularly fulfils such a lofty aim in practice. Too often, the factually innocent defendant 'self-convicts' for instrumental reasons, where the hidden cost is a loss of self-respect. It remains to be seen whether the sentencing community will succeed in forging a robust defence of the guilty plea as a defining feature of the sentencing process for the 2020s, despite mixed motivations for its use and the material risk it poses to a defendant's intrinsic worth.

* For insightful comments and critique, I thank the participants at the Oxford Guilty Plea and Sentencing Seminar in March 2022.

[1] 'Sentence reduction' is the term in use in England and Wales but the same differential (between the sentence if pleading not guilty compared to pleading guilty) is known in other jurisdictions as a 'sentence discount', 'allowance in respect of a guilty plea', 'adjustment', 'trial tax,' 'trial premium' and 'trial penalty' (Gormley, McPherson and Tata 2020).

II. Thinking Ethically about the Guilty Plea

The literature on the guilty plea has escaped harsh criticism in England and Wales when contrasted with the US plea bargaining system (Helm 2018). It has focused on three key themes: first, its statutory basis and the role of the Sentencing Guidelines; second, its role in securing a plea-based sentence discount; and, third, its prevalence (70 per cent of defendants in the Crown Court entered a guilty plea in 2021).[2] No doubt this scholarship is rich and extensive, but it is also inescapably pragmatic. The guilty plea calls out for analysis in ethical terms.

What might this task involve? The traditional but arguably deficient approach in the field of applied ethics is simply to 'apply' an ethical theory, such as utilitarianism or deontology, in a particular context – in our case, the entering of a guilty plea – to 'solve' the ethical problems it generates. This top-down approach to ethical reasoning adheres to the idea that ethics is akin to geometry, presupposing a solid foundation from which principles and general rules can be inferred and then applied to concrete cases independent of context. But there are limits to this narrow focus on *ethics as problem solving* that the sentencing community would do well to avoid. An ethical analysis of the guilty plea need not be reduced to an exercise in identifying the failures in sentencing law and practice. Rather, it ought to be a means by which to identify its successes too, especially if we subscribe to the idea of the ethical as 'good', 'right' or 'desirable' in a sense which evokes modernist moral and political theory (see, eg, Singer 2011: ch 1).

Furthermore, an ethical analysis need not be viewed as an exclusively abstract intellectual exercise, or an attempt at achieving a level of conceptual precision of interest only to the academic community. When we reconcile sentencing law and scholarship with concepts from ethics, it can be a concrete exercise too, with material implications for defendants and the sentencing process alike. Ethics, like law, is by its very nature a regulatory instrument for the proper direction of individuals towards the common good. As a system of moral concepts, it has the capacity to provide structured and systematic moral guidance, recommending what ought to be done or avoided. It too can be grounded and pragmatic.[3]

If there is a demand for ethical theory in the sentencing context, then ideas need to be presented carefully if they are to find their way into practice. Unsystematic criticism fuelled by moral intuition can call long-established practices into question, but explicit, stable and justifiable ethical principles provide a robust starting point and are essential to move forward.

[2] This represents a fall back from a peak of 79% in 2020. The high guilty plea rate reflects the restricted ability of courts to progress to jury trials as part of the COVID-19 response (Ministry of Justice 2021).

[3] On the practical demand for ethical theory, see Nussbaum (2000); Cueni and Queloz (2021).

III. The Guilty Plea in England and Wales

A plea of guilty is a formal reply to a criminal charge. While counsel may advise as to the appropriate plea, the decision is for the defendant alone, to be entered by him personally. It is essential that the plea be unequivocal, representing a clear acknowledgement of guilt (Ormerod and Perry 2021: Part D). If the court is satisfied with the plea, the prosecution is released from their obligation to bring evidence and prove the defendant's legal guilt beyond reasonable doubt. There is no need to assemble a jury and the defendant stands convicted simply by virtue of the word 'guilty' that he has uttered.

First established in English common law, sections 77(1) and (2) of the Sentencing Act 2020 now provide that, when determining what sentence to pass on an offender who has pleaded guilty, the court 'must take into account … (a) the stage in the proceedings for the offence at which the offender indicated the intention to plead guilty; and (b) the circumstances in which the indication was given'. However, the statute is otherwise silent on what approach a court ought to take when an offender pleads guilty. This gap is filled by the Sentencing Guidelines. By virtue of section 125 of the Coroners and Justice Act 2009, the court is required to follow the Guidelines unless 'satisfied that it would be contrary to the interests of justice to do so'. In 2017, the Sentencing Council issued a revised Guideline, *Reduction in Sentence for a Guilty Plea* (Sentencing Council of England and Wales 2017; see also Gormley, Roberts and Harris 2020).

A defendant who pleads guilty typically receives a reduction in sentence. Part D of the Guideline states that full credit amounts to a reduction of one-third where the guilty plea was entered at the first hearing at which a plea or indication of plea is sought and recorded by the court; one-quarter for a plea indicated after the first stage of proceedings; with a sliding scale of reduction thereafter, down to a maximum of one-tenth on the first day of trial. The reduction would normally be decreased further, even to zero, if the guilty plea is entered during the trial itself. The Guideline states that the benefits of a guilty plea apply regardless of the strength of the evidence against an offender, and so this matter should not be considered when determining the level of reduction. This is an important change from the earlier Guideline, where a reduced discount was often given in such cases (Sentencing Guidelines Council 2007).

A reduced sentence is not an automatic right for those who plead guilty. In *R v Darling and others* (2009), the Court of Appeal held that where the sentencing judge identifies circumstances which would make it unjust to impose the minimum sentence, the limited reduction permissible for a guilty plea no longer applies. Relatedly, *R v Ladbrook* (2022) confirmed that the effect of section 73 of the Sentencing Act 2020 and the Guideline is that it cannot be assumed that the defendant will inevitably be entitled to full credit for the guilty plea whenever a lesser or different offence is charged during proceedings, and he immediately pleads guilty to it. *R v Plaku and others* (2021) served as another reminder that a one-third discount for an early guilty plea will only be given if there is an '*unequivocal* indication' (paragraph 17) that the defendant wishes to plead guilty at the first stage of proceedings. An indication of a likely or probable plea is not enough since it keeps open the possibility of a not guilty plea and thus negates the advantages set out in the 'key principles' section of the Guideline.

There is an 'enhanced' discount available for defendants who assist the prosecuting authorities, for example, where an accomplice pleads guilty and gives evidence for the prosecution against his erstwhile co-defendants. In such cases, substantial credit should be given, particularly where that person's evidence leads to the conviction of a co-defendant or induces a co-defendant to plead guilty (*R v A (Informer: Reduction of Sentence)* 1999: 56).

The effect is that we have a negotiated form of justice in England and Wales, whereby the defendant essentially 'self-criminalises' or 'self-convicts'. Once a plea of guilty has been accepted, the court may then commence the procedure leading up to the passing of sentence. The fact that a plea of guilty has been considered must be made explicit in the sentencing remarks. The high rate of guilty pleas means that the contested trial, in theory the adversarial system's chosen mechanism for determining the question of legal guilt, plays no part in most criminal cases in this jurisdiction.

IV. Self-respect: An Interpretive Framework

Self-respect offers a means by which to interpret and assess the ethical issues associated with pleading guilty in England and Wales. What is self-respect? Despite the increasingly sophisticated accounts of self-respect to be found in the contemporary philosophical literature, disagreement persists as to precisely *how* the concept should be construed (see, eg, Bird 2010). It is possible, however, to detect some recurring themes in the literature and arrive at a working account of self-respect for the purposes of this chapter.

A. Two Kinds of Self-respect

Philosophers tend to agree that self-respect is something of great ethical importance. It is tied closely to an individual's sense of self-worth and is coupled with a desire to protect and preserve it. Suggesting that an individual has no self-respect or acts in a way that no self-respecting person would act amount to very strong moral criticisms. The notion that individuals must regard and treat themselves as deserving of respect is grounded in the Kantian claim that all human beings have a special moral value called dignity that is rooted in our capacity for autonomous rational agency (see, eg, Dillon 2021: Part 4).

There is a basic division in the way philosophers refer to self-respect. On the one hand, they invoke self-respect in the context of entitlements to due treatment from others, especially those required by justice. On the other hand, they describe self-respect as a character trait involving fidelity to certain standards or ideals of conduct (Dillon 2021: Part 4). Questions arise as to how distinct, if at all, these two notions are; about which is the primary concept of self-respect, and about how best to capture the contrast between them. We might, for example, distinguish between 'recognitional' and 'evaluative' conceptions of self-respect (Darwall 2009; Dillon 1995), or detect an opposition between Kantian and Aristotelian interpretations of the value (Dillon 2021: Part 4). It is striking, however, that none of the recent research has displaced the basic intuition that there is some distinction to be drawn between the two forms of self-respect: it runs through the otherwise unsettled literature on self-respect like a thread (Bird 2010).

Philosophers routinely point to the damage done to the self-respect of individuals who are marginalised, stigmatised or exploited by others. Its absence is painful and debilitating. Those with an injured self-respect cannot confidently view themselves as entitled to the very same respect they naturally extend to others. They are likely to see themselves as inferior or even deserving of mistreatment. Self-respect, then, is a central component of human well-being. This is illustrated by its connection to many other moral and social values such as rights, autonomy, dignity, freedom and equality (Bird 2010).

B. Self-respect as a Virtue of Individuals and Institutions

Philosophical scholarship on self-respect is not restricted to individuals. It is routinely proposed that legal institutions and practices are to be judged just or unjust – at least in part – by their impact on an individual's self-respect. Sometimes known as the 'dependency thesis', the idea is that self-respect is not self-sufficient (Bird 2010). Rather, it depends on the respectful attitudes of others or of institutions. A person or institution that permits or encourages disrespect for others will therefore be one that objectionably undermines or damages an individual's self-respect.

Margalit's conception of the dependency thesis is noteworthy here. According to Margalit, the conduct and attitudes of others pose a threat to our self-respect when they involve humiliation and, by extension, disrespect. He defines a 'decent' society as one in which major social institutions do not humiliate their members and a 'civilised' society as one whose members do not humiliate each other. Margalit understands humiliation as a form of disrespect for individuals that supplies 'victims with a sound reason for viewing their self-respect as having been injured' (Margalit 1996: 120). Given this construal of humiliation, Margalit naturally concludes that decent and civilised societies are the only ones that can fully preserve their members' self-respect. Societies that are indecent or uncivilised necessarily threaten their members' self-respect by tolerating and, in extreme cases, encouraging acts of humiliation.

Rawls' *A Theory of Justice* is similarly instructive. For Rawls, self-respect is an entitlement that institutions are required by justice to support and maintain. He argues that individuals' access to self-respect is largely dependent on how the basic institutions of society operate. This includes messages about the relative worth of citizens that are conveyed in the structure and functioning of these institutions, including legal ones. For Rawls, justice requires that social institutions and policies be designed to support and not undermine an individual's self-respect. The value of self-respect, he claims, lies in the fact that no institution can fully achieve its aims adequately without it (Rawls 1971; see also Stark 2012). Like Margalit, Rawls also subscribes to the dependency thesis, claiming that even under ideal conditions, the continuing reassurance of respect from others is still required for individuals to maintain their self-respect. On this view, our self-respect always remains vulnerable to others' disrespect.

C. Why Self-respect at Sentencing?

This chapter proposes self-respect as a concept of critical enquiry for sentencing law and practice. What are the attractions of self-respect for the sentencing scholar? The key motivation behind making respect central to an account of the guilty plea is as follows.

For too long, the guilty plea has been viewed narrowly as a means by which to expedite the criminal process, secure convictions and save public money. The sentencing community has been held hostage to the empirical question of whether it is successful in achieving these outcomes. In requiring that the State treats defendants well and prioritises their self-respect, we overcome the framing of the guilty plea process as a value-free instrumental exercise. The intrinsic case for self-respect is that it is to be valued irrespective of whether it is implicated in the pursuit of certain instrumental outcomes because it builds into sentencing law and practice an ethical sensitivity that we ought to value in a liberal democracy. Self-respect speaks to the idea that it matters *how* we support individuals in the entering of a guilty plea and not simply that the process itself is effective. The court must relate meaningfully to defendants – by recognising their moral standing or affording them a baseline moral status – in a manner that reaffirms that there are non-instrumental reasons to protect and support them (Watson 2020).

There is a further reason for recourse to self-respect in the sentencing context. When we appeal to mid-level principles that are central to sentencing scholarship (such as justice or proportionality), we may require guidance in weighing, balancing and adjudicating between them. A commitment to affirming a defendant's self-respect could provide such guidance, by setting a normative standard for the sentencing community which places defendants at the centre.

V. Pleading Guilty: Conflicting Interpretations

Self-respect is a value whose importance in contemporary criminal justice many would endorse in principle. It is a notion that is capable of justifying, or calling into question, the entering of a guilty plea in exchange for a sentence reduction in England and Wales. As I argue here, its value is in its capacity to offer an interpretive framework for sentencing and capture the conflicted nature of the guilty plea. Although it is not yet clear whether and, if so, how, that conflict is resolvable, it might be articulated as follows.

A. The Idealistic View

An idealistic view of the guilty plea procedure is one that prioritises and preserves a defendant's self-respect. For the defendant, the guilty plea is a mere option, and he has the right to require the State to prove the case against him to a criminal standard. According to the Sentencing Council of England and Wales, 'nothing in the Guideline should be used to put pressure on a defendant to plead guilty' (Sentencing Council of England and Wales 2017; see also Gormley, Roberts and Harris 2020). The aim is to influence the timing of guilty pleas, not to influence the rate of guilty pleas entered. On this view, the entering of a guilty plea ought to be viewed as a reliable indication of criminal responsibility. The presence of an incentive to plead guilty may not always, or even typically, be treated as an admission made against one's own interest.

The redeeming features of the guilty plea process are well rehearsed in the literature but might be summarised as follows. Without a trial, crime victims and witnesses are spared the experience of attending court to testify. For many victims and others with a personal stake in the offence, testifying in a public forum can be emotionally distressing and is ideally avoided. Victims often benefit from knowing that the offender has accepted responsibility by admitting guilt and might even view the plea as indicative of remorse (even though this matter is dealt with separately by the court).

The utilitarian argument is that the guilty plea is in the public interest since it drives more efficient and expeditious processing of criminal cases (Roberts and Pina-Sánchez 2021). If the plea is entered at an early stage of proceedings, the length of time between charge and conviction is significantly shortened. The guilty plea process also generates significant savings. Aside from court costs, there will also be savings to the prosecution and defence and, by extension, in legal aid expenditure. No doubt the utilitarian arguments are powerful: if every individual charged with a criminal offence elected to proceed to trial, then the system would likely grind to a halt.

Finally, the guilty plea serves a symbolic role for the defendant as a gesture of contrition, a form of atonement, and a public acceptance of legal responsibility. When defendants admit their guilt, they affirm the court as a legitimate form of authority. In practical terms, the plea might even constitute an important step towards a law-abiding life (Leverick 2013).

B. The Instrumental View

The alternative view is that the guilty plea process has been designed principally for the pragmatic benefit of the State. The efficiency rationale is regularly used as the basis for the sentence reduction (Leverick 2013). Yet efficiency is a flimsy basis upon which to justify a sentence reduction when weighed against the risks for the defendant. It is possible, for example, that the guilty plea process serves less to create scope for the cultivation of values such as self-respect than to marginalise or displace them.

As far as self-respect is concerned, a defendant who pleads guilty does not truly have his voice heard. This is suggestive of a transactional – even disinterested – form of adjudication. The defendant is required to utter a single word: 'guilty'. Even the word itself has a certain indeterminacy. Usually, it is deemed by the court to mean 'I acknowledge the prosecution case is true'. If there is a basis of plea, then the word might be deemed to mean 'I acknowledge the basis of plea is true'. Yet the plea will often be a deliberate construction, a strategic decision, or a compromise between conflicting accounts honed through negotiation (Watson 2021).

C. Incentivisation or Inducement?

There is a fine line between incentivisation and inducement where the guilty plea is concerned. The practice of plea-based sentence reductions could easily attract criticism from ethicists, not least because it might persuade a defendant to act against his own best interests. As part of that process, the defendant must come to terms with the fact that the public may perceive a lack of equivalence between the reduced sentence he receives and the gravity of his crime and its effect on the victim.

Arguably, the guilty plea procedure has been designed in such a way as to institutionalise the notion of inducement. McConville and Marsh coined the term 'state-induced guilty plea' (2014), implying that the guilty plea can be a tactical move facilitated by a practitioner rather than a mere admission of guilt on the part of the defendant. The current process assumes that plea decisions are truly autonomous and consensual, but there is good reason to believe that even the factually innocent defendant might be induced into pleading guilty in the face of weighty evidence against him.

The notion that defendants have complete freedom of choice over a guilty plea is a myth. There is mounting evidence to suggest that aspects of that process are non-consensual. It is difficult to accept that strategic pleading does not form part of some practitioners' everyday working practices and that this may lead to manipulation of a client's plea. That behaviour is clearly unethical if matters such as self-interest or convenience compromise the best interests of the defendant. In *R v Turner (Frank Richard) No. 1* (1970) the court was reluctant to acknowledge that counsel may exert undue pressure on a defendant and that legal advice on plea could itself overwhelm the defendant's free choice. The Court of Appeal maintained that this was an 'extravagant proposition', which would only be made out in an extreme case (325). Yet, since *Turner*, there have been several noteworthy appeals from defendants claiming to have been pressured into pleading guilty (see eg, *R v Herbert (Stephen)* 1992; *R v Bargery* 2004).

D. The Innocent Defendant

It would be naive to assume that factually innocent defendants never plead guilty given the prospect of a sentence reduction (Royal Commission on Criminal Justice 1993). Horder in *Ashworth's Principles of Criminal Law* reminds us:

> A guilty plea may simply be accepted … at face value, as proof beyond a reasonable doubt of the allegation in question. A guilty plea is not automatically subject to vigorous testing for its veracity, in the way that a plea of not guilty is tested. (Horder 2016: 11)

The straightforward acceptance of the plea as a reliable indication of legal guilt is deeply problematic for the innocent defendant, whose self-respect will already be at risk. Self-respect – together with Horder's equation of the guilty plea with the beyond-reasonable-doubt standard of proof – paints a rather inconclusive picture of the guilty plea's ethical plausibility.

Nonetheless, some commentators maintain that pleading guilty while factually innocent is a remote possibility (Gormley and Tata 2021). Surely, the argument runs, no person would plead guilty to a crime they did not commit; not least because defendants choose rationally and freely how to plead. Moreover, some commentators maintain that skilled lawyers hold steadfastly to legal values such as the presumption of innocence, which would supersede any interest in the uncontested administrative processing of such cases (Gormley and Tata 2021).

Yet the argument will only hold if we are confident in the quality of criminal defence and the functionality of the system. Research shows a pervading cynicism among legal aid lawyers, who routinely assume guilt. Practitioners – even the defendant's own lawyer – are themselves routinely involved in directing cases towards guilty pleas (Newman 2013; McConville et al 1994). The literature on the relationship between criminal defence lawyers and their clients shows that although, in formal terms, defendants *instruct* their lawyers, the reality is much more complex. Research has consistently highlighted the relative passivity of most clients, whose often weak educational, social and personal resources can severely limit their ability to control the progression of their cases. The power differential in the professional–client relationship, which is especially acute in criminal cases, exacerbates the situation further (Gormley and Tata 2021).

E. The Vulnerable Defendant

State inducement to plead guilty is likely to play on the individual weaknesses of a defendant, treating him as anything but a person of profound and intrinsic moral worth. A defendant's vulnerability might be internal or external: the former relating to cognitive impairments, illness, age and various kinds of personality disorder that may make him more suggestible; and the latter relating to his primary responsibility for the care of children or older people, or economic or time pressures. Even if greater proportions of the vulnerable are induced to plead guilty, that would be regarded as a positive outcome by the State because of the net benefits that accrue to the system.

No doubt it can be difficult for vulnerable defendants to take firm command of their cases. Even where a defendant knows what he has done, he may not be fully aware of what crime in law it may constitute, which calls into question the assumption that guilty pleas are made freely and are always fully informed. It is conceivable too that vulnerable defendants may struggle with the demands of the court process and the personal costs it inflicts, and so regard a plea of guilty as a lesser evil (Feeley 1979). This reality is hardly conducive to a flourishing sense of self-respect.

VI. Reimagining the Guilty Plea

This chapter has been driven by a conviction and a problem. The conviction is that reflecting on the ethical dimensions of the guilty plea is a worthwhile intellectual and practical endeavour. The problem is that a defendant's self-respect – described by Rawls as 'perhaps the most important' primary good (Rawls 1971: 396) – is at risk of being undermined whenever a defendant waives his right to a trial and enters a guilty plea in exchange for a sentence reduction.

A. Against Instrumentalism

Controversy around the guilty plea sentence reduction is not new, having long tapped into deep and ingrained tensions between due process and crime control models of criminal justice (Packer 1964). A recurring criticism of the guilty plea is that it has been designed according to narrow instrumental concerns, such as the efficient and expeditious processing of criminal cases through the system, financial savings on investigations and trials, and the saving of court time (Sentencing Council of England and Wales 2017; see also Gormley, McPherson and Tata 2020).

While it is inevitable that the process of entering a guilty plea will be grounded, at least in part, in a form of means-end reasoning, it is important that it is contained, or held in its proper place. Efficiency is, of course, a laudable goal for the sentencing process with which no one would reasonably disagree. However, implicit in the debate about the guilty plea is profound disagreement about what it means to be efficient. Efficiency in criminal justice should not be a value-free exercise. It is not simply about the number of cases processed, but also implies a normative claim about what is just. When there is a lasting preoccupation with instrumental outcomes, there is a risk of apathy towards a range of non-instrumental issues, including how best to affirm a defendant's self-respect. The implications of this approach are significant if we recall the Rawlsian claim that the presence or deficiency of self-respect in an institution is one indicator among many that it is just or unjust (Rawls 1971; Stark 2012).

The first step towards taking the guilty plea seriously from an ethical point of view will be to reorient the debate away from a marked preoccupation with instrumental outcomes and towards an increased concern with the defendant's intrinsic worth. This is not to discredit the instrumental functions that the sentencing process purports to perform. These functions must simply be contained, and scholars and practitioners alike must look afresh at the nature of the guilty plea, how it operates, and what it is for.

I propose that we treat self-respect as a side-constraint on the pursuit of instrumental outcomes at sentencing.[4] In other words, we should pursue instrumental outcomes such as the swift processing of cases *only* insofar as they preserve a defendant's self-respect. Side-constraints are not inherently weak or liable to be overwhelmed by instrumental considerations.[5] If a side-constraint is strong – like a Dworkinian trump right – then it is, in fact, a very powerful limit on the pursuit of other goals (Dworkin 1977). If side-constraints are framed in adequately robust terms (Watson 2020), they might even infuse the very foundations on which sentencing practices are based.

B. Rethinking Credit

If we were to commit to treating self-respect as a side-constraint on the pursuit of instrumental outcomes, what might that mean in practical terms? While there is no need to abandon the awarding of credit altogether, as Tonry (2009) contemplates, or implement a presumption against awarding credit unless justified by convincing reasons, as in the Scottish case (Leverick 2013; 2014), there is a need to rethink its purpose and operation. This is especially important in view of the systemic and personal pressures exerted on defendants to act quickly, often at the expense of their own self-respect, which, given their involvement in the criminal process, is likely already to be fragile.

[4] The term 'side-constraint' is attributable to Nozick (1974: 28–29).

[5] See, eg, Hart's approach to incorporating the principle of distributive fairness into his otherwise instrumental theory of punishment (Hart 1968).

The stage at which a defendant must plead guilty to receive full credit is simply too early to be consistent with the requirements of self-respect. It does not allow a defendant to reflect meaningfully on legal advice or the weight of the evidence against him. And following *R v Plaku and others* (2021), the process is arguably more prescriptive than ever. There is very little scope to argue that a defendant could not have offered an unequivocal plea at first appearance at the magistrates' court, except for the most exceptional of circumstances, such as not having been provided any papers by the prosecution prior to the hearing.

The Guideline, *Reduction in Sentence for a Guilty Plea* (Sentencing Council of England and Wales 2017), is stricter than its predecessor and too tightly drawn (see further House of Commons Justice Committee 2016). It offers certainty at the expense of flexibility and fairness, for example, in replacing the concept of the 'first reasonable opportunity' with clearly defined stages of the court process. It is hard to believe that the emphasis on a precipitous reduction in the discount was not designed to place pressure on the defendant, despite the Council's assurances to the contrary (Peay and Player 2018). In sum, the Guideline increases the risk that the defendant will act against his own self-interests, which is problematic where his self-respect is concerned.

The exception set out in the Guideline at F1 (further information, assistance, or advice necessary before indicating plea) would, in certain circumstances, retain the maximum one-third discount for a defendant who enters a plea of guilty *after* the first stage of proceedings. In considering whether this exception applies, sentencers are advised to distinguish between cases in which it is necessary to receive further advice or have sight of the evidence in order to understand whether the defendant is in fact and in law guilty of the offence charged, and cases in which a defendant merely delays the entering of a guilty plea in order to assess the strength of the prosecution evidence and the prospects of conviction or acquittal. As currently drafted, the exception is confined to rare cases. Its limited scope is especially insensitive to vulnerable defendants, such as those with mental health conditions, who may feel pressured to plead. It has the potential to detract attention from systemic coercion and to fix responsibility for the plea on the defendant alone. The vulnerable defendant must have sufficient time to process legal advice, engage in careful decision making, and take ownership of the decision.

In sum, the process is much less straightforward than the Sentencing Council presupposes. The Council has not fully recognised that a sentence reduction, substantial or not, offered against a diminishing time frame can be experienced as a coercive gamble for defendants, where the risk averse may choose to cut their losses. The F1 exception also implies a significant disregard for the defendant's self-respect, when he is already distanced from the protections afforded by trial. The exception should be expressly extended to any situation where the defendant wishes to obtain further legal advice before deciding whether to plead guilty, with a concerted effort to protect those deemed vulnerable. At the very least, the F1 exception might be applied more flexibly.

There is scope, then, to rethink the purpose and operation of awarding credit to defendants who plead guilty (see, eg, Bagaric and Brebner 2002). Of note is the need for greater flexibility in the Guideline, whose framing is unaccommodating to defendants facing the complex decision as to whether and, if so, when to plead guilty. This seems especially urgent in a system increasingly defined by its deficits in legally aided advice and representation.

Overall, the guilty plea process is currently at risk of undermining – or even directly violating – a defendant's self-respect. This is true however we classify self-respect: as a moral duty connected with the duty to respect all persons, as something to which all persons have a moral right, or as a moral virtue essential to morally good living. When self-respect is treated as a peripheral concern at sentencing, it will become increasingly difficult for the criminal process to protect its liberal credentials.

VII. The Limits of Self-respect

At the core of the guilty plea procedure there exists a fundamental – and possibly irresolvable – tension. In principle, the plea can promote a defendant's self-respect but – if State induced, as is often the case – it is likely to have the opposite effect. At best, then, the guilty plea is ethically suspect.

The immanent capacity of self-respect to function as a concept of critical enquiry for sentencing theory and practice, while notable, must not be overstated. The sentencing process is defined by a plurality of values, which are not ordered in a fixed or definite way and are not derivable from a single fundamental value. These are values which, even within one person, can conflict in ways that are not resolvable without loss (see, eg, Jacobs 2011; Zedner 1994). As such, it would be naive to propose self-respect as an overarching analytic category and suggest that we can make sense of the guilty plea exclusively in these terms. Likewise, we should not assume that self-respect can generate straightforward answers to every ethical dilemma in sentencing law and practice. Nonetheless, self-respect has great promise and there is much to be gained by foregrounding the concept, refining it, and then redirecting it in such a way that prompts deeper reflection about the guilty plea as it operates in England and Wales.

VIII. Conclusion

If we are to continue to afford the guilty plea a privileged role in the sentencing process of England and Wales, it is essential that we can explain and endorse it in ethical terms. With a sense of modest realism, we must recognise the redeeming features of the guilty plea, while viewing it more cautiously as a non-ideal form of 'negotiated justice' (Baldwin and McConville 1977) and a flawed means by which to expedite the criminal process, which too often benefits the State at the expense of defendants.

It would be difficult to imagine the sentencing of offenders in the total absence of ethical theory. If modestly conceived as a set of organising assumptions about how we relate to each other, we might even claim that ethical theory is indispensable to sentencing and criminal justice. One way of deepening our ethical understanding of the guilty plea is to appeal to the concept of self-respect: celebrated in moral philosophy, but scarcely discussed – even elusive – in sentencing and criminal justice. Self-respect is an effective tool for moderating the ethics of pleading guilty and might even be viewed as a critical and regulative ideal for criminal justice. The flexibility of the concept is such that it provides a means by which to sharpen our critique of the guilty plea, as well as a means by which to reimagine its use.

But self-respect is not merely an analytic tool. It is also a matter of material significance. For every defendant confronted with the opportunity to enter a guilty plea, self-respect is a precious commodity to be fiercely protected. It is gained slowly but may be lost in an instant. For Rawls (1971), self-respect is an entitlement that institutions are required by justice to support and maintain.

Once the foundations for an ethical understanding of the guilty plea have been laid, it is essential that these ideas are not restricted to the legal academy. Self-respect is sufficiently fine-grained to influence policy-making, provided it is complemented by structured political deliberation. One way forward for the sentencing community would be to redesign the guilty plea process to affirm – rather than erode – the defendant's sense of self-respect and consign the State's narrow instrumental concerns to their proper place.

References

Bagaric, M and Brebner, J (2002) 'The Solution to the Dilemma Presented by the Guilty Plea Discount: The Qualified Guilty Plea – I'm Pleading Guilty only because of the Discount …' 30 *International Journal of the Sociology of Law* 51.

Baldwin, J and McConville, M (1977) *Negotiated Justice: Pressures on Defendants to Plead Guilty* (London, Martin Robertson).

Bird, C (2010) 'Self-Respect and the Respect of Others' 18 *European Journal of Philosophy* 17.

Cueni, D and Queloz, M (2021) 'Whence the Demand for Ethical Theory?' 58 *American Philosophical Quarterly* 135.

Darwall, S (2009) *The Second-Person Standpoint: Morality, Respect, and Accountability* (Cambridge, MA, Harvard University Press).

Dillon, RS (1995) *Dignity, Character, and Self-Respect* (London, Routledge).

—— (2021) 'Respect' in EN Zalta (ed), *The Stanford Encyclopedia of Philosophy* (California, Metaphysics Research Lab, Stanford University).

Dworkin, R (1977) *Taking Rights Seriously* (Cambridge, MA, Harvard University Press).

Feeley, M (1979) *The Process is the Punishment: Handling Cases in a Lower Criminal Court* (New York, Russell Sage Foundation).

Gormley, J and Tata, C (2021) 'To Plead or Not to Plead? "Guilty" is the Question. Re-thinking Plea Decision-making in Anglo-American Countries' in C Spohn and P Brennan (eds), *Handbook on Sentencing Policies and Practices in the 21st Century* (London, Routledge).

Gormley, J, McPherson, R and Tata, C (2020) *Sentence Discounting: Sentencing and Plea Decision-Making* (Edinburgh, Scottish Sentencing Council).

Gormley, J, Roberts, JV and Harris, L (2020) *Sentence Reductions for Guilty Pleas: A Review of Policy, Practice, and Research* (London, Sentencing Academy).

Hart, HLA (1968) *Punishment and Responsibility: Essays in the Philosophy of Law* (Oxford, Clarendon Press).

Helm, R (2018) 'Conviction by Consent? Vulnerability, Autonomy, and Conviction by Guilty Plea' 83 *The Journal of Criminal Law* 161.

Horder, J (2016) *Ashworth's Principles of Criminal Law*, 9th edn (Oxford, Oxford University Press).

House of Commons Justice Committee (2016) *Reduction in Sentence for a Guilty Plea Guideline*. First Report of Session 2016–17 HC 168 (London, House of Commons).

Jacobs, J (2011) 'Criminal Justice and the Liberal Polity' 30 *Criminal Justice Ethics* 173.

Leverick, F (2013) 'The Rise and Fall of the Sentence Discount' 38 *Scots Law Times* 259.

—— (2014) 'Sentence Discounting for Guilty Pleas: An Argument for Certainty over Discretion' 5 *Criminal Law Review* 338.

Margalit, A (1996) *The Decent Society* (Cambridge, MA, Harvard University Press).

McConville, M and Marsh, L (2014) *Criminal Judges: Legitimacy, Courts, and State-induced Guilty Pleas in Britain* (Cheltenham, Edward Elgar).

McConville, M, Hodgson, J, Bridges, L and Pavlovic, A (1994) *Standing Accused: The Organisation and Practices of Criminal Defence Lawyers in Britain* (Oxford, Oxford University Press).

Ministry of Justice (2021) *Criminal Court Statistics Quarterly: April to June 2021* (London, Ministry of Justice).

Newman, D (2013) *Legal Aid Lawyers and the Quest for Justice* (Oxford, Hart Publishing).

Nozick, R (1974) *Anarchy, State, and Utopia* (New York, Basic Books).

Nussbaum, M (2000) 'Why Practice Needs Ethical Theory – Particularism, Principle, and Bad Behavior' in SJ Burton (ed), *The Path of the Law and Its Influence* (Cambridge, Cambridge University Press).

Ormerod, D and Perry, D (eds) (2021) *Blackstone's Criminal Practice 2022* (Oxford, Oxford University Press).

Packer, HL (1964) 'Two Models of the Criminal Process' 113 *University of Pennsylvania Law Review* 1.

Peay, J and Player, E (2018) 'Pleading Guilty: Why Vulnerability Matters' 81 *The Modern Law Review* 929.

Rawls, J (1971) *A Theory of Justice* (Cambridge, MA, Belknap Press of Harvard University Press).

Roberts, JV and Pina-Sánchez, J (2021) 'Sentence Reductions for a Guilty Plea: The Impact of the Revised Guideline on Rates of Pleas and "Cracked Trials"' *The Journal of Criminal Law*. Online First.

Royal Commission on Criminal Justice (1993) *The Report of the Royal Commission on Criminal Justice* (London, HMSO).

Sentencing Council of England and Wales (2017) *Reduction in Sentence for a Guilty Plea* (London, Sentencing Council of England and Wales).

Sentencing Guidelines Council (2007) *Reduction in Sentence for a Guilty Plea* (London, Sentencing Guidelines Council).
Singer, P (2011) *Practical Ethics*, 3rd edn (Cambridge, Cambridge University Press).
Stark, CA (2012) 'Rawlsian Self-Respect' in M Timmons (ed), *Oxford Studies in Normative Ethics: Volume 2* (Oxford, Oxford University Press).
Tonry, M (2009) 'Abandoning Sentence Discounts for Guilty Pleas' in A von Hirsch, A Ashworth and JV Roberts (eds), *Principled Sentencing: Readings on Theory and Policy* (Oxford, Hart Publishing).
Watson, G (2020) *Respect and Criminal Justice* (Oxford, Oxford University Press).
—— (2021) 'Ethics at Sentencing, Guilty Pleas, and the Case for Respect' 2 *Sentencing News* 6.
Zedner, L (1994) 'Reparation and Retribution: Are They Reconcilable?' 57 *The Modern Law Review* 228.

Legislation

Coroners and Justice Act 2009
Sentencing Act 2020

Cases

R v A (Informer: Reduction of Sentence) [1999] 1 Cr App R 52
R v Bargery [2004] EWCA Crim 816
R v Darling and others [2009] EWCA Crim 1610
R v Herbert (Stephen) [1992] 94 Cr App R 230
R v Ladbrook [2022] EWCA Crim 113
R v Plaku and others [2021] EWCA Crim 568
R v Turner (Frank Richard) No.1 [1970] 2 QB 321

8

Why Should Guilty Pleas Matter?

THOM BROOKS*

I. Introduction

Punishments are mostly agreed through defendants making a guilty plea rather than post conviction after a trial by judge or jury.[1] Submitting a guilty plea is normally accompanied by a reduced sentence.[2] It has been said that 'no doubt some version of this practice is justifiable, even necessary' (Clark 2006: 95). The making of guilty pleas is so commonplace that we are thought to live in a 'guilty-plea culture' (McConville 1998: 572–76). This is borne out by the US Supreme Court's remark in *Lafler v Cooper* that 'criminal justice today is for the most part a system of pleas, not a system of trials'.[3] The guidance for determining reduced sentences for a guilty plea has been described as 'one of the most important principles in sentencing … and of the greatest practical importance' given its widespread, entrenched use (Wasik 2014: 71; see Wasik 2004: 298–99). Guilty plea discounts are 'a well-established principle of common law' as it has been practised for 'decades' and is very likely to remain for many more decades to come (Beard 2017: 4; see Royal Commission on Criminal Justice 1993: 10; Wright 2012).[4]

The prevalence of guilty pleas and the sentence reductions for pleading guilty raise the issue of *why* pleading guilty should matter in sentencing. For example, first, it might be argued that two individuals who commit the same offence should

* My thanks to feedback from all conference participants, with extra thanks to Andrew Ashworth, Rebecca Helm, Zach Hoskins and, most especially, Julian Roberts and Jesper Ryberg.

[1] I will refer to the individuals charged with crimes as 'defendants' throughout rather than offenders. This is to highlight the categorical difference between them – not all defendants are offenders, including not all defendants who plead guilty as discussed below.

[2] It should be noted that while guilty pleas *can* lead to reduced sentences, it is not a requirement that sentences *must* be reduced, eg in cases where there is a mandatory sentence such as life imprisonment for murder found in several jurisdictions. This will be discussed further in later sections. I will refer to 'punishment' and 'sentencing' interchangeably.

[3] *Lafler v Cooper* (2012).

[4] Guilty plea sentencing discounts in England and Wales were placed on a statutory footing in s 48 of the Criminal Justice and Public Order Act 1994. This was later replaced by s 144 of the Criminal Justice Act 2003 and then by s 18 of the Sentencing Act 2020. See Vogel (1999) on the American origins of the discount.

receive the same sentence, but yet the making of a guilty plea could lead one individual to receive less punishment than the other. This raises issues about desert in punishing people differently for the same crime, creating an 'awkwardness' in drawing the distinction (see Walker 1980: 128).[5] Secondly, it might also be argued that making a guilty plea is not proof of guilt as it avoids important safeguards, such as scrutiny of evidence and the jury trial, with many examples of individuals confessing to crimes they did not commit. This raises issues about whether the use of pleas undermines the duty to avoid punishing the innocent and ensuring evidentiary standards more generally. Thirdly, it might be claimed that the use of guilty pleas for sentence reductions is purely instrumental and damaging to other factors, such as supporting the victims of crimes being punished.

This chapter examines each of these issues. It will focus specifically on the use of plea bargaining in the United States and the use of guilty plea discounts in England and Wales, as each presents us with different ways of thinking about how and why a guilty plea can matter for sentencing reductions (see Baldwin and McConville 1979). The chapter will raise serious objections to the way plea bargaining is done in the United States and rejects its use. However, the chapter will provide a qualified defence of sentence reductions for guilty pleas as used in England and Wales. This qualified defence rests on the need for more robust safeguards to be put in place in order to ensure greater consistency and fairness for the use of guilty plea reductions to be justified more substantially. So, this is not a defence of how the system is, but rather for a reformed system in future.

II. The Problem with Plea Bargaining

This section will examine the American model for sentencing discounts for guilty pleas. In the United States, only 3 per cent of defendants stand trial – the others agree to a plea bargain and avoid trial (Rakoff 2021: 23). Plea bargaining is where a defendant admits guilt usually for a lesser charge in return for the prosecutor dismissing more serious charges that might otherwise be brought. Both sides are thought to benefit from the bargaining over the charge: the defendant receives a reduced sentence, often avoiding prison time, and the prosecution is able to resolve criminal cases swiftly without the need for a time-consuming and costly trial (Rakoff 2021: 21). These bargains *usually* lead to lesser charges, but there can be constraints relating to mandatory minimum sentences among other relevant factors, such as judicial discretion.

American plea bargaining is problematic on several grounds. The first is plea bargaining fails to respect desert (Lippke 2011). This objection can be portrayed as creating a justice gap between the sentence a defendant should have received and

[5] For views on desert, see Brooks (2020); von Hirsch and Ashworth (2005); von Hirsch (2017).

the lesser punishment that was, in fact, received. For example, a defendant might have committed a crime punishable by five years' imprisonment; but, in return for making a guilty plea and avoiding the need for a trial, the defendant accepts a conviction for a less serious offence with a less serious sentence. The concern is that the defendant receives a sentence that is less than that defendant deserves.[6]

It is undoubtedly difficult to know with precision exactly how many days is required for most desert-based accounts. As Aristotle (1984: 1730) has argued, we should only 'look for precision in each class of things just so far as the nature of the subject admits'. Relatedly, Hegel (1991: 245) argues that 'It is impossible to determine … whether the just penalty for an offence is … imprisonment for a year or for 364 days … And yet an injustice is done if there is even … one day in prison too many or too few'.[7] While there might be limits to how precise we can distinguish punishments for every crime, we should aim to gain as much clarity as possible notwithstanding the various challenges in doing so noted by Aristotle, Hegel and others.[8]

Nonetheless, the issue here is not only that a defendant is sentenced less than they would be punished without agreeing a plea bargain, but that the defendant is usually sentenced for a lesser charge than they would be otherwise (Spohn 2009: 280). In other words, plea bargaining is about more than receiving a lesser punishment for a crime; but, instead, it is about receiving a lesser punishment for a *different kind* of crime typically entailing a lesser charge. Therefore, American plea bargaining can be about changing both the *kind* of crime that is punished and not only the *amount* of punishment in relation to that crime.[9]

This sharpens the objection to guilty plea sentencing reductions from desert. Plea bargaining fails to respect desert because even if defendants could be said to deserve less punishment for a crime because they admit guilt – which will be discussed separately below – they cannot be said to deserve any amount of punishment for a different crime because this is not the act or omission they are being held responsible for. In short, the bargains lead to defendants admitting to crimes they did not actually commit in return for lesser sentencing. Or, in other words, defendants are punished for crimes different from, and punished less than, the crimes they did. Defendants do not categorically receive their just deserts.[10]

[6] If the existing legal system overly punishes crimes, then it might be said that a reduced sentence for a guilty plea might better fit the crime.

[7] The full reference to the translated German text is *Elements of the Philosophy of Right*, §214 Remark.

[8] The full reference to the translated Greek text is *Nicomachean Ethics*, Book 1, 1094 lines 24–25. Andreas von Hirsch (1993: v) observes that 'Punishment is a fascinating but uncomfortable question … No one should delude themselves that there are neat solutions'.

[9] While he does not discuss plea bargaining, this desert-based objection to different *kinds* of crime arising from a plea bargain also has its roots in Hegel's discussions about retributivist punishment (Hegel 1991: 127 [§101 Addition]; see Brooks 2001; 2004a; 2012; 2013; 2017a; 2017b).

[10] Furthermore, this justice gap might be seen as distorting the proportionality between the seriousness of an offence and the severity of its penalty (see von Hirsch 1993: 29).

This problem is exacerbated by common American prosecutorial practices. For example, some, such as Douglas Husak (2011: 216), claim that defendants who are found guilty at trial can be thought to pay a so-called 'trial tax' in failing to benefit from a sentencing reduction if they had pleaded guilty before trial. But, again, the primary issue is about the *kind*, not merely the *amount*, of punishment involved. Rachel Barkow (2019: 52) has exposed the practice of many prosecutors bringing *additional charges* for defendants who refuse to plea bargain (see Jaconelli 2002: 56–58; McConkie 2015: 68; Tonry 2011: 117–18). This is a further affront to any desert-based considerations. The difference between a plea bargain and trial is not only the possibility of receiving more punishment, but the prosecutor attempting to convict for different, and sometimes additional, crimes. The plea bargain arrangement can be of an entirely different character from the crime(s) that actually took place.

A second problem for plea bargaining is its patented unfairness. As senior judge of the US District Court for the Southern District of New York Jed Rakoff (2021: 20) argues, American plea bargaining takes place almost exclusively 'behind closed doors and with no judicial oversight'. How prosecutors present and agree a deal in one case can vary considerably with another thanks to the wide discretion they have to reach a plea deal creating inconsistent outcomes across similar cases.

While there is a pressing need for more empirical studies of how prosecutorial discretion is used, the outcomes seem to speak for themselves. Racial discrimination is endemic in the American criminal justice system with wide disparities in the rate of conviction and length of sentences for convicted defendants by race – and plea bargaining does not appear to reduce these injustices (Tonry 2009: 352–53; Kutateladze et al 2014; Berdejo 2018; Goncalves, Jr 2022).

Some of these issues arise from the decisions to charge offences with required minimum sentences for capital crimes. For example, there are racial disparities in decisions to prosecute where capital punishment is considered. This is impacted further by the fact that most accused of capital crimes choose to go to trial and avoid possible execution exacerbating known disparities (Tsai 2019: 83). Without judicial oversight and a lack of empirical information, there are insufficiently robust safeguards to counter any implicit bias and discrimination in plea bargaining.

To conclude this section, American defendants can receive a lesser sentence by plea bargaining. This practice faces two problems. The first is that defendants can be offered lesser, but also different, charges than what actually happened leading to lesser punishment than might otherwise be received. But if they refuse, they could also face additional charges beyond what is discussed in plea bargaining. The second problem is the use of American prosecutorial discretion seems so wide as to be unfair lacking robust safeguards to protect against bias and discrimination. Unsurprisingly, various disparities are sadly a commonplace in the US criminal justice system. This is not a unique feature, but its size and scale is alarming.

III. A Plea for an Alternative: The English Discount

This section examines an alternative to the American model of plea bargaining found in England and Wales.[11] Whereas the US process is prosecutor led and conducted beyond the gaze of the judiciary, the English process is very different – and, I will claim, more compelling in comparison.

Instead of plea bargaining before trial, the English system grants sentencing discounts for charged offences on an early guilty plea to that charge.[12] As a result, defendants that plead guilty are accepting their responsibility for this charge – and not for some different offence(s) as in the United States. In 2020/21, nearly 80 per cent of cases in magistrates' courts and about 78 per cent of cases in the Crown Court were resolved by guilty pleas (Crown Prosecution Service 2021: 41, 43).

Whereas American plea bargaining can reduce sentences by charging for a lesser and different offence, the English system provides a sentencing discount of one-third if a defendant pleads guilty at the first opportunity (Sentencing Council 2017a). The first opportunity is considered to be the earliest time a defendant appears in court to enter a plea – and so takes place in open court, not behind closed doors.[13] The sentencing discount is applied to all English courts and forms of sentence, not only any time in custody (see Ashworth and Kelly 2021: 172). Nearly nine out of 10 defendants plead guilty at the first reasonable opportunity (Ashworth and Roberts 2017: 861).

The key factors for determining this 'English discount' for reduced sentencing are the stage in the proceedings for an offence at which a defendant pleads guilty and the circumstances in which this indication was given.[14] A defendant may receive a discount on a declining scale after a first appearance in court where a one-third reduction is possible. A guilty plea at a second hearing could lead to a one-quarter reduction in sentence, followed by a one-tenth reduction if a defendant pleads guilty on the day of trial. If circumstances prevented a defendant from reasonably indicating a guilty plea sooner, then exceptions can be made to award a more generous sentence discount but this cannot be more than one-third (Leveson 2015; Sentencing Council 2020).

The English discount is taken into consideration after the appropriate sentence for the crime(s) is determined using any available sentencing guidelines accounting for harm and culpability. The sentencing reduction is then determined, in part, in light of its timing and circumstances as above – the amount of the reduction is stated and applied (Sentencing Council 2017b). As a result, the English discount

[11] For ease of reference, I will speak of the 'English' discount when referring to the plea discount in the legal system of England and Wales.

[12] See s 144(1) of the Criminal Justice Act 2003 and s 73 of the Sentencing Act 2000. See also House of Commons Justice Committee (2016).

[13] See *R v Caley* (2013).

[14] See s 73(2)–(3) of the Sentencing Act 2000.

is explicitly a discount subject to a common procedure relevant for most offences that is explicit and transparent.

This discount is subject to limits, such as mandatory minimum tariffs that can constrain sentence discounts and mandatory sentencing. For example, murder is subject to imprisonment for life. If the court determines a whole life minimum tariff is mandated, then an early guilty plea will receive no discount (Sentencing Council 2017b). Therefore, guilty pleas do not always lead to a reduced sentence for all offences.

Moreover, English judges are *not* required to grant a one-third discount in every instance.[15] The context matters. In *Simpson*, an offender pleaded guilty to aggravated vehicle taking, which had a maximum sentence of two years.[16] Despite pleading guilty at the first opportunity, the judge gave the defendant a 23-month sentence discounting only one month because it was noted that a much higher sentence than two years could have been warranted in that case. While judges have discretion not to grant discounts in full and may exercise some discretion where warranted, they cannot increase discounts under any circumstances.

To conclude this section, the English discount has advantages over US plea bargaining. Whereas the latter can lead to a defendant being charged with a lesser offence than was committed (and receiving a lesser sentence depending on the bargain agreed), the English discount is only for the offence charged.[17] As Lord Justice Hughes says in *Caley*, 'it is particularly important that unrealistic bases of plea should receive no incentive'.[18] While US plea bargaining takes place behind closed doors, lacks consistency and appears to contribute to alarming levels of disparity, the English discount is acknowledged in open court and follows sentencing guidelines providing greater consistency in application linked to the time a plea is made.

But this is *not* to say the English discount is unproblematic. Similarly high numbers of defendants plead guilty as in the United States and yet there are serious problems of bias and discrimination in the United Kingdom's criminal justice system too (Lammy Review 2017). In this volume, Mike Hough and Jessica Jacobson (Chapter 11) point out that the offences for which a defendant is charged can be a product of pre-trial, 'largely hidden' negotiation. They are correct. There is much effort made pre trial in the Crown Prosecution Service to ascertain

[15] See *R v Wilson* (2012).

[16] See *R v Simpson* (2009).

[17] This important feature about the place of guilty plea reductions in English sentencing might be strengthened further by following the prosecution guidelines in New Zealand which state that 'the number or seriousness of charges should not be inflated to increase the likelihood of an offer by the defendant to plead guilty to a lesser charge'. These guidelines forbid bargaining about the charge(s) and, thus, ensure that any guilty plea is an acceptance of guilt for the crime(s) committed (see Solicitor-General 2013: para 8.2).

[18] *R v Caley* (2013): para 26. Lord Justice Hughes became Lord Hughes of Ombersley shortly afterwards when appointed to the UK Supreme Court on 9 April 2013. See Simester et al (2019: 89) who note: 'The very notion of the trial, of a plea, assumes putative answerability *for something*' (emphasis added). This underscores the importance of securing a realistic basis for a plea.

the likelihood of defendants pleading guilty to probable charges. So, the English system is not immune from US-like negotiations over charge and pleas, albeit this transpires in a more limited context where prosecutors have less power than in America.[19]

The criminal justice system does not operate in a vacuum or an ivory tower. Issues about discrimination require a solution beyond the means of the criminal justice system alone. Nonetheless, however less problematic the English discount is in comparison with American plea bargains, three important questions remain that I will address. The first is: do guilty plea discounts bargain away innocence and contribute to punishing the innocent? The second is: does accepting guilty pleas lower evidentiary standards? The third is: how much of a discount is too much? The remaining sections focus on these questions in light of the two models for guilty plea-related sentencing discounts from the United States and England considered here.

IV. Do Guilty Plea Discounts Bargain Away Innocence?

The previous sections considered two different approaches – American and English – to determining how sentence reductions should work for pleading guilty. In this section, attention is turned to an important set of issues regarding both evidentiary standards and the risk that the use of offering sentencing discounts for guilty pleas could perversely incentivise defendants in some circumstances to plead guilty to crimes they did not commit.

Both the legal systems in the United States and England champion the importance of a fair trial. The United Kingdom recognises 'fundamental British values', including democracy, the rule of law, and tolerance, with a centuries-old tradition of using jury trials for serious offences, with early roots in the Magna Carta of 1215.[20] The Fifth Amendment of the US Constitution guarantees 'no one can be compelled to be a witness against himself' and its Sixth Amendment guarantees 'in all criminal prosecutions, the accused shall enjoy the right to a speedy and public trial, by an impartial jury'. The right to a fair trial has an important role in safeguarding individual rights through the law of evidence, judicial oversight and other measures (see Brooks 2004b; 2009). Yet, the trial is increasingly rare, with most avoiding trial through pleading guilt – and receiving a reduced sentence for doing so.

[19] See *McKinnon v USA* (2007): para 54 ('viewed from the perspective of an English court the notion that a prosecutor may seek to induce a plea of guilty on the basis that substantial benefits will be withdrawn if one is not forthcoming is anathema') and Padfield (2009: 13) ('Surely the power of the prosecutor to influence not only the length of sentence, but also the conditions in which it is to be served, causes concern').

[20] On fundamental British values, see Department for Education (2014). On Magna Carta and trial by jury, see Library of Congress (2014). On fair trials and the right to trial by jury, see Brooks (2004b; 2004c; 2009).

This begs the question of whether the use of guilty plea sentence reductions undermines safeguards found at trial. After all, making a guilty plea can stop other events from happening that would normally be a part of any trial process. For example, evidence is not subjected to the full scrutiny it would receive at trial, no witnesses are cross-examined and issues relating to whether any evidence should be downgraded, if not excluded, become moot (Sanders and Young 2000: 397). In cutting the time to conclude a criminal case (and its associated costs), it might appear that corners are being cut relating to relevant evidentiary and procedural safeguards. Some scholars go further and claim that these plea bargains are merely 'transactional', with a focus only on concluding a deal, not delivering justice (see Chapter 12).

Of course, merely pleading guilty by itself is insufficient for establishing guilt. Some scholars have argued that innocent defendants have pleaded guilty to crimes they did not commit due to some degree of coercion, especially impacting more vulnerable persons (Helm 2019). Jed Rakoff (2021: 28, 31) observes that in the United States as many as 10 per cent of guilty pleas are made by innocent people.[21] Sometimes this is because someone is accused of a capital crime facing the possibility of execution if wrongly convicted (where pleading guilty avoids that possibility), but others are thought to lack confidence in the system and so cut their losses by making a guilty plea. However, there is no comparative data to test whether a similar or different number of innocent defendants pleaded guilty to crimes they did not commit before plea bargaining became the norm.

There is undoubtedly pressure on defendants to plead guilty. Some of this pressure is overt, such as with plea bargaining. In this US approach, there is a strong power imbalance created whereby often elected prosecutors are incentivised to push for long sentences to score points for future election campaigns (Barkow 2019: 51). Prosecutors hold most of the cards threatening more severe punishment to compel defendants into pleading. This imbalance of power favouring the American prosecutor has been described as giving cause for 'concern' and 'undermining the role of other supposedly "independent" players in the process' (Padfield 2009: 13).

Moreover, American prosecutors will be richly experienced given the prevalence of plea bargaining, whereas the defendant may be a relative novice, inexperienced and anxious about the impact of failing to strike a bargain. According to George Fisher (2000: 859), the dominance of plea bargaining owes much to its having 'served the interests of the powerful', making easier the work of concluding cases for prosecutors and judges (see Balbus 1973; Brunk 1979). Thus, 'there is no glory in plea bargaining' within the shadows behind closed doors (Fisher 2000: 859).

Some of the pressure on defendants to plead guilty is less emphatic. One such example is the possible benefit of receiving a sufficiently enticing sentencing discount. For instance, in England, Ashworth and Kelly (2021: 174) claim

[21] See *US v Quinones* (2002) on the conviction of innocent defendants and, in relation to *Quinones*, Brooks (2004d: 2011).

that 'a substantial reduction of up to one-third of the sentence … amounts to a very powerful incentive to plead guilty' (see also Ashworth 2009: 14–15). Some argue that such benefits should be much reduced to a 10 per cent reduction so that defendants do not face undue pressure to plead guilty when they are innocent (see Lippke 2008: 241). While I will turn to the issue of how much of a discount is too much in Section VI, suffice to say that most of these concerns about the influence of the discount amount in compelling innocent defendants to plead guilty require much more empirical work.

The State must not deliberately punish the innocent – nor create conditions where the punishment of the innocent is made more likely, such as through unjustified inducements (see Helm 2021; Chapter 4). No one should be egged on to admit guilt for a crime they did not commit. US-style plea bargaining seems deeply flawed on this issue given the deep power imbalances between the State and the individual and the lack of sufficiently robust safeguards, such as through judicial oversight. While judges could challenge pleas, this almost never happens. McConkie (2015: 63) observes trial judges only rarely challenge guilty pleas as 'they often have little information about the case beyond what is stated in the indictment'. Turner (2006: 202) claims judges are 'passive verifiers of plea bargains'. So, guilty pleas are mostly accepted when received.

English-style plea discounts work differently. The defendant has more control over what sentencing discount they are likely to receive. This is because – as noted in the previous section – sentencing discount possibilities are known in advance and consistently applied. If the defendant wishes to receive an indication of a likely sentence, they may ask the judge, who will advise, but only if requested by the defendant.[22] These factors create a better balance between prosecution and defence than with America plea bargaining. Interestingly, Sentencing Council research found that 'the main factor determining whether or not offenders plead guilty was the likelihood of being found guilty at trial' (Dawes et al 2011: 32). This suggests that, in the English model, the likelihood of conviction, not the potentially enticing magnitude of any sentence reduction, 'was the primary determinant in the decision to plead guilty' (Gormley et al 2020: 15).

A judge is unable to accept a defendant's guilty plea if it is based on 'an unreal and untrue set of facts'.[23] If a plea is based on a statement found to be untrue, then any credit for making a guilty plea would be withheld.[24] The relevant guidance notes correctly that 'illogical or unsupportable' bases for a plea will lead to 'inappropriate' sentences with the potential to damage 'public confidence in the criminal justice system' and so must be avoided (Attorney General 2012). Moreover, if the

[22] See *R v Goodyear* (2005) and limits on indications per *R v Kulah* (2008). Since *Goodyear*, Nicola Padfield (2009: 13) notes 'the case law following this decision shows the practical advantages of the process, but also the dangers: the judge is bound by his indication even if the full facts are only revealed at a later stage'.

[23] *R v Beswick* (1996: 346).

[24] See *R v Elicin and Moore* (2009).

judge is unconvinced of the accused's plea of guilt, the accused can be challenged – so it is not the case that the accused can make any guilty plea they wish and have it accepted automatically with a guaranteed sentencing discount for doing so.[25] In the English system, a guilty plea should not be taken at face value and it may, where appropriate, be refused.

The above highlights the necessary role of judicial oversight of the acceptance of guilty pleas for the purposes, in part, of reducing sentences. Subjecting pleas to such scrutiny and challenge is necessary to help protect defendants from pleading guilty to offences they did not commit – and it is necessary that this is an active aspect of confirming any plea deal.

The trial standard is proving a guilt 'beyond a reasonable doubt' (Crown Prosecution Service 2022). This standard is imperfect – and reasonable doubt is different from absolute certainty (Laudan 2006: 12–13). Understandably, juries frequently request that judges explain this standard to them at trial (Laudan 2006: 49). Nevertheless, the English (and American) legal systems are adversarial in nature. Where the State via the prosecutor charges a defendant and that defendant pleads guilty, there is at least a prima facie lack of reasonable doubt when both sides are in agreement. Such a guilty plea agreement has been likened to a kind of 'bargain' whereby both sides strike a mutually agreeable deal (Kipnis 1976: 104; see Bowers 2008).

Crucial to this agreement being understood as beyond reasonable doubt more substantively, not merely at face value, is whether the defendant makes a plea without coercion. Most legal systems recognise that a defendant is responsible for their plea and free to choose whether to plead guilty or not guilty, irrespective of how relatively strong or weak others might find the case against the defendant (Wasik 2014: 11).[26] Robust judicial oversight – and, where appropriate, judicial challenge – is critically necessary to help ensure that the reasonable doubt standard is sound. While guilty pleas might avoid trial and some of the checks in place at trial to ensure safe convictions, we can maintain the standard if robust measures were in place.

Furthermore, it is right that there are additional checks to ensure any accepted plea leads to a safe conviction. A defendant who pleads guilty could challenge their conviction and claim innocence, although this requires a high standard being met such as establishing that the original guilty plea entered into was not 'knowing, voluntary or intelligent'.[27] It might also be possible to overturn a conviction if new evidence came to light casting sufficient doubt on the defendant's guilt, such as can transpire via innocent projects (Brooks 2004d; 2011). Pleading guilty does not end the matter. Safeguards are in place to continue the possibility of appropriate challenge to ensure outcomes are sound.

[25] See *R v Tolera* (1999).
[26] See *R v Nightingale* (2013).
[27] See *Boykin v Alabama* (1969).

In conclusion, this section considered evidentiary standards for guilty plea sentencing reductions, including the concern that this practice might lead innocent defendants to plead guilty to offences they did not commit. American-style plea bargaining is problematic. There is evidence that a number of innocent defendants are pleading guilty in a system dominated by prosecutorial discretion exercised behind closed doors.

In contrast, the English-style plea discounts provide for greater control by defendants and, therefore, improved balance. There is no clear evidence this system is contributing to innocent defendants pleading guilty, or at least not to the extent observed in the United States.[28] The process of making a plea is more transparent, systematic and consistently applied. Pleas can more regularly be subjected to challenge to help ensure convictions are beyond a reasonable doubt. So, while trial is avoided, scrutiny is not.[29]

While the English plea discount deals with this issue better, it is imperfect. Judicial oversight must be more robust and it should be more commonplace for any guilty pleas to be subjected to greater scrutiny to ensure the safety of convictions, and promote public confidence in the criminal justice system overall.[30] The key issue is that we must have confidence that '"guilty" means "proved guilty"' (Duff et al 2006: 11). We can achieve a standard of beyond reasonable doubt without a trial, subject to satisfactory safeguards working effectively (see Ho 2021: 151). More robust judicial oversight will help enable this.[31]

V. Are Sentencing Discounts Justified *Only* Instrumentally?

This section considers the objection that sentencing discounts – whether plea bargained or through guilty plea reductions – are justified primarily, if not solely, instrumentally. Agreeing less punishment for a guilty plea is a means of concluding

[28] A possible reason for this difference is the prevalence of innocence projects challenging convictions for individuals sentenced for a capital offence.

[29] Scrutiny and challenge may be far less rigorous in a guilty plea than at trial, but a crucial difference is that the guilty plea is normally accepted – and so the parties to the adversarial dispute are in broad agreement and therefore not in dispute over the facts as they might be if not in agreement and at trial.

[30] It is a noteworthy problem that not all defendants can afford legal representation, raising additional questions about the role of the judge in such cases. Ideally, all defendants would have access to legal representation in court.

[31] Ashworth and Redmayne (2010: 318) note 'the overriding assumption that is necessary to increase the proportion of guilty pleas and of early guilty pleas and any reference to the greater involvement of judges in assessing case papers and in ascertaining that innocent defendants were not being pressured into pleading guilty would probably be dismissed as too costly. But even if this were true – and until it has been thoroughly investigated, it would be unwise to make the assumption – then the question is plainly one of expense rather than respect for rights'. My recommendation of an English model of guilty plea sentence reductions with greater judicial oversight is intended to address this imbalance and respect for rights.

criminal cases more quickly and cheaply – and this is why the practice has become endemic. Whatever else might be said about these discounts, they have facilitated a more efficient system able to handle additional cases more quickly and it would make the system exponentially more expensive, and prohibitively so, to require full trials in every case.[32] This raises the question of whether this a problem and, if so, why?

This objection is usually based on the assumption that an instrumental, or otherwise consequentialist, justification is somehow deficient and a substandard foundation for criminal justice – and, thus, such a justification is insufficient to defend guilty plea sentence reductions. Unsurprisingly, the practice has come under fire from various retributivists (see Lippke 2011; Chapter 12; see also Brooks 2021: 30, 168–69, 283). Of course, not all philosophers of punishment are retributivists or share this concern with many other penal theories defended on consequentialist grounds, including most theories of deterrence.[33] While some be unpersuaded by instrumental justifications, it is important to note that they are justifications nonetheless, whatever their other merits – although I will bracket this issue here.[34]

The instrumental objection is also stated in terms of efficiency. For example, some argue that 'the only plausible justification for sentencing discounting is that of efficiency' (Leverick 2004: 384). This view is spelled out by Lord Taylor CJ in *Buffrey*:

> Some reduction must be made, as frauds of this kind were so complex and took such a long time to unravel, that they became a burden to the criminal justice system. They were costly in time and money, and caused stress to jurors who had to try them, judges who had to try them, and to witnesses and defendants themselves.[35]

The use of sentencing discounts in return for guilty pleas is about saving time and money on this view rather than about setting sentences in proportion to just deserts (Kipnis 1976; see Heumann 1977). Curiously, there is no argument here that sentencing discounts is an *ideal* practice that we should accept or even encourage if time and resources were not an issue. The ends of efficiency justify the means.

It is far from clear how much time or money is saved through sentencing discounts. It has been called the stuff of 'lore' to claim that the criminal justice system would grind quickly to a halt if these discounts were ended, as a result of the unbearably greater workload, but there is insufficient evidence to substantiate

[32] Richard Lippke (2022: 185) claims 'observers of US-style plea bargaining routinely note that many judges are reluctant to confound plea deals … this is because judges, like prosecutors, face caseload pressures which discourage them from second guessing the plea deals presented to them for fear of slowing down the work of the courts'.

[33] For a critical survey of penal theories and ethics, see Brooks (2021).

[34] For an insightful analysis on instrumental justifications (addressing the topic of strict liability offences), see Simester (2005: 25–37).

[35] *R v Buffrey* (1992: 515).

these claims (Ashworth and Kelly 2021: 176–77). Nevertheless, it is clear that cases would take longer to resolve and greater resources would be required without sentencing discounts. Lord Justice Hughes notes in *Caley* that 'various public benefits which underlie the practice of reducing sentence for plea of guilt apply just as much to overwhelming cases as to less strong ones'.[36] While the full effects are uncertain, there is no dispute that guilty pleas make the system more efficient, with a greater number of cases being concluded and more cheaply.[37]

The Sentencing Council (2016: 15) has claimed that 'the guilty plea reduction is in place to provide an incentive … not a reward'. The offering of incentives is the very definition of an instrumental usage, of course. However, we should not see anyone being rewarded for admitting their guilt. Sentence discounts are never intended to be a prize or special achievement. Instead, the sentence reduction primarily acts as a form of *recognition*, at least in the English system. There the plea is publicly stated and then acknowledged through a transparent, systematic and consistently applied procedure. Defendants are not rewarded for admitting guilt, but receive public recognition. And note that, in the English system, minimum sentencing or required outcomes could mean that no discount may be available, or at a much reduced rate.

Pleading guilty does not automatically mean that a defendant must receive a sentence reduction to a certain degree for any offence. But there is always a public recognition of their plea – and it is this recognition that is central. There is non-instrumental value in having, and encouraging, citizens to admit and take responsibility for their crimes. It is better for a guilty defendant to make an early plea of guilt than for them to know their guilt but hope that they would be found innocent at trial. This is because it is critical for the criminal justice system to detect and acknowledge breaches of the criminal law. If no one was permitted, let alone encouraged, to admit wrongdoing outside of a completed trial, this would likely undermine social solidarity and the trust required for a healthy democracy (Brooks 2022). This is because a failure of the State to take seriously such admissions of guilt fails to fully respect persons in disregarding their claims. The issue is not whether guilty pleas can ever be accepted, but whether they are sufficiently sincere and accurate (see Dennis 1995).

Sometimes guilty plea reductions are justified for the non-instrumental reason of acknowledging repentance (see McConville 1998: 563). The idea is that when a defendant admits guilt, they accept that they should not have broken the criminal law. Pleading guilty benefits deterrence aims – at least in its formulation as specific deterrence tailored to the individual – as these persons come to accept their conviction and punishment for it.[38] Rehabilitative aims are met as well where

[36] *R v Caley* (2013: para 24); see *R v Paul Wilson* (2012: para 29) ('even in an overwhelming case the guilty plea has a distinct public benefit').

[37] This scenario is described by Easterbrook (1992) as a 'compromise' from which offenders, victims and society benefit overall.

[38] On specific deterrence (or 'micro-deterrence'), see Brooks (2021: 43, 49, 58).

defendants acknowledge their wrongdoing so they can avoid it in future (see Brooks 2021: 62–75).

Moreover, there are desert-related benefits as well of accepting the use of guilty plea discounts. There is a difference between the defendant who publicly acknowledges their crime and someone who did commit a crime, but does not admit it when asked. Rights against self-incrimination and the need for the State to prove guilt beyond reasonable doubt are honoured where we do not systematically increase sentences for those who are only convicted at trial. At the same time, probable, but qualified, reductions for making an early guilty plea that take account of each individual charge and circumstance beforehand can be consistent with desert-based accounts. This is, in part, because addressing someone's moral responsibility and their public acceptance of this responsibility has non-instrumental value in making their 'confession of public wrongdoing' (Duff 2007: 177). The different and lesser punishment as a result of this acceptance is a way to acknowledge this fact. It must be emphasised that this discount is qualified and may not be granted in every instance.[39] This addresses the possible objection that accepting guilt before trial should never lead to a change in sentence from that which might be confirmed post trial, as exceptions are made.[40]

The Sentencing Council (2017a) also justifies guilty plea discounts for more than instrumental reasons linked to efficiency. Noting its purpose of encouraging 'those who are going to plead guilty to do so as early in the court process as possible', the Council says – in addition to promoting 'the public interest', as the discounts 'save public time and money on investigations and trials' – that a policy of encouraging early guilty pleas aims to reduce the impact of crime on victims and to save victims and witnesses from the need to testify.

These additional reasons are non-instrumental. They speak to the anxiety and distress that victims and witnesses can experience in attending trials and being called on to testify (see Manikis 2023). Not all such individuals wish to engage in those ways and, thus, accepting a guilty plea, subject to satisfactorily robust safeguards, could facilitate this benefit for them. It has been argued that 'guilty pleas are good not just for the system's accounting, but for victims and other witnesses who need not take the time, the trauma or the physical risk of giving evidence'

[39] It might be objected that any discount undermines the presumption of innocence stated in Article 6.2 of the European Convention on Human Rights. The concern is that pleading innocence, if a protected right, should not lead to someone always being punished more when exercising that right in relation to someone who pleads guilty before trial. In reply, it could be said that there is no systematic maltreatment as early guilty pleas do not always lead to any reduction taking into account individual context and circumstances. Someone who pleads guilty or someone else found guilty for the same crimes can receive the same punishment in some circumstances.

[40] For lack of space, I leave open the question of when exceptions should be made whereby a guilty plea reduction should not be allowed. I note these exceptions are already listed in practice. Their existence is important for highlighting the principled point made above that making a guilty plea can matter for sentencing discounts, but that it is right that this is qualified, allowing for exceptions where appropriate. I do not argue that simply admitting guilt should always, and in an unqualified way, lead to sentence reductions. Context matters when making any such determinations.

(Dripps 2011: 427). Research conducted for the Sentencing Council found victims to be more supportive of guilty plea sentencing than the general public (Dawes et al, 2011). Victims are key stakeholders and their broad support matters – and has non-instrumental value (Brooks 2014; 2016).

Of course, not all victims (or witnesses) wish to avoid such interaction. For example, the increasing interest in, and use of, restorative justice speaks to this need for victims and their communities to have a say in matters of justice (see Brooks 2021: 76–101; 2017c). A possible concern with plea arrangements is that those victims who would like to have a voice could lack the means, if they wanted that opportunity. As the criminal justice system has become increasingly reformed to bring the victim back in, it would seem contrary to such reforms to shut victims out completely (see Gardner 1998).

The use of victim impact statements can be helpful. Victims need not take up this opportunity if they do not want to. However, if they do, this information about their experiences might not make much, if any, difference to a judge's decision about sentencing although it can be suitably meaningful for victims to express publicly the impact they felt and for offenders to better understand the consequences of their wrongful actions (Brooks 2021: 84; see Jackson 2003). So, the voice of victims need not be lost if trials are averted – and victims are generally favourable to the guilty plea discount system overall.

In conclusion, some object to the use of sentencing discounts because they are instrumentally justified only. It is true that these discounts save significant time and resources, even if the exact amounts are difficult to pin down. Nor is it obvious, at least to me, that instrumental justifications cannot be valid although I do not explore this point for want of space. The concern about sentencing discounts as only instrumental is a criticism mostly voiced by scholars supportive of desert-based accounts.

In response, it is argued that sentencing discounts should be seen more as forms of acknowledgement than purely incentives. This is partly because the incentives are not available in every case, whereas the recognition of a public acknowledgement of guilt is available always. Moreover, such acknowledgement is positive for social trust, supports various penal aims, not least deterrence and rehabilitation, and can be consistent with a desert-based approach as well because defendants accept responsibility in public for their actions. Guilty plea discounts save time and resources but have a value we should retain even if society could afford a full trial for every charge.

Finally, guilty plea discounts have support from victims. As stakeholders in the process, their voices matter, too. However, it is important that there should be some opportunity, should any victims want it, to express publicly the impact a crime had on them. The use of victim impact statements and the like can allow this.

In these ways, guilty plea sentencing discounts have non-instrumental value that we should promote – and even if we could afford to hold trials in every instance instead. However, this requires that there are robust safeguards in place to ensure guilty pleas are made sufficiently sincere and accurate. It has already been argued that these safeguards could be more robustly enforced and so it is not claimed that the guilty plea procedures, as they are found in England, are ideal or should be uncritically accepted, but rather that discounts can be justified with satisfactory safeguards in place – and that this would not be justified only instrumentally.

VI. How Much of a Discount Is Too Much?

Thus far, this chapter has focused on the justification of having a guilty plea discount. I have favoured the English guilty plea over American plea bargaining and argued that it can be justified, subject to having in place robust safeguards such as greater judicial oversight and challenge.

A third and final issue to be considered here concerns the size of the discounts. It has already been noted above that not every plea necessitates a reduction, as a minimum sentence requirement might forbid it. But if a discount can be justified, what price should be paid?

There is a wide array of different practices ranging from modest discounts to no limit (see Chapter 5).[41] In response, academics claim that discounts range from 'may appear reasonable and modest' to 'too great' (Helm 2019: 171; Campbell, Ashworth and Redmayne 2019: 343). As Julian Roberts (2013: 119) observes, with 'no clear statutory yardstick for determining departures from the Guilty Plea guideline … conclusions about the acceptable degree of judicial compliance with this guideline are likely to be subjective'. This situation calls for more – and better – empirical evidence from different plea-discounting jurisdictions about the uses of discounts for different offences, noting impacts on individuals with varying protected characteristics. This would help provide a more definitive snapshot of the practice of discounts and their distribution to different groupings of people. It would also support clearer comparative studies across jurisdictions than at present.

Nevertheless, we can still address the principled sentencing issue even if more data is needed. One possible issue is defining what relative discount amount would count as excessive. Gormley et al (2020: 14) note that 'it is unclear what form of evidence would resolve the question of whether current levels of reduction are excessive'. For example, someone pleading guilty at the first opportunity could have a sentence of eight months reduced to six. Given half this amount would normally be served in prison, the difference a plea might make is spending three months in custody rather than four (Gormley et al 2020: 14). As Hegel (1991: 245) has noted before, while one day in prison or one dollar fine too much may be an injustice, there is a limit to the precision a theoretical approach can make to

[41] The UK government considered a discount of up to half in a Green Paper, but this was rejected because it was thought to 'erode public confidence', amongst other factors (Cameron 2011).

determining the exact quantity of punishment in every case – it is instead a project of setting 'a general limit within which variations are also possible'.[42]

Therefore, it is challenging to state categorically that a discount of, say, one-third for pleading guilty at the first opportunity is too excessive in comparison with a one-quarter or one-fifth discount beyond relying on subjective intuitions in the absence of clearer data. One issue raised above is where a discount is deemed excessive because a sentence reduction is so great that it can effectively compel an innocent defendant to plead guilty to a crime they did not commit. In addition to requiring more data to establish this claim, our aim should be to ensure that any plea entered is sound and compelling. It should not be taken at face value and left unchallenged, which is why greater judicial oversight and robust scrutiny is required for our having confidence that a defendant's guilty plea is sufficiently sincere and accurate.

A second issue is that a discount is deemed excessive because the sentence reduction justified by the discount might be reduced further by factors intrinsic to the discount's justification. In short, discounts can count for more in reducing sentences than they should. For example, some scholars, such as Hough and Jacobson (Chapter 11), claim that, in fact, defendants can gain much more than a one-third sentencing discount from receiving more favourable treatment of their personal mitigation linked to their having pleaded guilty early. So, a defendant pleading guilty receives a one-third discount and a further bonus discount for little more reason than a kind of reward for the early guilty plea. Arguments of this variety can often appeal to the place of remorse playing a role in justifying the original discount, but then also serving as a mitigating factor reducing sentences still further. Remorse is counted twice.

In response, it is not obvious that every guilty plea is intended to be, in fact, a sign of remorse rather than mostly a desire to avoid a more severe punishment (see Sanders and Young 2000: 401). This is another matter for further, careful empirical investigation. However, as a formality, remorse is not assumed in pleading guilty. For example, the Sentencing Council guidance emphasises that remorse is a separate issue from the guilty plea – and remorse has a separate value too (see Maslen and Roberts 2013: 127).

It might be that some academics would wish to argue that remorse should be bound up with the making of a plea agreement. This view is found in *Harper*, in which it was said that 'It is … of course proper to give a man a lesser sentence if he has shown genuine remorse, amongst other things by pleading guilty'.[43] Restorative justice proponents have long argued for the importance of the offender's admission of guilt and apology as a critically important feature of any restorative framework, with the benefits it brings to improved victim and offender satisfaction, for fostering a sense of closure and reducing future offending (see Brooks 2021: 76–101).

[42] The full reference to the translated German text is *Elements of the Philosophy of Right*, §214 Remark.
[43] *R v Harper* (1967). See Tasioulas (2011) for his 'internalist' interpretation of mercy.

While remorse can bring many positives, it is unclear that the State should be in the business of requiring defendants to exhibit remorse because that would impact on individual conscience, even if remorse might be encouraged and promoted.[44]

Perhaps a guilty plea renders a defendant more likeable by judges or magistrates. It is likely sentencers take some account of an offender's demeanour and conduct in court, however difficult it might be to gauge (Shapland 1987). The main issue is whether the appropriate sentencing guidelines are followed faithfully, likeability or not. Remorse or other appropriate factors, including dangerousness, may appear more than once in the process. What matters is that each stage is appropriate, not that factors might reappear per se. Unless quantified, it is difficult to discern how excessive, or even different, a conveyance of remorse is supposed to be in making a plea in these circumstances.[45]

In conclusion, this section has considered the issue of, if a guilty plea reduction can be justified, how we can guard against its being excessive. When examining various claims about excessiveness, each are non-compelling. It is unclear what, if any, discount will not compel defendants, especially vulnerable persons, to plead guilty to crimes they did not commit. This is especially true if more robust judicial oversight is taken into account. It is further unclear that making a guilty plea and receiving a sentence reduction (which itself might be justifiable) leads to excessive reductions as a result of favourability with judges or magistrates. Again, perhaps a defendant is more likeable, but the only problem is not that but rather whether other steps in confirming a sentence are determined in a way that breaches relevant guidance – and this is unproven.

Furthermore, the claim that remorse can be counted twice as a necessary factor in making a plea is, at least formally, untrue. This is because, as remorse is considered separately, it may be in fact untrue as it should not be assumed every defendant only pleads guilty to express remorse and, again, there seems no prohibition in any factor having some bearing on different stages in determining a sentence provided each stage is handled appropriately. The excessiveness of guilty plea discounts is not established – even though it is a difficult, complex matter trying to discern where a line should be drawn.

This is not to say that no discount is, or can be, excessive. If we had improved data, this would help facilitate clearer thinking around the impact of different quantitative measures. What is required is an English-style guilty plea discount subject to more robust judicial oversight and challenge. This reform of the current system would appear to address concerns about the use of guilty plea discounts in a satisfactory way – and without any clear use of excessive discounts.

[44] See von Hirsch (1993: 10–11) ('Censure gives the actor the opportunity for so responding, but it is not a technique for evoking specified sentiments').

[45] It is acknowledged that expressing remorse can play some role in the sentencing part of a capital trial (Eisenberg, Garvey and Wells 1998).

VII. Conclusion

In his history of the adversarial criminal trial, John H. Langbein (2003: 19) notes that seventeenth-century trial judges in England 'actively discouraged criminal defendants from tendering guilty pleas' (see McConville and Mirsky 2005: 311–14). Today, the overwhelming majority of defendants plead guilty to the charges brought before them. Their guilty pleas normally lead to lesser punishment. The issue is then how these discounts might be justified, if at all. This chapter has considered two different forms of sentencing reductions for guilty pleas: American plea bargaining and the English sentencing discount. The latter was found more compelling because it better ensured that defendants were convicted for the crimes they did (rather than for lesser offences they did not commit), the sentencing discount used is more transparent and consistently applied and there is greater judicial oversight.

The chapter then considered several specific issues. The first was whether the use of sentence discounts led to innocent defendants pleading guilty to crimes that they did not commit. It was argued that guilty pleas cannot be accepted at face value and, where appropriate, they should be refused. More robust judicial oversight and challenge can help ensure guilty pleas are sufficiently sincere and accurate. The second issue was whether the sentencing discounts are justified primarily, if not solely, instrumentally as a means of concluding criminal cases more quickly and cheaply. It was argued that there is substantial non-instrumental value in accepting guilty pleas and granting sentencing reductions, but only if following more stringent judicial safeguards.

The third and final issue was about the magnitude of discount for a guilty plea. This is a complex matter to unpack given the limited data available. Claims of excessiveness appear to be based more on subjective intuition than empirical findings or claims that sentencing guidelines have been misapplied. This is not to argue that the current discount system is perfect within a criminal justice system very far from perfection. Rather, the case for discounts being excessive is unproven, and, without compelling evidence, the current sliding scale of guilty plea discounts in England is satisfactory even if procedural safeguards are not – these must be more robust if the use of guilty plea discounts is to be justified. Guilty pleas matter. This chapter has attempted to explain why and how.

References

Aristotle (1984) 'Nicomachean Ethics' in J Barnes (ed), *The Complete Works of Aristotle*, vol 2 (Princeton, Princeton University Press).

Ashworth, A (2009) *Principles of Criminal Law*, 7th edn (Oxford, Oxford University Press).

Ashworth, A and Redmayne, M (2010) *The Criminal Process*, 4th edn (Oxford, Oxford University Press).

Ashworth, A and Roberts, JV (2017) 'Sentencing: Theory, Principle, and Practice' in A Liebling, S Maruna and L McAra (eds), *The Oxford Handbook of Criminology*, 6th edn (Oxford, Oxford University Press).
Ashworth, A and Kelly, R (2021) *Sentencing and Criminal Justice*, 7th edn (Oxford, Hart Publishing).
Attorney General's Office (2012) *The Acceptance of Pleas and the Prosecutor's Role in the Sentencing Exercise: Guidance* (London, TSO).
Balbus, ID (1973) *Dialectics of Legal Repression: Black Rebels before the American Criminal Courts* (New York, Russell Sage Foundation).
Baldwin, J and McConville, M (1979) 'Plea Bargaining and Plea Negotiation in England' 13 *Law and Society Review* 287.
Barkow, RE (2019) *Prisoners of Politics: Breaking the Cycle of Mass Incarceration*. (Cambridge, MA., Belknap Press of Harvard University Press).
Beard, J (2017) 'Reduction in Sentence for a Guilty Plea', *House of Commons Library: Briefing Paper*, No 5974 (London, House of Commons).
Berdejo, C (2018) 'Criminalizing Race: Racial Disparities in Plea-Bargaining' 59 *Boston College Law Review* 1189.
Bowers, J (2008) 'Punishing the Innocent' 156 *University of Pennsylvania Law Review* 1117.
Brooks, T (2001) 'Corlett on Kant, Hegel and Retribution' 76 *Philosophy* 561.
—— (2004a) 'Is Hegel a Retributivist?' 49/50 *Bulletin of the Hegel Society of Great Britain* 113.
—— (2004b) 'The Right to Trial by Jury' 21 *Journal of Applied Philosophy* 197.
—— (2004c) 'A Defence of Jury Nullification' 10 *Res Publica* 401.
—— (2004d) 'Retributivist Arguments against Capital Punishment' 35 *Journal of Social Philosophy* 188.
—— (ed) (2009) *The Right to a Fair Trial* (Aldershot, Ashgate).
—— (2011) 'Retribution and Capital Punishment' in MD White (ed), *Retributivism: Essays on Theory and Policy* (Oxford, Oxford University Press).
—— (2012) 'Hegel and the Unified Theory of Punishment' in T Brooks (ed), *Hegel's Philosophy of Right* (Oxford, Blackwell).
—— (2013) *Hegel's Political Philosophy: A Systematic Reading of the Philosophy of Right*, 2nd edn (Edinburgh, Edinburgh University Press).
—— (2014) 'Stakeholder Sentencing' in JV Roberts and J Ryberg (eds), *Popular Punishment: On the Normative Significance of Public Opinion for Penal Theory* (Oxford, Oxford University Press).
—— (2016) 'Justice as Stakeholding' in K Watene and J Drydyk (eds), *Theorizing Justice: Critical Insights and Future Directions* (New York: Rowman and Littlefield).
—— (2017a) 'Hegel on Crime and Punishment' in T Brooks and S Stein (eds), *Hegel's Political Philosophy: On the Normative Significance of Method and System* (Oxford, Oxford University Press).
—— (2017b) 'Hegel's Philosophy of Law' in D Moyar (ed), *The Oxford Handbook of Hegel* (Oxford, Oxford University Press).
—— (2017c) 'Punitive Restoration and Restorative Justice' 36 *Criminal Justice Ethics* 122.
—— (2020) 'Retribution' in F Focquaert, E Shaw and B Waller (eds), *The Routledge Handbook of the Philosophy and Science of Punishment* (London, Routledge).
—— (2021) *Punishment: A Critical Introduction*, 2nd edn (London, Routledge).
—— (2022) *The Trust Factor: Essays on the Current Crisis and Hope for the Future* (London, Methuen).

Brunk, CG (1979) 'The Problem of Voluntariness and Coercion in the Negotiated Plea' 13 *Law and Society Review* 527.
Cameron, D (2011) *PM's Press Conference on Sentencing Reforms*, www.gov.uk/government/speeches/pms-press-conference-on-sentencing-reforms
Campbell, L, Ashworth, A and Redmayne, M (2019) *The Criminal Process* (Oxford, Oxford University Press).
Clark, SJ (2006) '"Who Do you Think You Are?" The Criminal Trial and Community Character' in RA Duff, L Farmer, S Marshall and V Tadros (eds), *The Trial on Trial: Judgment and Calling to Account*, vol 2 (Oxford, Hart Publishing).
Crown Prosecution Service (2021) *Annual Report and Accounts 2020–21* HC 430 (London, TSO).
—— (2022) *The Verdict and Sentencing* (London, TSO).
Dawes, W, Harvey, P, McIntosh, B, Nunney, F and Phillips, A (2011) *Attitudes to Guilty Plea Sentence Reductions* (London, Sentencing Council of England and Wales).
Dennis, I (1995) 'Instrumental Protection, Human Right or Functional Necessity? Reassessing the Privilege against Self-Incrimination' 54 *Cambridge Law Journal* 342.
Department for Education (2014) *Guidance on Promoting British Values in Schools* (London, TSO).
Dripps, DA (2011) 'The Substance-Procedure Relationship in Criminal Law' in RA Duff and SP Green (eds), *Philosophical Foundations of Criminal Law* (Oxford, Oxford University Press).
Duff, RA (2007) *Answering for Crime: Responsibility and Liability in the Criminal Law* (Oxford, Hart Publishing).
Duff, RA, Farmer, L, Marshall, S and Tadros, V (2006) 'Introduction: Judgment and Calling to Account' in RA Duff, L Farmer, S Marshall and V Tadros (eds), *The Trial on Trial: Judgment and Calling to Account*, vol 2 (Oxford, Hart Publishing).
Easterbrook, FH (1992) 'Plea Bargaining as Compromise' 101 *Yale Law Journal* 1969.
Eisenberg, T, Garvey, SP and Wells, MT (1998) 'But Was He Sorry? The Role of Remorse in Capital Sentencing' 83 *Cornell Law Review* 1599.
Fisher, G (2000) 'Plea Bargaining's Triumph' 109 *Yale Law Journal* 857.
Gardner, J (1998) 'Crime: In Proportion and in Perspective' in A Ashworth and M Wasik (eds), *Fundamentals of Sentencing Theory: Essays in Honour of Andrew von Hirsch* (Oxford, Clarendon).
Goncalves, Jr, WI (2022) '"How Much Time Am I Looking At?" Plea Bargains, Harsh Punishments and Low Trial Rates in Southwest Border Districts' 59 *American Criminal Law Review* 293.
Gormley, J, Roberts, JV, Bild, J and Harris, L (2020) *Sentence Reductions for Guilty Pleas: A Review of Policy, Practice and Research* (London, Sentencing Academy).
Hegel, GWF (1991) *Elements of the Philosophy of Right*, AW Wood (ed) (Cambridge, Cambridge University Press).
Helm, RK (2019) 'Conviction by Consent? Vulnerability, Autonomy and Conviction by Guilty Plea' 83 *Journal of Criminal Law* 161.
—— (2021) 'Cognition and Incentives in Plea Decisions: Categorical Differences in Outcomes as the Tipping Point for Innocent Defendants' *Psychology, Public Policy and Law*, forthcoming (doi.org/10.1037/law0000321).
Heumann, M (1977) *Plea Bargaining: The Experiences of Prosecutors, Judges and Defense Attorney* (Chicago, IL, University of Chicago Press).

Ho, HL (2021) 'Justification, Excuse, and Proof Beyond Reasonable Doubt' 31 *Philosophical Issues* 146.
House of Commons Justice Committee (2016) *Reduction in Sentence for a Guilty Plea Guideline: First Report of Session 2016–17*, HC 168 (London, TSO).
Husak, D (2011) 'Retributivism, Proportionality, and the Challenge of the Drug Court Movement' in M Tonry (ed), *Retributivism Has a Past, Has It a Future?* (Oxford, Oxford University Press).
Jackson, JD (2003) 'Justice for All: Putting Victims at the Heart of Criminal Justice' 30 *Journal of Law and Society* 309.
Jaconelli, J (2002) *Open Justice: A Critique of the Public Trial* (Oxford, Oxford University Press).
Kipnis, K (1976) 'Criminal Justice and the Negotiated Plea' 86 *Ethics* 93.
Kutateladze, BL, Andiloro, NR, Johnson BD and Spohn, CC (2014) 'Cumulative Disadvantage: Examining Racial and Ethnic Disparity in Prosecution and Sentencing' 42 *Criminology* 515.
Lammy, D (2017) *The Lammy Review: An Independent Review into the Treatment of, and Outcomes for, Black, Asian and Minority Ethnic Individuals in the Criminal Justice System* (London, Ministry of Justice).
Langbein, JH (2003) *The Origins of Adversary Trial* (Oxford, Oxford University Press).
Laudan, L (2006) *Truth, Error and Criminal Law: An Essay in Legal Epistemology* (Cambridge, Cambridge University Press).
Leverick, F (2004) 'Tensions and Balances, Costs and Rewards: The Sentence Discount in Scotland' 8 *Edinburgh Law Review* 360.
Leveson, B (2015) *Review of Efficiency in Criminal Proceedings* (London, Judiciary of England and Wales).
Library of Congress (2014) *Magna Carta: Muse and Mentor* (Washington, DC, Library of Congress).
Lippke, RL (2008) 'To Waive or Not to Waive: The Right to Trial and Plea Bargaining' 2 *Criminal Law and Philosophy* 181.
—— (2011) *The Ethics of Plea Bargaining* (Oxford, Oxford University Press).
—— (2022) 'Plea Bargaining, Principled Sentencing, and Artificial Intelligence' in J Ryberg and JV Roberts (eds), *Sentencing and Artificial Intelligence* (Oxford, Oxford University Press).
Maslen, H and Roberts, JV (2013) 'Remorse and Sentencing: An Analysis of Sentencing Guidelines and Sentencing Practice' in A Ashworth and JV Roberts (eds), *Sentencing Guidelines: Exploring the English Model* (Oxford, Oxford University Press).
McConkie, DS (2015) 'Judges as Framers of Plea Bargaining' 26 *Stanford Law and Policy Review* 61.
McConville, M (1998) 'Plea Bargaining: Ethics and Politics' 25 *Journal of Law and Society* 562.
McConville, M and Mirsky, CL (2005) *Jury Trials and Plea Bargaining: A True History* (Oxford, Hart Publishing).
Padfield, N (2009) 'Shining the Torch on Plea-Bargaining' 68 *Cambridge Law Journal* 11.
Rakoff, JS (2021) *Why the Innocent Plead Guilty and the Guilty Go Free: And Other Paradoxes of Our Broken Legal System* (New York: Picador).
Roberts, JV (2013) 'Complying with Sentencing Guidelines: Latest Findings from the Crown Court Sentencing Survey' in A Ashworth and JV Roberts (eds), *Sentencing Guidelines: Exploring the English Model* (Oxford, Oxford University Press).
Royal Commission on Criminal Justice (1993) *Report* Cm 2263 (London, TSO).

Sanders, A and Young, R (2000) *Criminal Justice*, 2nd edn (London, Butterworths).
Sentencing Council (2017a) *Reduction in Sentence for a Guilty Plea: Definitive Guideline* (London, Sentencing Council).
—— (2017b) *Reduction in Sentence for a Guilty Plea: First Hearing on or After 1 June 2017* (London, Sentencing Council).
—— (2020) *Assessing the Impact and Implementation of the Sentencing Council's Reduction in Sentence for a Guilty Plea Definitive Guideline* (London, Sentencing Council).
Sentencing Council of England and Wales (2016) *Reduction in Sentence for a Guilty Plea Guideline: Consultation* (London, Sentencing Council of England and Wales).
Shapland, J (1987) 'Who Controls Sentencing? Influences on the Sentencer' in D Pennington and L Lloyd-Bostock (eds), *The Psychology of Sentencing* (Oxford, Centre for Socio-Legal Studies, University of Oxford).
Simester, AP (2005) 'Is Strict Liability Always Wrong?' in AP Simester (ed), *Appraising Strict Liability* (Oxford, Oxford University Press).
Simester, AP, Spencer, JR, Stark, F, Sullivan, GR and Virgo, GJ (2019) *Simester and Sullivan's Criminal Law: Theory and Doctrine*, 7th edn (Oxford, Hart Publishing).
Solicitor-General (2013) *Solicitor-General's Prosecution Guidelines* (Auckland, Crown Law Office).
Spohn, C (2009) 'Criticisms of Mandatory Minimums' in A von Hirsch, A Ashworth and JV Roberts (eds), *Principled Sentencing. Readings on Theory and Policy*, 3rd edn (Oxford, Hart Publishing).
Tasioulas, J (2011) 'Where is the Love? The Topography of Mercy' in R Cruft, MH Kramer and MR Reiff (eds), *Crime, Punishment and Responsibility: The Jurisprudence of Antony Duff* (Oxford, Oxford University Press).
Tonry, M (2009) 'Abandoning Sentence Discounts for Guilty Pleas' in A von Hirsch, A Ashworth and JV Roberts (eds), *Principled Sentencing. Readings on Theory and Policy* 3rd edn (Oxford, Hart Publishing).
—— (2011) 'Punishment' in M Tonry (ed), *The Oxford Handbook of Crime and Criminal Justice* (Oxford, Oxford University Press).
Tsai, RL (2019) *Practical Equality: Forging Justice in a Divided Nation* (New York, W. W. Norton).
Turner, JI (2006) 'Judicial Participation in Plea Negotiations: A Comparative View' 54 *American Journal of Comparative Law* 199.
Vogel, ME (1999) 'The Social Origins of Plea Bargaining: Conflict and the Law in the Process of State Formation, 1830–1860' 33 *Law and Society Review* 161.
von Hirsch, A (1993) *Censure and Sanctions* (Oxford, Clarendon).
—— (2017) *Deserved Criminal Sentences* (London, Bloomsbury).
von Hirsch, A and Ashworth, A (2005) *Proportionate Sentencing: Exploring the Principles* (Oxford, Oxford University Press).
Walker, N (1980) *Punishment, Danger and Stigma: The Morality of Criminal Law* (Oxford, Basil Blackwell).
Wasik, M (2004) 'What Guides Sentencing Decisions?' in A Bottoms, S Rex and G Robinson (eds), *Alternatives to Prison: Options for an Insecure Society* (Cullompton, Willan).
—— (2014) *A Practical Approach to Sentencing*, 5th edn (Oxford, Oxford University Press).
Wright, RF (2012) 'Charging and Plea Bargaining as Forms of Sentencing Discretion' in J Petersilia and KR Reitz (eds), *The Oxford Handbook of Sentencing and Corrections* (Oxford, Oxford University Press).

Legislation

Criminal Justice Act 2003
Criminal Justice and Public Order Act 1994
Sentencing Act 2000
Sentencing Act 2020

Cases

United Kingdom

McKinnon v USA [2007] EWHC 762 (Admin)
R v Beswick [1992] 14 Cr App Rep (S) 343
R v Buffrey [1992] 14 Cr App Rep (S) 511
R v Caley [2013] 2 Cr App R (S) 305
R v Elicin and Moore [2009] 1 Cr App R (S) 561
R v Goodyear [2005] 1 WLR 2532
R v Harper [1967] 52 Cr App R 21
R v Kulah [2008] 1 WLR 2517
R v Nightingale [2013] EWCA Crim 405
R v Simpson [2009] 2 Cr App R (S) 492
R v Tolera [1999] 1 Cr App Rep (S) 25
R v Wilson [2012] EWCA Crim 386

United States

Lafler v Cooper, 566 US 156, 170 (2012)
US v Quinones, 205 F Supp 2d 256 (2002)

9

Victim-related Assumptions Underlying Plea-based Sentence Reductions: A Communicative and Experiential Framework

MARIE MANIKIS

I. Introduction

Common law sentencing regimes rest on a series of assumptions around guilty pleas to justify sentence reduction. Several of these assumptions relate to the beneficial effects on victims suggesting that guilty pleas have a beneficial impact on victims, by either reducing process-related harms or contributing to their welfare (see Chapter 5). Others also focus on these effects on victims but are framed within a desert-based logic (see further discussions on desert and retributivism in Chapter 3), suggesting that the guilty plea diminishes the offender's level of blame since it is tied to remorse and to a desire to diminish the harms suffered by victims and increasing their welfare. This chapter analyses the Canadian context following an analysis of case law[1] on guilty pleas and victim-related assumptions and suggests that these assumptions are often readily made without careful consideration or engagement with the underlying sentencing rationales and individualised contexts. This risks affecting the process of censure and its dialectical value by blurring the underlying rationales and communicating inaccurate statements to the polity.

Building on a communicative and relational theory of punishment, the chapter proposes a dynamic and principled understanding of guilty pleas by ensuring that the assumed grounds for mitigation are (1) rooted within clear and principled

[1] Over 3,000 cases have been analysed and some are relied upon as illustrations. Some general tendencies of these cases are discussed in this chapter. There is a clear tendency in most of these judgments to assume that testimony is harmful to victims without seeking participative input from victims about this dimension. Similarly, these judgments also show a tendency that lower individual blame of the offender is assumed on the basis of a guilty plea without further evidence.

sentencing rationales and (2) understood and weighed in relation to contextual grounds that justify pleas rather than formulated in abstract and predetermined assumptions. This can in part be achieved through dialectical engagement with victims, the accused, communities and the State. This engagement ensures that the underlying assumptions that relate to victims are clear and accurate. This proposition will enable a more nuanced, relational and individualised understanding of each plea, similar to that reserved to other mitigating factors, which in turn can offer a more accurate message to the public, victims and the offender. Finally, this proposed approach also challenges current sentencing schemes that prioritise an automatic fixed reduction based on the timing of the plea, since doing so glosses over context by assuming these underlying assumptions about pleas.

A. Overview

The chapter is divided into three sections. The next two sections discuss victim-related assumptions and expose some of their underlying issues in the Canadian context of guilty plea reduction. Section II discusses and classifies the main underlying victim-related assumptions around plea-based sentence reduction and suggests that these assumptions are not always tied to clearly articulated sentencing rationales. Section III suggests that these main assumptions are often relied upon without consideration of the individualised context. Section IV builds on a communicative and experiential theory of punishment to argue in favour of greater clarity and a more contextualised and individualised approach towards victim-related assumptions for plea-based sentence reduction.

II. The Underlying Victim-related Assumptions Around Plea-based Sentence Reduction: Desert Based or Harm Reductionist/Cathartic?

Within common law jurisdictions, including Canada, and England and Wales, there are several assumptions that underlie plea-based sentence reduction that relate to victims. An analysis of case law in Canada suggests that these assumptions can be grouped into three categories.

The first category of assumptions is premised on the idea that guilty pleas are considered mitigating in sentencing because they save victims from testifying in open court, and thus save them from additional traumatic experiences,[2] help to protect their privacy, and save victims from embarrassment (*R v S.S.* 1990: 11).

[2] See various Court of Appeal decisions in Canada that affirm this: *R v Martineau* (2021: 24); *R v Salehi* (2022: 1); *R v Kreutziger* (2005: 10); *R v Johnston and Tremayne* (1970: 783), citing *R v de Haan* (1967); *R v Bernardon* (2021).

This set of assumptions is rooted in a view that victim testimonial participation in the criminal process is harmful to them in a number of different ways and therefore the defendant's plea of guilt needs to be rewarded since it reduces or eliminates that harm.

A second set of assumptions relates to the idea that guilty pleas reduce or eliminate some of the additional harms suffered by victims in the hands of the criminal justice process, notably that they eliminate the uncertainties for victims inherent in the trial process (see *R v Ruddick* 2008; *R v Poepl* 2021) minimises the victim's stress associated with the legal process (see *R v S.W.* 2021) and that it reduces community speculation and censure experienced by complainants in sexual assault matters until the outcome of the trial is known (*R v P.A.C.* 2020). These arguments rest on a recognition that the criminal justice process itself is very harmful for victims and that a plea of guilty is a laudable action that diminishes systemic harms to victims.

A third set of assumptions suggests that guilty pleas provide victims with a wider sense of justice and well-being. Indeed, courts have highlighted the claim that guilty pleas ensure justice is done from the victim's perspective, bring closure to the victim (see *R v Kapolak* 2020: 24) and provide a degree of finality that would otherwise not exist (*R v A.C.* 2017: 41[3]). Other courts note that guilty pleas imply 'sincere remorse' (*R v S.W.* 2021: 85) and acceptance of legal responsibility from the offender, which is considered to be of great importance for victims. Within this set of rationales, the guilty plea is not only considered to reduce the harms suffered by victims in the hands of the system, but is also understood as something cathartic that enables victims to achieve some of their needs in relation to the criminal justice system.

Within the case law in this jurisdiction, the underlying sentencing rationale that underpins these assumptions remains unclear and inconsistent. This is particularly the case with the first set of assumptions that relate to sparing victims from testifying. Specifically, it is unclear whether this assumption is premised on the idea that the accused is less blameworthy because he has *intended* to spare the victim from the testimonial ordeal by pleading guilty (desert based) or whether the reduction is predominantly grounded on the plea's effect on the victim, regardless of the accused's desired consequence or intention vis-à-vis the victim (harm reductionist) (Roberts and Dagan 2019: 143). Some decisions have hinted towards the first possibility by citing the academic literature which associates guilty pleas with remorse, highlighting that 'avoiding the need to have a victim testify is a legitimate dimension of remorse but gets little credence if a guilty plea is entered only after hearing the witness at a preliminary hearing' (Manson 2001[4]). In contrast, in another case where the evidence pointed towards the defendant's lack of remorse

[3] Citing *R v Faulds* (1994), which states the guilty plea provides a degree of finality that would otherwise not exist.

[4] Cited in *Deng v La Reine* (2003: 30) and *R v Nicholson* (2008: 11). See also *R v McArthur* (2019).

despite his guilty plea, the guilty plea was seen as substantially mitigating since it saved victims from the harms of testifying (*R v Mattess* 2021).

The main circumstance that judges examine in this set of assumptions is the timing of the plea and whether victims have had to testify. The message that the focus on timing sends to the public is also unclear. Is an earlier guilty plea meant to show lesser blame and thus tied to the defendant's mental state (desert) or is the timing meant to be considered from a victim harm-reductionist perspective, which suggests that the earlier the plea the less harm victims will have suffered in relation to their potential testimony in the process? Most decisions seem to hint at the latter harm-reductionist perspective by highlighting that even a late plea on the date of the trial is considered to have some mitigating effect because it relieves victims of the need to testify (*R v Burback* 2012; *R v Martineau* 2021: 24). In other cases it has been suggested that its effect should be non-existent or diminished when it does not 'save the complainant from much stressful anticipation' (*R v MacArthur* 2018: 22; see also *R v Campbell* 2014; *R v CMC* 2016; *R v D.O.* 2021; *R v Salehi* 2022). If this is the case, where does that leave cases where the defendant nevertheless intends to reduce victim harms? To what extent is the plea-based reduction premised on the effects on victims vs the offender's desert?

Being clear about the specific sentencing rationales that underpin these assumptions is particularly relevant since they can signal different messages and lead to different results. Indeed, a clear articulation of these rationales – whether they are premised on reduced individual blame from the accused or a harm-reductionist-cathartic perspective for victims – is especially important from a communicative perspective since the sentencing process as a public forum of communication needs to be clear to the public about the message behind a plea-based sentence reduction.

Further, as will be discussed in the next section, assumptions about harms suffered by victims as an inherent part of the process are often stated automatically without much consideration of variations within contexts. This can be particularly challenging when plea-based reductions benefit from an automatic predetermined reduction based on the timing of the plea. Indeed, it may be the case that for some victims, the testimonial process is cathartic and therefore an early plea of guilt is detrimental to their well-being and causes additional harms. In such cases, how does one measure individual desert in the case of an early plea of guilt? Which rationale should prevail?

Some of these issues were raised in the case of *S.W.*, in which a trial judge diminished the weight afforded to the early guilty plea on the basis that the victims were denied the 'cathartic effect' of testifying at trial (*R v S.W.* 2021: 85). This portion of the decision was reversed on appeal on the basis that the mitigating effect of a guilty plea would be rendered nugatory and an accused would insist on a preliminary inquiry to afford victims an opportunity to testify and would only then plead guilty. It is worth highlighting that the Court of Appeal did not challenge the fact that testifying can be cathartic for victims (*R v Nicholson* 2008). These different perspectives bring forward the varied experiences of victims when testifying and the potential unethical aspects of automatic sentence reduction based on the timing of the plea. Ultimately, the appellate court's reasoning in this decision raises ethical questions about the authenticity of these assumptions. By reading this passage, one may wonder whether at the end of the day, reductions for guilty pleas are an incentive to avoid trials (see further discussion in Chapter 4) rather than rooted on actual effects on victims or the offender's level of blame.

III. A Lack of Contextualised and Verified Assumptions

In addition to a lack of clarity around the rationales underpinning plea-based sentence reduction, an analysis of Canadian case law suggests that the victim-related assumptions discussed above are generalised, abstract and decontextualised[5] – often reached without seeking participative perspectives that take into account reality on an individualised basis, including those that include the accused's level of blame or the effects of pleas on victims. Indeed, despite mentioning the effects of a plea of guilt on victims, these assumptions are often made without seeking and considering the victim's actual perspectives, characteristics or experiences, including any increased vulnerabilities that may generate greater systemic harms, or the actual effect of the guilty pleas on victims.

Similarly, when the sentence reduction relates to the defendant's desire to minimise victim harms, there is a generalised assumption that this is automatic with the plea of guilt, but there is very rarely any contextual analysis that seeks to determine whether the guilty plea is made with an actual desire on the part of the accused to spare the victim additional harms. Indeed, in most analysed cases, the mental element related to the accused's intent to save victims from testifying is assumed and there is no contextual evidence that is required. For instance, in *McArthur*, where the defendant was accused of a brutal killing, the accused's guilty plea was seen as taking responsibility for the killing and 'extremely mitigating' since it was considered as 'saving the families and the community the nightmare of a trial' (*R v MacArthur* 2019). Despite this framing, there was no evidence of this dimension present in the case.

Notwithstanding these generalised claims, it is worth noting that there are some exceptions within Canadian case law, in which judges have considered more contextualised dimensions within individualised cases.[6] Relating to the first type of assumption about saving victims from testifying, there are some cases that

[5] For instance, see appellate court cases such as *R v Frenette* (1999: 6); *R v C.R.H.* (2021). Lower court cases include *R v Alexandruk* (2003); *R v Adrian* (2001); *R v Schneider* (2016: 52); *R v Stover* (2018: 54); *R v Irwin* (2017: 22); *Ontario College of Teachers v Clarke* (2019: 17); *R v Blackplume* (2020). It is worth highlighting that there are many more cases within those surveyed.

[6] Whether this is more common or available in regimes that do not rely on automatic numeric reductions based on the timing of guilty pleas is an important question and is left for another day.

have taken into account the type of offence or the victim's personal characteristics to confirm that assumption. For instance, in *Smith* the court decided that the assumption related to saving victims from testifying as a factor for mitigation will be less relevant for certain victims (*R v Smith* 2016). It stated that fraud against a large corporation will be less relevant than in offences such as the present case, which was an attempted murder of a vulnerable victim. Within this case, there seems to be an assumption that the extreme level of violence and the impact of the offence on the victim, which was severe, was a good indicator of the experience related to testifying in the case. Further, in some cases the age of the victim was considered a relevant characteristic that supposed the need to be saved from testifying (*R v Smith* 2016; *R v Anagnostaras* 2019). It is worth highlighting that even in these cases, the assumptions rest on certain victim characteristics perceived as greater vulnerabilities and suppose more harms related to testimonial participation, which may not be the case in reality.

Only a handful of cases from the ones surveyed seem to directly engage with individual victims' experiences and their perspectives about testifying. Indeed, very few indicate that prosecutors consulted with them on various aspects prior to stating these assumptions. For instance, in *Boychuk*, the evidence was clear that the prosecutor had to manage conflicting victims' and family dynamics as well as evidentiary issues from victims who did not want to testify (*R v Boychuk* 2020: 58). In this case, perspectives of harm from testifying were rooted in experiential evidence which suggested that the guilty plea saved the victims who did not wish, or were reluctant, to testify from the need to do so.

Other cases are less clear but seem to suggest that the prosecution consulted with individual victims about the effect of the guilty plea and the harm they would suffer from the prospect of testifying. For instance, in *Witvoet* the judge highlighted that the reduction of the victims' stress relating to not having to testify following a guilty plea was due to the importance of certainty and privacy in their specific context (*R v Witvoet* 2020). Specifically, privacy was an important consideration for them since many had not disclosed to their partners and family the crime that they had suffered. Testifying would result in a significant intrusion into their lives in a very public way, given the media attention these proceedings would engender. This would not just be revealed to family and a publication ban would not prevent them from having to take time off work and revealing this to their employer. The judge concluded that 'being spared the necessity of testifying helped protect their privacy and save them from embarrassment' (*R v Witvoet* 2020: 48). Further, in *P.A.C.* the prosecutor described the specific fear and anxiety experienced by the victim in anticipation of having to testify, as well as the time spent reliving the details of the offence during preparation for trial testimony (*R v P.A.C.* 2020). Finally, in *D.O.*, it was argued by the prosecution that since the victims in this case had already been through the trouble of preparing their testimony, in addition to other reasons, little mitigating weight was placed on the guilty plea (*R v D.O.* 2021).

Similarly, when it comes to contextualising remorse and the assumption that relates to the defendant's desire to spare victims from testifying, in *Mattess* the judge took into account the individual context of the accused to suggest that given the defendant's lack of expressed remorse or concern for the victims, it seemed unlikely that his guilty plea was motivated by a desire to save the victim from the harm of testifying (*R v Mattess* 2021). Despite this grounded perspective, contextualisation was nevertheless partial, since no inquiry was made about the effects of the plea on victims and their desire or need to be freed from the harm or burden of testifying. Instead, the plea was considered a substantial mitigating factor on the basis of a generalised assumption related to victim testimonial harm.

To conclude, it is apparent from the case law that there is rarely any communicative engagement that seeks to contextualise the guilty plea and verify the underlying assumptions behind plea reductions. As will be seen below, this can be problematic from a communicational perspective since guilty pleas can signal wrongful messaging when resting on inaccurate and unverified assumptions (see a similar argument about inaccuracy in common law discussed in Chapter 12).

IV. A Communicative and Experiential Framework for Clarifying and Contextualising Victim-related Assumptions about Plea-based Sentence Reduction

Addressing the two issues with the victim-related assumptions discussed above is important if one is concerned about the criminal justice process's adherence to communicative theories of punishment.

Over the years, sentencing systems have afforded greater space for individualised, experiential and contextualised assessments of aggravating and mitigating factors, whether these relate to victims' or defendants' experiences (Dancig-Rosenberg and Dagan 2019). In Canada it has long been recognised that the sentencing process is not meant to be formulaic and therefore does not involve simply ticking off mitigating and aggravating factors without considering the circumstances of the case (*R v R.M.* 2019). As seen above, this has yet to be the case with assumptions that are used to justify plea-based sentence reductions, particularly those that are rooted in assumptions about the experiences of criminal justice participants, such as accused and victims.

An important rationale for clarifying sentencing rationales and contextualising assumptions about guilty plea reduction can be located within communicative theories of punishment. These theories consider punishment to be a communicative enterprise in which the punishment engages with citizens and their shared values. Specifically, Duff's communicative theory is rooted in common law, understood as a space where citizens engage as a political community with themselves through a rational process. In this sense, 'the voice of the law is (or aspires to be) the voice of the community addressing itself, the voice of all citizens addressing one another and themselves' (Duff 2001). For Duff, censure as communication[7] is to give meaning to the declaration that certain kinds of conduct are public wrongs. To remain silent in the face of crimes would be to undermine – by implication to go back on – its declaration that such conduct is wrong. Censure of conduct declared to be wrong is owed to victims, as members of the community, and as manifesting that concern for them and for their wronged condition that the declaration itself expressed. It is also owed to society whose values the law claims to embody, as showing that those values are taken seriously, and it is owed to offenders themselves since an honest response to another's wrongdoing, a response that respects him as a responsible moral agent, is criticism or censure of that wrongdoing. Accordingly, for Duff communication involves a reciprocal and rational engagement. He highlights that communication requires someone to or with whom we try to communicate. It aims to engage that person as an active participant in the process, who will receive and respond to the communication as it appeals to the other's reason and understanding. The response it seeks is one that is mediated by the other's rational grasp and its content.

Building on Duff's responsive censure, certain retributivists have reconceptualised censure and punishment as a more dynamic form of communication (Roberts and Dagan 2019: 143). While they suggest that the communicative dimension of punishment is not aimed at provoking a response, they nevertheless highlight that if the offender takes the opportunity to respond, this can be considered at sentencing and during the administration of the sentence. This responsive view of censure suggests that the sentence may evolve in response to certain acts of the offender (Roberts and Dagan 2019). Contrary to traditional desert theory, the offender is recognised as a responsive agent who partakes in a dialogue and cannot be ignored (Maslen 2015). Accordingly, this approach, primarily rooted in desert, enables authorities to review the original censuring decision over the years in order to account for the prisoner's response to the sentence's message in relation to the offence (Roberts and Dagan 2019).[8]

Building on the idea of dialogue and dynamic engagement, if the aim of criminal justice processes is to signal or communicate messages to citizens and amongst them, then it is important that these messages are clearly articulated and that opportunities be provided to the various participants to communicate in

[7] An important discussion around censure is the question of whether hard treatment is necessary or whether a purely symbolic punishment can suffice. Duff essentially sees hard treatment as a prerequisite for repentance while just-deserts theorists highlight a dual dimension: a neutral sanction embodying no blame would not just be a (possibly) less efficient preventive device but would also fail to treat the actor as a moral agent answerable for his behaviour. For Duff, a purely prudential sanction, aimed at preventing crime and not conveying blame, would fail to recognise the defendant as capable of moral deliberation. While these are important queries, they remain outside the scope of this chapter.

[8] Examples of responsive offence-related factors include the way the person addresses the harm inflicted by compensating the victim's loss; showing sincere empathy, remorse; apologising; taking responsibility for the harm. Responsive factors unrelated to harm and culpability should be excluded from this account since they may rely on utilitarian aims such as diminishing reoffending.

order to ensure that these messages and signals are accurate and rooted in actual experiences and facts rather than mere assumptions. This dialectical engagement, which sees citizens as rational agents, should apply at the various communicative moments of the criminal justice process, which include processes that lead to the guilty plea and sentencing.

Similar to sentencing, the guilty plea, and the processes leading to it, are important dialectical moments that help construct and send messages to citizens, which include victims. This message needs to be rooted in clear sentencing underpinnings and, to the extent possible, accurately depict reality in order to respect the agency of citizens. In the current system, this dialogue is often pursued with a State response by way of sentence reduction that is not attentive to experiential realities, which risk depicting inaccurate experiences and disrespecting individuals in the process. In its signalling, the State needs to ensure as much accuracy as possible, as well as respect towards its citizens, by including their perspectives when they are meant to form the underlying premises of these assumptions.

A. Engaging the Victim

It is doubtful that assumptions about guilty plea reductions that relate to the impact of testifying on victims can ethically and accurately be made without engaging the victim, namely by verifying (1) their perception about testifying in the process and (2) the effects of a guilty plea on them. This is particularly important in light of the literature on victim participation, which highlights that for some victims, participation is therapeutic and important in order to have their experiences, and harms acknowledged in criminal justice (Roberts and Manikis 2011). Contrary to the underlying assumptions that suggest that victims need to be spared from testifying, it may be that in some cases, victims may want to testify and allowing them to do so can be therapeutic or provide a positive experience for them. In such cases, relying on the first set of assumptions about guilty pleas and the effects of testimony on victims to mitigate a sentence would not be an accurate depiction of the victim's experience and therefore risks giving rise to a defect in communication.

In addition, the failure to consider victim perspectives and simply assuming that testimonial participation is harmful to them also risks creating additional system-created harms towards victims and broader citizenship values, as their views and experiences would be discarded or misrepresented within the public process.

Moreover, seeking the victim's perspective on the impact of guilty pleas in relation to testimonial participation is important to understand and distinguish the source and types of harms some may be experiencing. This inquiry would enable a greater understanding of where some of the harm about testifying might be coming from and thus attributing responsibility relationally and more accurately. In this sense, when most of the harms experienced by victims come from the system itself (State) or society, the mitigating dimension of the plea would need to be understood differently than if it merely arose from the offender's intended conduct. Indeed, as will be examined in greater depth below, in some cases, if anyone is to blame for the harms caused by testifying at the trial or wider harms related to the process or victim embarrassment, it is the State and society rather than the accused. Within a relational communicative framework these nuances would need to be articulated.

Finally, in addition to verifying victim-related assumptions that underpin plea-based sentence reduction, it is important to verify the accuracy of another assumption that often underpins the plea itself, namely that it accurately communicates the offence that occurred and the harm suffered by the victim. While this assumption may be accurate in some cases, there are times when the guilty plea and its accompanying statement of facts do not reflect the harms suffered by victims (see *R v Epinoza-Ortega* 2019[9]) or those described by victims in the victim impact statement (VIS) (*R v Nickerson* 2019).

There are many possible explanations for these discrepancies. The first is the failure to consult victims prior to the plea and take into account the harms that result from the offence. From a communicative and dialectical perspective, inviting victim perspectives on the harms they suffered as a result of the offence and their desire to testify can be a useful way to maximise the chances of a rational[10] and accurate depiction of reality. The failure to do so can be problematic from a communicative and dialectical perspective since the plea may gloss over the harms suffered as a result of the offence and fail to accurately represent the gravity of the offence, particularly psychological aspects that relate to the offence that may not be as evident to decision makers.[11]

A second possibility may also be that victims were consulted on the harms they suffered as a result of the offence prior to the plea, but for a variety of reasons, the agreement on facts which is part of the guilty plea does not reflect present harms and was reached based on other considerations. Reasons for reaching such pleas can be varied and include a lack of evidence on the part of the prosecution, transient harms suffered by victims at the time of plea that may have changed later on (see, eg, *R v Nickerson* 2019), or a guilty plea for a lesser charge in exchange for a sentence reduction. Communicating with the victim and the public at sentencing to explain the reasons for these discrepancies allows for greater transparency and accuracy of pleas.

This communicative endeavour is illustrated in *Nickerson*. This case involved a drunk driver who pled guilty for impaired driving and dangerous operation following a car crash that injured a victim. The judge in this case noted the discrepancy

[9] The judge in this case rightly rejected a joint submission because the victim did not have the opportunity to present a victim impact statement. Once the victim did, the judge rejected the joint submission on the basis of public interest.

[10] As discussed above, dialectical and communicative perspectives in sentencing highlight that individuals' contributions to deliberation are considered, analysed and rationally scrutinised.

[11] The literature on VISs has revealed that decision makers are not always aware of the harms that victims have suffered in relation to the offence (see Roberts and Manikis 2011).

between the VIS, which described greater harms suffered by the victim, and the statement of facts that relied on information obtained by the Crown in advance of the plea of guilt. The judge explained this discrepancy at sentencing by highlighting the transient nature of the victim's injury, which initially was minor and was not considered to be bodily harm by the Crown. To deal with this discrepancy, he highlighted that

> I can take into account the impact of Mr Nickerson's offences on the victims as an aggravating factor on sentencing. However, the contents of the VIS were inconsistent with the agreed statement of facts and the information obtained by the Crown in advance of the plea of guilt. The Crown is required to prove any disputed aggravating facts beyond a reasonable doubt. Mr. Nickerson has not been convicted of impaired bodily harm or dangerous driving causing bodily harm nor did he accept the aggravating factors contained in the VIS. (*R v Nickerson* 2019: 15–16)

This case is an example of some communicative commitment since there was a public explanation as part of the sentencing process as to why the parties agreed on a guilty plea for a lesser offence than impaired bodily harm or dangerous driving causing bodily harm. Further, the victim had the possibility to express the harms suffered within a VIS afterwards even if the harms described in this statement did not ultimately affect the sentence.

Although this case illustrates some commitment to communicative values, the case law to date suggests that in most cases of discrepancy the VIS portion will be discarded and described by the judge as irrelevant if it does not reflect the statement of facts agreed upon as part of a guilty plea (see, eg, decision of Hill J in *R v Gabriel* 1999[12]). While some courts have considered aggravation as separate and allowed the victim to include this evidence at sentencing if proven beyond a reasonable doubt by the prosecution, others have explicitly stated that these portions of the statement are irrelevant and disregarded this information (see, eg, *R v Hemmaway* 2021). Instead of formulating such statements as irrelevant, it may be more accurate from a communicative perspective to allow them for expressive purposes and explain the discrepancies. Indeed, the failure to adequately acknowledge such harms can lead to the system perpetuating an incomplete and inaccurate message that can itself create additional harms to victims and society.

In brief, an overall ethical and communicative approach in those contexts would first require that victims are consulted prior to the guilty plea to ensure that the plea reflects victim harms. If there are valid reasons that warrant a guilty plea that is not reflective of the harm at that stage, then at the very least these reasons should be articulated clearly to victims and to the public. Further, in such scenarios, rather than being referred to as irrelevant, victims should be afforded the possibility to communicate these harms at sentencing even if they do not influence the sentence (see *R v Swift* (2007), cited also in *Hardwick v Tasmania* (2020),

[12] See *R v Bremner* (2000), highlighting that 'attempts to state, or presumably restate, the facts of the offence usurp the role of the prosecutor and risks inconsistency with, or expansion of, prior trial testimony, or facts read in, and agreed to, on the guilty plea appearance'.

which offers this more flexible approach to communicating harms at sentencing). This nuance between the functions of VISs can be understood as serving expressive functions which differ from instrumental functions (Manikis 2015). Indeed, within an expressive aim, the main goal is to communicate a message to the various participants in the process without necessarily having a direct impact on the quantum of the sentence.

In sum, a communicative engagement with victims on guilty pleas would be twofold. First, it would need to seek out victim perspectives on the consequences of a guilty plea rather than relying on an untested or unclear assumption about mitigation. Secondly, to ensure adequate communicative censure of the offence, the victim would also need to be provided with opportunities at the various communicative stages of the process, including prior to guilty pleas as well as sentencing to communicate the harms suffered as a result of the offence.

B. Engaging the Accused

A communicative and experiential framework would also seek to contextualise the guilty plea by engaging the accused in a dialectical process in order to hear and determine the defendant's motivations behind the guilty plea rather than relying on generalised assumptions relating to the plea (for the importance of hearing the offender, see Chapter 11). This suggests a more active communicative process that seeks to understand whether there is remorse or a desire to reduce actual harms experienced by victims.

This is particularly important as there are notable situations where a person pleads guilty but has no interest, is indifferent to the effects on victims, or may even plead guilty in order to prevent victims from being heard, particularly in relation to their emotional harm.[13] This situation is seen in *Humphries v Director* (2021), a case in which the defendant alleged that his counsel failed to inform him about the possibility of victim participation via VIS even once a plea of guilt was made. Hearing the defendant's perspective in this case revealed that had he known that VISs were going to be made despite the guilty plea, he would not have pleaded guilty and insisted on going to trial instead.[14] This suggests that a guilty plea does not necessarily equate to a desire of victim harm reduction, welfare or remorse, and instead engaging with the offender can enable a more accurate perspective on personal mitigation (and potentially a greater moral relevance of courtroom performance, as highlighted in Chapter 6) than merely assuming remorse and specific intentions towards victims.

[13] It is worth highlighting that even when remorse is found not to be genuine and the defendant seeks to retract the plea, there is still a discount offered on the sole assumption that the guilty plea saves victims from the harms of testifying.

[14] 'Humphries fails to explain how his counsel's alleged failure to advise him that such statements would be made was ineffective; nor has he shown a reasonable probability that, had he known of the process, he would not have pleaded guilty and insisted on going to trial' (*Hill* 1985).

Further, in some cases, it may also be that hearing directly from the accused can reveal remorse and the desire to limit victim harms in the process. This was the case in *Lacelle Belec v R* (2019), in which the court was able to mitigate the sentence on the basis of post-offence conduct towards the victim only once the accused provided specifications on his actions and intentions.

In addition to contextualising and verifying assumptions around the guilty plea, a communicative framework would also suggest that the rationale underpinning the sentence reduction would need to be very clearly articulated and signalled within the public process. This engagement with the defendant and evidence related to this dimension of blame would allow for a more accurate signalling and assignment of blame.

If there is evidence suggesting that the accused is interested in improving the victim's experience, then this would be a reason for signalling personal mitigation. This desire would need to truly engage with how the victim's situation may be improved rather than simply assuming that the plea of guilt will necessarily improve the situation. This engagement may even give rise to a context in which the interests of victims and defendants align and expose the ways that the harms experienced by victims in the process are attributable to the State, thus engaging with 'State blame', discussed in greater depth in the next section. Further, it is worth highlighting that to benefit from personal mitigation, an actual improvement of the victim's situation should not be required. Instead, a desire that shows genuine interest in understanding the victim's experience and improving their situation would be sufficient.

Further, if the accused who pleads guilty is not genuinely interested in achieving any positive effects on victims, or reducing harms, any sentence reduction that would arise from an improved victim experience resulting from the guilty plea would need to signal that the sentence reduction is not premised on personal mitigation but rather a reduction of systemic harms suffered by victims as a result of the process. This, in turn, might also create discursive opportunities for shifting the focus on the State's contribution in creating these harms that relate to the process.

Engaging with what is conceptually referred to as 'State blame' would be more accurate and appropriate in some of these contexts as it recognises that guilty pleas are in part relied upon by the system to diminish the harms suffered by victims in the hands of this system. This can indeed allow a more accurate depiction and dynamic response since there will be a discussion about the source of these harms and the State's potential contributory role in creating some of them.

C. Engaging the State and Relational Blame

As argued elsewhere, communicative theories of punishment can be expanded to include the State as a relevant subject of censure and blame (Manikis 2022). This is rooted in a recognition that the State can be a fallible institution to various degrees, as highlighted in Chapters 2 and 8, and can contribute to various forms of harms. Accordingly, an assignation of blame and harms needs to take that into account by signalling that censure is not only individual, but also relational and systemic. Indeed, the criminal justice system has often attributed responsibility to the offender for harms suffered by victims. It has also been conceptualised in a way where the State is the victim and therefore is not understood as having any share of responsibility in the process. However, reality highlights that many harms suffered by victims and witnesses can be attributed to the State. Within a communicative and relational approach to criminal justice, harms that are in part attributable to the State need to be incorporated into the conversation.

For instance, many of the harms that are the focus of assumptions around plea-based sentence reduction, including the harms experienced by certain victims when testifying, can in certain contexts be partly attributed to the State. Examples of these contributions include State policies, practices and decisions that have enabled and continue to foster myths and stereotypes around certain types of victims in the process, and have given rise to inherent suspicion and forms of mistreatment towards them.[15] They also include specific legislative policies and decisions that allow certain problematic forms of cross examination tactics, or a failure to offer services and structures that can enable victims to bring forward their accounts (Brennan and Brennan 1989;[16] Beaudry 2017;[17] Seelinger et al 2011;[18] further, see Washington State Administrative Office of the Courts 2015[19]).

A typology of State blame has been formulated elsewhere and highlights the various types of State contributions and harms that can occur. (Manikis 2022). Those described in this chapter that relate to victims can be classified as State contributory harms that result from aspects of the criminal justice process itself (type 3);[20] and those more broadly related to social attitudes and inequalities can be classified as State criminogenic contributions by the creation and maintenance of social inequalities (type 1).

A communicative theory underpinned by responsive censure and relational blame would require these considerations to be incorporated into the conversation, which can be done at important dialectical moments, including the guilty plea or the sentencing process.

[15] For discussions of the treatment of certain victims within the criminal justice process, particularly those from marginalised groups, see Murphy-Oikonon et al (2021). McGarry and Walklate (2015) also highlight the ways that processes of victimisation are cultural, structural and social.

[16] Discussing the language barriers encountered by children in sexual assault trials.

[17] Discussing the lack of state mechanisms to offer victims with disabilities appropriate testimonial aids.

[18] Highlighting issues with government-funded testimonial aids.

[19] Which highlights that other reasons for the harms felt by some victims to testify include the State's failure to offer adequate protective measures and services (including socio-economic) for victims who may still be threatened and manipulated by their abusers, and feelings of shame or guilt in relation to the offence. Arguably, the latter also has an element of State and community contribution due to the historical inequalities surrounding sexual violence.

[20] Conceptually, this can take the form of collateral consequences of the punishment process that have also been documented in the context of crime victims (see Manikis 2022; Condry and Minson 2020).

Within these processes, the State would recognise its share of responsibility in producing these harms and its potential failings in its duties,[21] along with justifications for and responses to any of its contributions that inflict additional harms that are not justified as punishment, as part of individuals' prima facie moral right not to be harmed by the State (Bulow 2014; Zedner 2017). A dynamic understanding of censure, which includes State censure, would require that these harms be signalled as part of the sentencing process to the public, including victims and the accused, and responded to with strategies of harm reduction across longer periods of time.

When the State relies on rationales other than personal mitigation to reduce the sentence in the context of a guilty plea, it needs to contextualise and clearly signal them to the various participants. This includes harm-reduction/victim-welfare rationales that relate to victims. Specifically, some of the harms that victims identify in the context of the testimonial process can be attributed to the State, and therefore from a communicative and relational perspective, the State needs to signal this reality within the public process. By communicating the State's contributory role in the creation of these harms, the State also signals its responsibility in responding to this situation in the long run. Indeed, the State has a role, through its processes, to ensure as much as possible that it offers a space for citizens to engage in dialogue in a way that does not create further harms to its participants.

V. Conclusion

In conclusion, while guilty pleas routinely arise in busy and rushed criminal justice systems, they also trigger sentence reductions that are often abstract and rooted in unverified assumptions. Indeed, these rationales are rarely discussed and examined as part of communicative processes such as guilty pleas and sentencing. Within a process that seeks to communicate clear and accurate messages to the public as well as treat interested participants with respect (see further discussions in Chapter 7), the current treatment of guilty pleas and sentence reduction falls short of delivering these principles and aims.

A commitment by the State to communication and respect towards its citizens would entail a clearer articulation of the rationales that underpin these sentence reductions, along with a contextual analysis and engagement of the underlying assumptions, by ensuring that they take into account the actual experiential perspectives of individuals that the system purports to portray. Moreover, in

[21] Arguably, as part of its communicative commitments, the State has a duty to ensure as much as possible that it offers a space for citizens to engage in dialogue in a way that does not create further preventable harms to its participants, including victims. This would also apply to accused who are in unequal socio-economic contexts. Accordingly, it would be important to find ways to incorporate 'State blame' by discussing the ways that inequitable criminal justice policies affect them (see, eg, the impact of guilty plea reductions as incentives (and pressures) in Chapter 10).

light of these commitments it would be important that sentence reductions also took into account context instead of solely being based on the timing of the plea without any additional engagement. Failure to include a more communicational and contextual analysis risks delegitimising the process by sending unclear and potentially inaccurate messages to the public, disrespecting participants, and contributing to additional systemic harms perpetuated by the State.

References

Beaudry, JS (2017) 'The Intellectually Disabled Witness and the Requirement to Promise to Tell the Truth' 4 *Dalhousie Law Journal* 239.

Brennan, M and Brennan, R (1989) *Strange Language – Child Victims Under Cross Examination* (Washington DC, US Department of Justice).

Bulow, W (2014) 'The Harms Beyond Imprisonment: Do We Have Special Moral Obligations Towards the Families and Children of Prisoners?' 17 *Ethical Theory and Moral Practice* 775.

Condry, R and Minson, S (2020) 'Conceptualizing the Effects of Imprisonment on Families: Collateral Consequences, Secondary Punishment, or Symbiotic Harms?' 25 *Theoretical Criminology* 540.

Dancig-Rosenberg, H and Dagan, N (2019) 'Retributarianism: A New Individualization of Punishment' 13 *Criminal Law, Philosophy* 129.

Duff, RA (2001) *Punishment, Communication and Community* (Oxford, Oxford University Press).

Manikis, M (2015) 'Victim Impact Statements at Sentencing: Towards a Clearer Understanding of Their Aims' 65 *University of Toronto Law Journal* 85.

—— (2022) 'Recognising State Blame in Sentencing: A Communicative and Relational Framework' 81 *Cambridge Law Journal* 294.

Manson, A (2001) *The Law of Sentencing* (Toronto, Irwin Law).

Maslen, H (2015) *Remorse, Penal Theory and Sentencing* (Oxford, Hart Publishing).

McGarry, R and Walklate, S (2015) *Victims: Trauma, Testimony and Justice* (London, Routledge).

Murphy-Oikonon, J, Chambers, L and Miller, A (2021) 'Sexual Assault: Indigenous Women's Experiences of Not Being Believed by the Police' 28 *Violence Against Women* 1.

Roberts, JV and Manikis, M (2011) *Victim Personal Statements: A Review of Empirical Research* (London, Office of the Commissioner for Victims and Witnesses of England and Wales).

Roberts, JV and Dagan, N (2019) 'The Evolution of Retributive Punishment: From Static Desert to Responsive Penal Censure' in A du Bois-Pedain and A Bottoms (eds), *Penal Censure: Engagements within and Beyond Desert Theory* (Oxford, Hart Publishing).

Seelinger, KT, Silverberg, H and Mejia, R (2011) *The Investigation and Prosecution of Sexual Violence* (California, Sexual Violence & Accountability Project: UC Berkeley).

Washington State Administrative Office of the Courts (2015) *DV Manual for Judges* (Washington, WA, Washington State Administrative Office of the Courts).

Zedner, L (2017) 'Penal Subversion: When Is a Punishment Not a Punishment, Who Decides and on What Grounds?' 20 *Theoretical Criminology* 1.

Cases

Australia

Hardwick v Tasmania [2020] TASCCA 2

Canada

Deng v La Reine (2003) CanLII 75168
Lacelle Belec v R (2019) QCCA 711
Ontario College of Teachers v Clarke (2019) ONOCT 84
R v A.C. (2017) ONCJ 317
R v Adrian (2001) ABPC 40
R v Alexandruk (2003) ABPC 19
R v Anagnostaras (2019) QCCS 5065
R v Bernardon (2021) ONCJ 438
R v Blackplume (2020) ABPC 90
R v Boychuk (2020) SKQB 302
R v Bremner (2000) BCCA 345
R v Burback, 2012 ABCA 30
R v Campbell (2014) ABPC 297
R v CMC (2016) ABQB 196
R v C.R.H. (2021) BCCA 183
R v D.O. (2021) BCPC 171
R v Espinoza-Ortega (2019) ONCA 545
R v Faulds (1994) 20 OR (3d) 13 (CA)
R v Frenette (1999) ABCA 225
R v Gabriel (1999) CanLII 15050 (ONSC)
R v Hemmaway (2021) ABPC 246
R v Irwin (2017) ONSC 4492
R v Johnston and Tremayne [1970] 2 OR 780
R v Kapolak (2020) NWTTC 12
R v Kreutziger (2005) BCCA 231
R v MacArthur (2018) PECA 10
R v Martineau (2021) ABCA 401
R v Mattess (2021) BCPC 164
R v McArthur (2019) ONSC 963
R v Nicholson (2008) ABCA 256
R v Nickerson (2019) ONCJ 756
R v P.A.C. (2020) BCPC 284
R v Poepl (2021) BCSC 725
R v R.M. (2019) BCCA 409
R v Ruddick (2008) NSSC 350
R v Salehi (2022) BCCA
R v Schneider (2016) BCPC 268
R v Smith (2016) ONCJ 565
R v S.S. (1990) CanLII 12393

R v Stover (2018) BCPC 198
R v S.W. (2021) QCCQ 3732
R v Swift (2007) VSCA 52
R v Witvoet (2020) BCPC 128

United Kingdom

R v de Haan [1967] 3 All ER 618 (CA Crim Div)

United States

Hill v Lockhart 474 US 52 (1985)
Humphries v Director TDCJ-CID (2021)

10

Plea-based Sentence Reductions: Legal Assumptions and Empirical Realities

REBECCA K HELM

I. Introduction: Masking Plea Complexity

In 2014, the European Court of Human Rights passed judgment in the case of *Natsvlishvili and Togonidze v Georgia* (2014). In that case the court determined the validity of guilty pleas that had been made by one of the applicants, Amiran Natsvlishvili. A relevant question in making this determination was whether Mr Natsvlishvili had chosen to plead guilty voluntarily. Essentially, Mr Natsvlishvili had faced a choice between pleading guilty and paying a fine or going to trial and facing a near certain lengthy custodial sentence (given Georgia's 98 per cent conviction rate at trial) in poor conditions.[1] The European Court of Human Rights concluded that Mr Natsvlishvili's decision to plead guilty in these circumstances was 'undoubtedly' conscious and voluntary.

In one way, it is easy to understand this conclusion. It is likely that if faced with the choice of a fine or a near certain lengthy sentence in prison, most people would accept the fine without facing external pressure, and would do so regardless of factual guilt or innocence. In the same way it could be said that someone who hands over all their money to a thief who threatens to shoot them if they do not, hands over the money voluntarily. Given that they would be shot otherwise, they will choose to hand over the money without facing external pressure to do so (see also Kipnis 1976). But accepting these decisions as conscious and voluntary misses the point. The terms of a choice itself can, in reality, undermine or even eliminate voluntariness. Framing the choice to plead guilty in *Natsvlishvili* as undoubtedly conscious and voluntary masks a high degree of complexity present in real decisions in a way that is common in systems incentivising guilty pleas through the use of sentence reductions.

[1] In fact, he was in very poor conditions when deciding whether to plead – sharing a cell with a murderer who had previously abducted him.

The complex influence of sentence reductions on guilty plea decision making is largely due to the fact that these sentence reductions act as incentives – encouraging often vulnerable defendants to waive their right to trial.[2] Decisions to plead guilty have traditionally been regarded as morally positive admissions, worthy of recognition or reward (see Chapter 5). However, sentence reductions can change plea decisions into tactical decisions motivated by a far greater range of influences than factual guilt and innocence (see Helm 2018). The influence of sentence reductions on behaviour is complicated by the fact that the State, the body that benefits the most when defendants plead guilty, can set sentence reductions that can essentially cause defendants to do so. When reductions begin to result in guilty pleas through creating strong incentives for defendants to plead guilty, it becomes problematic to describe those reductions as recognitions or rewards for positive behaviour. Where a person performs what would otherwise be a morally positive behaviour, such as owning up or telling the truth, as a result of strong incentivisation, that behaviour is no longer performed for morally positive reasons worthy of reward and instead becomes self-interested behaviour or, in extreme cases, mere compliance (see also Chapter 12).

The contention that plea-based sentence reductions change defendant behaviour rather than just recognising morally positive behaviour is supported by an examination of the history of guilty pleas – before guilty pleas were incentivised, evidence suggests that very few defendants chose to plead guilty (see Alschuler 1979). Perhaps more importantly, the fact that plea decisions can represent self-interested behaviour or even compliance rather than morally positive behaviours can be seen by the fact that innocent as well as guilty defendants plead guilty, known as the 'innocence problem' (note that at least in non-dystopian systems, guilty pleas from innocent defendants could actually be seen as morally wrong due to frustrating the interests of justice and the victim, see Chapter 2). Incentives to plead guilty, including sentence reductions, result in innocent people pleading guilty and being convicted of crimes with no independent scrutiny of the evidence against them (see, eg, Baldwin and McConville 1978; Blume and Helm 2014; Helm 2019; Nash, Dioso-Villa and Porter 2021; Chapter 4).

In this context, regardless of whether sentence reductions are intended to influence defendant choice or whether they are rewards that have a side effect of influencing defendant choice, it is crucially important to understand the influence that they have on that choice. In fact, the nature and reality of that choice plays a key role in determining whether convictions via guilty plea are legitimate from a normative perspective. The innocence problem associated with guilty pleas combined with the lack of enquiry into the veracity of resulting convictions, suggest that self-conviction via guilty plea can no longer be legitimised in the same way as convictions at trial are – through being *accurate* as well as fair and respecting human rights (see Dennis 2017: ch 2). Commentary now suggests that

[2] I focus in this chapter on sentence reductions, although many jurisdictions also allow charge reductions offered prior to conviction, which can have similar or stronger effects.

convictions via guilty plea are justified on the basis of the autonomous choice of a defendant (Bowers 2007; Nobles and Schiff 2019).

Imposing a trial on a defendant who does not want one might be seen as paternalistic or wasteful, and offering incentives to plead can be seen as providing opportunities for both innocent and guilty defendants as well as benefits for the State (Bowers 2007). This idea that convictions via plea are justified by being consistent with the choice of accused people is in line with existing legal regulation, which typically does not require guilty pleas to be accurate or based on any particular amount of evidence, but does require that choices made by defendants are *voluntary* and made *autonomously* (ie on the basis of informed consent), free from *constraint* or *pressure*. On the basis of this freedom, systems typically impose far less regulation on processes surrounding guilty pleas than on those surrounding full trial.

Therefore, concepts such as voluntariness, autonomy, constraint and pressure are crucially important in the context of guilty pleas. These concepts are complex psycho-legal constructs. They can be enhanced or depleted in subtle and psychologically intricate ways, and their definitions are debated in philosophical and psychological literatures. Importantly, the operation of these kind of constructs in a system where sentence reductions actively incentivise decisions to be made a certain way is complicated.

In this chapter, I consider a series of three empirically incorrect assumptions relating to these psycho-legal constructs that are currently relied on in maintaining and regulating plea-based sentence reduction regimes: the assumption that sentence reductions cannot undermine voluntariness, the assumption that there is a dichotomy between incentivisation and pressure, and the assumption that giving all defendants a choice ensures equality. I demonstrate the impact of these assumptions through explorations of plea-based sentence reductions in England and Wales and the United States and suggest that legal systems need to move away from reliance on superficial conceptions and confront the question of precisely what impact of sentence reductions on defendant choice is acceptable. I conclude by laying out suggested criteria for acceptable sentence reductions based on meaningful engagement with psycho-legal constructs, and by making some brief suggestions as to how sentence reductions might be structured and regulated to meet these criteria.

II. Exploring the Assumptions

A. Assumption 1: Sentence Reductions cannot Undermine Voluntariness

Voluntariness is an important psycho-legal concept in criminal convictions via guilty plea. Jurisdictions that allow convictions via guilty plea generally have some requirement that essentially means that to be valid, guilty pleas must be entered voluntarily. For example, laws in the United States and Canada require that to be valid, guilty pleas must be entered voluntarily (*Brady v United States* 1970: 748; s 606 Canadian Criminal Code), and in England and Wales a guilty plea that is shown to be involuntary will be considered a nullity (see Nobles and Schiff 2020: 524). In applying these requirements, states have tended to assume that allowing sentence reductions does not undermine the voluntariness of defendant choice, even in relatively extreme cases. In the US context, in a case holding that the threat of life imprisonment if convicted at trial compared to a five-year term of imprisonment from pleading guilty did not compromise the voluntary nature of a defendant's decision, the United States Supreme Court explicitly stated that the determination of whether a plea agreement is truly voluntary does not depend on the terms or generosity of the bargain involved (ie the discount offered, see *Bordenkirtcher v Hayes* 1978). Essentially, the court reasoned that it was inherent in the nature of offering sentence reductions to incentivise guilty pleas (through plea bargaining in that context) that guilty pleas are *induced* by promises of a more lenient sentence and fear of the possibility of a greater penalty upon conviction after a trial. In fact, the US Federal Rules of Criminal Procedure suggest that a guilty plea should only be considered involuntary where it is the result of force or threats or of promises apart from the plea agreement (Federal Rules of Criminal Procedure s 11(b)(2)).

The UK House of Lords (the predecessor to the current Supreme Court) adopted a relatively similar approach in an extradition case involving consideration of whether the right to a fair trial would be compromised by incentives to plead guilty in the United States, appearing to suggest that almost any discounts from a justifiable sentence upon conviction at trial would not undermine the right to a fair trial. In that case, Lord Brown, delivering the judgment of the court, acknowledged that 'In one sense all discounts for pleas of guilty could be said to subject the defendant to pressure' but suggested that this pressure would not be unlawful in the absence of very significant discounts ('very substantially more generous than anything promised here') and consequences of trial that go 'significantly beyond what could properly be regarded as the defendant's just deserts' (*McKinnon v United States* 2008).

These discussions of voluntariness (and, relatedly, pressure) rely on relatively superficial conceptions of what voluntariness is from a psychological and philosophical perspective. The current interpretation of voluntariness in plea decision making, illustrated by the examples given above, suggests that whether a decision is voluntary depends not on the availability of alternative choices for the person making the choice, but on the acceptability of any limitations on alternative choices. So, voluntariness is measured by reference to the actions of the State rather than the actual choice of the defendant (see also Kisekka 2020). This interpretation is in line with what have been called 'rights-based' conceptions of voluntariness. For example, in defining the limits of voluntariness, philosopher Robert Nozick stated:

> Whether a person's actions are voluntary depends on what it is that limits his alternatives … Other people's actions place limits on one's available opportunities.

> Whether this makes one's resulting action non-voluntary depends upon whether these others had the right to act as they did. (Nozick 1974: 262)

While consideration of the legitimacy of the action of someone placing limits on the opportunities of others may be appropriate in cases in which limits on voluntariness are balanced with other considerations (see, eg, *R v Howe* 1987 in England and Wales outlining the law on duress), the legitimacy of limits has little to no bearing on the actual impact of those limits on defendant choice itself and therefore is inappropriate in many contexts. Serena Olsaretti has used the example of a prisoner to demonstrate how voluntariness can be undermined even by legally permissible action (Olsaretti 1998: 54–60). Imagine a prisoner who decides to escape from prison and is recaptured. When the prisoner is recaptured, it would clearly be wrong to say that they voluntarily stay in prison, even though the prisoner has no right to be outside prison and the guards have a right to keep them in prison. Although the limits on voluntariness are acceptable, the prisoner remaining in custody is not voluntary.

In the context of guilty plea decisions, what is important is the reality of defendant choice rather than the legality of what constrains that choice. The defendant must truly have access to a fair trial since that access is a human right (recognised, eg, by the European Convention on Human Rights). Olsaretti provides an alternative definition of voluntariness that is more appropriate in this context. She argues that voluntariness should be determined by the presence of acceptable alternative choices, with a choice being non-voluntary where there is no acceptable alternative to that choice (Olsaretti 1998: 54). Thus 'things other than threats may undermine voluntariness. Choices made in response to offers, warnings, or other situations of constrained choice may all be non-voluntary where there is no acceptable alternative' (Olsaretti 1998: 54).

Adopting this conception of voluntariness in the context of guilty pleas, a guilty plea decision is only voluntary where taking a case to trial is an acceptable alternative choice (in light of the sentence available by pleading guilty). Since sentence reductions can prevent trial from being an acceptable alternative, sentence reductions can clearly undermine the voluntariness of defendant choice. Consider the Definitive Guidelines on Reduction in Sentence for a Guilty Plea in England and Wales (Sentencing Council 2017). These guidelines provide for a one-third sentence reduction when defendants plead guilty at the earliest opportunity, and explicitly allow this reduction to result in the imposition of a non-custodial rather than custodial sentence (Sentencing Council 2017: E1). Thus, defendants can end up facing a risk of a custodial sentence if they go to trial that can be definitively avoided by pleading guilty. For many defendants, ironically particularly defendants who are innocent, risking a custodial sentence may not be viewed as acceptable. As a result, defendants facing a choice of no risk of custody vs a risk of custody are left with no acceptable alternative but to plead guilty. This reality can be demonstrated in practice by looking at the recent Post Office scandal in the United Kingdom. The scandal involved the conviction of a large number of sub-postmasters and -mistresses (SPMs) on the basis of evidence from a computer system known as Horizon, which was later found to have been faulty (see Evidence-Based Justice Lab nd). Over 85 per cent of the 72 SPMs who have since been acquitted of all offences had initially pleaded guilty to those offences. Those who have discussed why they did so have explained that pleading guilty was their only option to avoid a risk of prison (see Helm 2021a).

Defendants in this situation may have children, precarious employment or difficult financial circumstances and feel unable to risk custody. Some work has argued that actually these reductions do not undermine voluntariness but provide defendants with a good deal that, should they accept it, benefits both themselves and the State (eg Bowers 2007). However, this argument neglects the fact that 'good deals' can deprive the defendant of what might be their ultimate aim and what they think they ultimately deserve – recognition of being not guilty. Defendants may want to take this risk, but feel that when they are offered certain reductions they can no longer personally justify doing so, for example due to obligations to family or work. Going to trial becomes a huge gamble that, in reality, only a privileged few may be able to take.

B. Assumption 2: There is a Dichotomy between Incentives and Pressure

Resolving cases through a guilty plea has become a necessary part of the administration of criminal justice in many legal systems because of perceived benefits to the State and trial participants (eg victims, see Chapter 9). Perhaps most important in this regard is the relative efficiency of resolving cases via plea compared to a full trial. As Lord Justice Hughes stated in the case of *R v David Caley and others* (2012) in England and Wales, if all defendants who pleaded guilty insisted on a full trial 'the administration of criminal justice would be in danger of collapse' (*R v David Caley and Others* 2012: 6). As a result, many jurisdictions explicitly recognise and allow sentence reductions as incentives to plead guilty. This motivation is recognised in the relevant sentence reduction guideline in England and Wales, which states that the rules surrounding sentence reductions seek to 'provide an incentive to those who are guilty to indicate a guilty plea as early as possible' (Sentencing Council 2017). So, states are seeking to modify the choices of defendants to plead guilty or go to trial by altering the risks and benefits involved in these choices. However, systems simultaneously require that the choices made by defendants are made in the absence of constraint or pressure leading them to make the decision a certain way. For example, the European Convention on Human Rights requires that guilty pleas must be made without constraint to constitute valid waivers of the right to a fair trial guaranteed by Article 6 of that convention (see *Deweer v Belgium* 1980). In England and Wales, the guideline discussed above also states that 'Nothing in the guideline should be used to put pressure on a defendant to plead guilty' (Sentencing Council 2017). However, the presence of any incentives to plead guilty increases the appeal of the plea option compared to the trial option, essentially creating pressure for a defendant to plead guilty. Saying that sentence reductions act as incentives but do not create pressure is appealing, but, in reality, it creates a false dichotomy between incentivisation and pressure, which refer to different aspects of the decision process. Incentivisation is a type of control over the behaviour of others. Pressure is the impact of this control.

Incentivisation refers to a method for influencing the behaviour of another person. An incentive is 'an offer of something of value, sometimes with a cash equivalent and sometimes not, meant to influence the payoff structure of a utility calculation so as to alter a person's course of action' (Grant 2006: 29). Incentives are effectively an exercise of power in the sense that they are a tool that can be used by one person or institution to influence the behaviour of another person or institution (see Grant 2006). While this tool can help push decision makers towards one option when they otherwise feel relatively indifferently towards their options, it can also put pressure on decision makers to act a particular way. Specifically, incentives can give a decision maker strong reasons to act against their better judgement or create a conflict between values such as obligations to family and protection of self.

A related argument suggests that offers (or promises) and threats can be distinguished based on the baseline against which they are made, and that offers are permissible while threats are not. According to this argument, incentives to plead guilty should be considered against the baseline position of a defendant's post-charge predicament, against which they likely appear a welcome and desirable prospect (eg Wertheimer 1979). However, while this distinction between an offer and a threat may have some impact on the level of pressure a defendant feels with all else being held equal (as discussed below), the form of constraint on decision making as an offer or a threat does not necessarily determine the pressure it places on a defendant. A threat of something that matters very little to a defendant (eg a threat of a small monetary loss) could create significantly less pressure than a hugely compelling incentive (eg the offer of no possible prison time). Incentives and offers may typically be seen as more ethically acceptable ways to influence the decision making of others than threats, but their impact is not always more benign in practice.

In the case of guilty plea decision making, the effect of sentence reductions as incentives is complicated. Absent any sentence reductions (and ignoring other pressures to plead guilty) a purely rational defendant would prefer the trial option to the guilty plea option, since trial involves a possible conviction and sentence but the guilty plea involves a certain conviction and sentence. As a result, guilty pleas have traditionally been considered admissions against a defendant's own interest. In that sense, any incentive that pushes people towards the plea option is an incentive pushing people against what would otherwise be in their best interests. Thus, any sentence reductions create some pressure for defendants to plead guilty rather than go to trial. The level of pressure created by reductions is likely to vary based on a number of factors, including those discussed below.

i. *The Magnitude of a Reduction in Sentence Length*

Clearly, the larger the reduction, the more pressure will be placed on a defendant to plead guilty. The size of a reduction can be influenced by both the specific reduction given in sentence length, and by the impact that this reduction might have on the ability of a person to end their sentence early, for example through eligibility for parole.

ii. *Any Categorical Difference between Plea and Trial Created by a Sentence Reduction*

Categorical differences have the potential to create more psychological pressure in pushing defendants towards a guilty plea, specifically in adults, due to decision processes thought to be relied on. One psychological theory of memory and decision making, Fuzzy Trace Theory (FTT), highlights the importance of meaningful categorical distinctions in adult decision making, suggesting that decisions are driven by these distinctions where possible (for more information and descriptions of tests of the theory, see Reyna 2012). Where a categorical distinction is created between plea and trial, this distinction is likely to drive decision making (and can do so even in innocent defendants). This suggestion has been discussed and supported in experimental work (Helm 2021b; Helm and Reyna 2017). Categorical distinctions could be made between different types of sentence (such as a custodial sentence, community sentence, and fine) but could also result where differences in sentence length become large enough to cross categorical boundaries (eg so that a sentence that is considered long or difficult becomes a sentence that is considered short or easy).

iii. *Whether a Sentence Differential is Seen as a Sentence Reduction when Pleading Guilty or a Penalty for Going to Trial*

Sentence differentials are likely to create more pressure for defendants to plead guilty when they are viewed as sentence penalties for going to trial, rather than sentence reductions for pleading guilty (Lippke 2011). Whether a differential is seen as a sentence reduction or trial penalty will depend on the assumptions of the default position, which will provide a reference point for the defendant (see, eg, Yan and Bushway 2018). Legal procedures have the potential to influence which sentence is seen as the reference point by a defendant. Importantly, procedures that allow a defendant to know the sentence if they plead guilty while leaving the sentence if convicted at trial uncertain, such as Goodyear hearings in England and Wales (see *R v Goodyear* 2005), increase the possibility that the guilty plea sentence will be seen as a reference point, and thus that defendants will perceive the likely additional sentence at trial as a trial penalty. Similar arguments based on reducing pressure on defendants underlay the previous law in England and Wales, according to which sentence indications could not be given (*R v Turner* 1970).

Recognising that any incentives to plead likely apply some pressure to defendants is important since it demonstrates the necessity of engaging in a meaningful discussion as to the amount of pressure that it is normatively acceptable to apply to defendants, and what sentence reductions that will apply that level of pressure look like. Procedure can then be tailored, bearing in mind the considerations above, to ensure that the pressure placed on defendants is not too high based on the level of pressure that is normatively justified.

C. Assumption 3: Choice can Ensure Equality

Equality of treatment for different defendants is an important normative goal in criminal justice systems (see, eg, *Griffin v Illinois* 1956 in the US context). By presuming that offering all defendants the same choice will ensure equality, systems make implicit assumptions about autonomy and freedom of choice that are not justified. Importantly, restrictions on voluntariness and levels of pressure created by sentence reductions, discussed above, will often differ depending on individual characteristics and circumstances.

While a significant amount of policy has aimed to ensure that all defendants have equal respect and protection in the trial process (see, eg, Fisher 2019; Bennett 2010; *R v Ford* 1989), equal respect and protection in guilty plea systems seems to be assumed where all defendants are offered the same choice (ie the same sentence discounts apply to all defendants). All defendants have an equal right to insist upon trial and therefore might be assumed to be equally protected by access to the protections afforded by trial (for a discussion on this issue see Nobles and Schiff 2019). However, the complex range of influences on human decision making, and differences in those influences among defendants, means that this presumption is unlikely to reflect reality.

Martha Finemann's Vulnerability Theory illustrates the limitations on human autonomy as a result of our embodiment (our existence as embodied beings that interact with the world) and embeddedness (our place within relationships and institutions in the world) (Fineman 2013: 20). The decisions that we make are not made in a vacuum. Instead, people's choices are influenced in both obvious and subtle ways by their positions within various institutions and relationships. Different people have different opportunities open to them, and different constraints on their decision making processes. As a result, Fineman concludes that absolute autonomy is a myth and that we must rely on the State to minimise harmful depletions of autonomy. In fact, the concept of autonomy as a myth is consistent with philosophical conceptions of the concept, which view it as a metaphysical ideal that is not attainable in practice (Dworkin 1988; Helm, Dehaghani and Newman 2022). The fact that the guilty plea decision is not a fully autonomous choice made in a vacuum means that a sentence discount offered to one defendant may well have a different impact on their decision making than a sentence discount offered to another defendant. A discount that might not have a strong influence on the decision making of one defendant may have a coercive impact on the decision making of another.

Consider, for example, the presence of a reduction that means a defendant can get a non-custodial sentence by pleading guilty but will face a short custodial sentence if convicted at trial. This reduction is likely to place greater pressure to plead guilty on defendants who cannot cope with a prison sentence, however short, for example defendants who have caring responsibilities or insecure employment. Thus, the decisions of those defendants will be more constrained than the decisions of defendants who are not in those circumstances. Some defendants may not be as free as others, despite having been offered the same choice. This reality is reflected in work showing that pressures to plead guilty, including those resulting from sentence reductions, may be greater for women than men. Work has suggested that women often have particularly strong reasons to want to avoid jail, including more frequently being primary caregivers who will suffer themselves and cause suffering to their families if incarcerated, and facing greater stigma if handed a prison sentence (Jones 2011). Research has also examined how vulnerabilities might influence guilty plea decision making, resulting in systematic differences in outcomes for defendants with enhanced vulnerability (Peay and Player 2018).

These limitations on true autonomy in decision making mean that guilty plea choices are likely to be determined by a range of complex factors, with the potential to lead to significant inequality in outcomes for different groups. Inequalities are also likely to result from internal differences in defendant cognition. One important set of differences that are not accounted for by current procedures are age-based cognitive differences. Research suggests that differences in cognitive style mean that children are more likely than adults to plead guilty on the basis of relatively short sentence discounts, even when they are innocent (Helm et al 2018a; Helm 2021c). Thus, utilising small sentence discounts to protect defendants from pleading guilty when innocent may protect adult defendants but not child defendants.

Equality in a system based on defendant choice cannot be ensured by treating people the same. Robust and individualised consideration must be given to sentence reductions that are appropriate for different classes of defendant, and which sentence reductions being offered are likely to result in group differences in decisions and to exacerbate inequalities and vulnerabilities. The protections of trial (and, relatedly, the decision to refuse to plead guilty) must be equally accessible to all defendants, should they wish to contest their guilt.

III. Case Studies: England and Wales and the United States

A. England and Wales

An examination of procedure in England and Wales shows how even a sentence discount system that appears quite modest, particularly in comparison to the US plea bargaining system (see Chapter 8), can end up operating in a way that has the potential to significantly constrain defendants and to result in unequal outcomes. In England and Wales, a relatively formal regime regulates sentence discounts granted when defendants plead guilty. The Definitive Guideline on Reduction in Sentence for a Guilty Plea, discussed above (Sentencing Council 2017), provides that the maximum level of reduction in sentence for a guilty plea is one-third. Generally, where a guilty plea is indicated at the first stage of proceedings, a reduction of one-third of the sentence should be made, subject to some exceptions. This reduction gets smaller the further along in proceedings a guilty plea is entered, up to a maximum reduction of one-tenth of sentence where a guilty plea is entered on the first day of trial.

The Guideline explicitly provides that this reduction in sentence can make a difference in sentence 'type', for example it can convert a sentence from a custodial sentence to a community sentence or from a community sentence to a fine. In reality, sentence reductions in exchange for a guilty plea may well end up being larger than this guideline suggests. Although there is no widely acknowledged charge-bargaining practice, prosecutors are able to accept a guilty plea to a lesser charge and as a result drop additional charges (often more serious charges) against a defendant. Doing so can have a significant impact on sentence. For example, a defendant charged with inflicting grievous bodily harm with intent (with a sentencing starting point of four to 12 years in custody) might be able to agree to plead guilty to a charge of simple grievous bodily harm (with a sentencing starting point of a high-level community order to three years in custody) (Sentencing Council 2011).

Therefore, under this sentencing regime, while some sentence reductions are relatively modest, others are more significant. Reports from real defendants highlight how these incentives can undermine voluntariness and place pressure on defendants to plead. A good example of the pressures defendants can face in this system is provided by the recent Post Office scandal, discussed briefly above. In that scandal, defendants who have now been acquitted pleaded guilty to offences against them based on financial shortfalls that they knew they were not responsible for. However, the sentence reductions that they could obtain by pleading guilty were compelling. One of the victims of what has now been acknowledged as a large miscarriage of justice who pleaded guilty, Christopher Trousdale, has described his decision to do so – he has reported that he would have to have risked seven years in prison if he went to trial but faced a community sentence if he was willing to plead guilty (Boëda 2022). The pressure that available sentence discounts placed on defendants is clear from the fact that some defendants were willing to forego any criticism of the Horizon system (the system we now know was faulty and produced misleading evidence against them) – something they would clearly not have done otherwise – so that they could obtain the discounts associated with pleading guilty (see *Hamilton and Others v Post Office* 2021). (Note that requiring them to forego this criticism has now been recognised as an affront to justice.)

Empirical research also supports these suggestions that incentives to plead guilty are undermining voluntariness and creating pressure in England and Wales, and suggests inequalities may be resulting from plea decisions. This work provides evidence that sentence length discounts (particularly where they are exacerbated by factors like eligibility for early release) and the ability to avoid a custodial sentence if they plead guilty, can dominate the minds of defendants making plea decisions (Helm, Dehaghani and Newman 2022: 151–55). In addition, this work suggests that plea-based sentence reductions can interact with sentence reductions for personal mitigation, to result in even more significant discounts (Chapter 11). Research in England and Wales also suggests that sentence discounts (and the guilty plea regime more generally) may be leading to disparate outcomes for defendants of different ethnicities. This research suggests that defendants from minority groups are pleading guilty less often than White defendants, potentially due to having less confidence in the system offering sentence discounts (Hood 1992; Lammy 2017). This difference has the potential to result in defendants from minority groups receiving longer sentences than White defendants.

B. The United States

The United States provides an example of a system in which benefits defendants receive for pleading guilty are far less regulated and consistent than they are in England and Wales. The system essentially involves negotiations on aspects of the case, including charge, sentence and plea, between the parties (ie the defence and the prosecution) (Brook et al 2016: 1163–64). In this system, the prosecution can offer a variety of benefits to a defendant in exchange for a guilty plea, including limiting the number of charges brought or changing the type of charges brought against a defendant. Changing the charges brought can have a significant impact on the sentence a defendant is given. For example, a prosecutor might agree to dismiss a drug distribution count carrying a mandatory minimum sentence of 10 years and to replace it with a charge of using a communication facility to further a drug crime, carrying a maximum sentence of four years and the possibility of probation (Brook et al 2016: 1165). In this system, defendants can agree to enter 'fictional' pleas, so that convictions via guilty plea involve offences which bear little or even no resemblance to the offences that they were initially charged with (Johnson 2019) and, in some jurisdictions, can plead guilty while explicitly maintaining innocence (see Shipley 1986).

Empirical research has examined the offers made to defendants and highlights the huge sentence reductions that can be obtained by defendants who plead guilty in this system. For example, in one survey response, a lawyer reported a client being charged with sexual assaults and being threatened with a 40-year prison sentence being able to plead guilty to disorderly conduct and being sentenced to pay only court costs (Helm et al 2018b: 923). Thus, for some defendants, going to trial is transformed into a gamble that many cannot afford to take. One lawyer surveyed in an empirical study articulated this sentiment, stating 'Faced with decades of prison and offered a year or two, rational people don't even gamble'

(Helm et al 2018b: 923). These decisions are not voluntary or free from pressure in a meaningful sense. While many defendants may feel they have done well out of guilty plea decisions (reducing a sentence they deserved based on factual guilt to a much lesser one), innocent defendants are unlikely to feel this way, particularly where they realise that the chance of conviction is low or that charges against them could even be dropped should they be able to pursue trial. This possibility is likely for innocent defendants since research suggests that more compelling offers are made to defendants where the probability of conviction is low (see Bushway, Redlich and Norris 2014). The National Registry of Exonerations has described the discrepancies between sentences at plea and trial as having 'virtually eliminated the constitutional right to a trial' (National Registry of Exonerations nd). The pressure to plead guilty in the US system can be seen by the huge number of defendants pleading guilty (around 98 per cent of defendants in Federal cases pleaded guilty in 2019, see United States Sentencing Commission 2019 Sourcebook of Federal Sentencing Statistics: Table 11) and the significant role of guilty pleas in wrongful convictions (National Registry of Exonerations nd).

As in England and Wales, evidence from the United States suggests that incentivised guilty pleas may also have a role in creating inequalities in the criminal justice system. For example, a recent analysis of data from the Maryland Commission on Criminal Sentencing policy found that Black and Latino defendants were substantially less likely to plead guilty than White defendants (Testa and Johnson 2020) and thus were less likely to benefit from sentence reductions. Thus, again, the presence of choice in guilty plea decision making does not appear to be ensuring true voluntariness, eliminating pressure or protecting equality.

IV. Conclusion: Taking Constraint on Choice Seriously

Sentence reductions have the potential to interfere with defendant choice, and their relationship with psycho-legal constructs of voluntariness, autonomy, pressure and constraint is complicated. Systems utilising plea-based sentence reductions tend to mask this complexity by relying on superficial definitions of relevant constructs and, as a result, assume that plea decisions are voluntary and free from pressure in all but the most extreme circumstances, and that giving all defendants a choice is protective of equal rights. This treatment has created a system in which legal rhetoric is increasingly detached from practical reality, where legal regulation appears to protect defendants but does very little in practice.

To provide defendants with meaningful protections in practice, rather than jury in theory, meaningful engagement with underlying constructs is necessary. In this chapter, I have suggested that (contrary to current assumptions) sentence reductions can undermine voluntariness, incentives to plead guilty create pressure to plead guilty, and merely giving everyone the choice of guilty plea or full trial does not ensure equality. Given these realities, it is important to closely consider the extent to which it is acceptable for sentence reductions to influence choice and to regulate sentence reduction regimes to ensure that they do not have an unacceptable impact on plea decisions.

The question of the extent to which it is acceptable for sentence reductions to influence choice is a difficult one. It is clear, as argued above, that decisions to plead guilty should be voluntary in the sense that defendants should have another acceptable option available to them. But, the amount of pressure that it is acceptable for reductions to create is less clear. A helpful way to determine what level of pressure should be considered acceptable is to consider the role that defendant choice plays in legitimising convictions via guilty plea. Essentially, defendant autonomy – the ability of a defendant to live their own life in accordance with their own second-order goals (the desires they have reflectively about what they want or what is good) – can justify allowing criminal convictions via guilty plea without meaningful scrutiny of the evidence against a defendant (and even in light of evidence showing innocent defendants plead guilty). This notion is in line with affirmation of the self-respect of defendants in the guilty plea process and the criminal justice process more generally (see Chapter 7). Sentence reductions can therefore be considered acceptable provided that they do not themselves deplete autonomy.

A sensible starting point is therefore one proposed by prior work – that sentence reductions are acceptable provided they do not prevent plea decisions from being driven by a defendant's relevant second-order goals (see Helm et al 2022). Importantly, second-order goals driving a plea decision should be those relating to the central plea decision itself – the decision to self-incriminate. Where sentence reductions draw defendants away from these second-order goals (eg by invoking a whole new set of second-order goals not relevant to the core plea decision), these reductions undermine rather than promote defendant autonomy and thus should be seen as creating impermissible pressure. On the other hand, reductions that assist a defendant in making a choice between two relevant second-order goals – eg the good of owning up and the good of avoiding punishment – can be seen as preserving autonomy while still nudging a defendant towards the guilty plea option. This approach also has the benefit of ensuring that reductions only influence defendants who are at least somewhat driven by the good of owning up, and thus are arguably more clearly eligible for some reward in the form of a sentence reduction.

Empirical work has the potential to inform the development of sentencing guidelines that operate in the way described above – nudging defendants between two second-order values relevant to the core plea decision rather than drawing defendants away from those second-order values. Two promising ways in which plea decisions might be brought more in line with relevant second-order values are (1) ensuring that discounts do not result in outcomes from pleading guilty that are categorically different from those received if convicted at trial (see Helm 2021b), and (2) avoiding the provision of concrete information to defendants prior to plea on the sentence they will face if they plead guilty. Providing this information has the potential to change the reference point that defendants work from when making plea decisions through providing a benchmark against which a sentence at trial can come to be viewed as a penalty. Providing this information also contributes to transforming the plea decision into a tactical one based on trading off risks and rewards, where pressure created by balancing those risks and rewards can draw decision makers away from the central plea decision. It is also necessary to closely consider equality when regulating incentives to plead guilty, recognising that offering all defendants a choice does not guarantee equality in a meaningful sense. Sentence reductions should be accompanied by individualised protection to retain the ability of all defendants to act in accordance with relevant second-order values. This protection might be provided in a number of ways, depending on defendant need, for example through the provision of robust financial support, legal advice from a trusted source, or greater utilisation of house arrest.

By drawing on these suggestions and taking psycho-legal constructs seriously, states can continue to benefit from defendant guilty pleas (although potentially not on the same scale), while providing appropriate protection for defendants in their criminal justice systems – protection that many states already claim to be providing in theory, but are not providing in practice.

References

Alschuler, AW (1979) 'Plea Bargaining and Its History' 79 *Columbia Law Review* 1.

Baldwin, J and McConville, M (1978) 'Conviction by Consent: A Study of Plea Bargaining and Inducements to Plead Guilty in England' 7 *Anglo-American Law Review* 271.

Bennett, MW (2010) 'Unravelling the Gordian Knot of Implicit Bias in Jury Selection: The Problems of Judge-dominated Voir Dire, the Failed Promise of Batson, and Proposed Solutions' 4 *Harvard Law & Policy Review* 149.

Blume, JH and Helm, RK (2014) 'The Unexonerated: Factually Innocent Defendants Who Plead Guilty' 100 *Cornell Law Review* 157.

Bowers, J. (2007) 'Punishing the Innocent' 156 *University of Pennsylvania Law Review* 1117.

Boëda, M (2022) 'Scandal of post office workers wrongly accused of thefts in the UK', *Le Parisien* (21 February) www.leparisien.fr/faits-divers/scandale-des-postiers-accuses-a-tort-de-vols-au-royaume-uni-si-je-navais-pas-ete-enceinte-je-me-serais-suicidee-20-02-2022-ZUOKZ27JV5E7LKRZ4FCDBXLA5Y.php

Brook, CA, Fiannaca, B, Harvey, D and Marcus, P (2016) 'A Comparative Look at Plea Bargaining in Australia, Canada, England, New Zealand, and the United States' 57 *William and Mary Law Review* 1147.

Bushway, SD, Redlich, AD and Norris, RJ (2014) 'An Explicit Test of Plea Bargaining in the Shadow of the Trial' 52 *Criminology* 723.

Dennis, I (2017) *The Law of Evidence*, 6th edn (Edinburgh, Sweet and Maxwell).

Dworkin, G (1988) *The Theory and Practice of Autonomy* (Cambridge, Cambridge University Press).

Evidence Based Justice Lab (nd) 'Post Office Project', https://evidencebasedjustice.exeter.ac.uk/current-research-data/post-office-project/#projectinformation

Fineman, MA (2013) 'Equality, Autonomy, and the Vulnerable Subject in Law and Politics' in MA Fineman (ed), *Vulnerability: Reflections on a New Ethical Foundation for Law and Politics* (London, Routledge).

Fisher, L (2019) 'Criminal Justice User Fees and the Procedural Aspect of Equal Justice' 133 *Harvard Law Review Forum* 112.
Grant, RW (2006) 'Ethics and Incentives: A Political Approach' 100 *American Political Science Review* 29.
Helm, RK (2018) 'Cognitive Theory and Plea-bargaining' 5 *Policy Insights from the Behavioral and Brain Sciences* 195.
—— (2019) 'Constrained Waiver of Trial Rights? Incentives to Plead Guilty and the Right to a Fair Trial' 46 *Journal of Law and Society* 423.
—— (2021a) 'False guilty pleas and the post office scandal', *Evidence Based Justice Lab Blog*, https://evidencebasedjustice.exeter.ac.uk/false-guilty-pleas-and-the-post-office-scandal/
—— (2021b) 'Cognition and Incentives in Plea Decisions: Categorical Differences in Outcomes as the Tipping Point for Innocent Defendants' 28 *Psychology, Public Policy, and Law* 344.
—— (2021c) 'Guilty Pleas in Children: Legitimacy, Vulnerability, and the Need for Increased Protection' 48 *Journal of Law and Society* 179.
Helm, RK and Reyna, VF (2017) 'Logical but Incompetent Plea Decisions: A New Approach to Plea Bargaining Grounded in Developmental Theory' 23 *Psychology, Public Policy, and Law* 367.
Helm, RK, Dehaghani, R and Newman, D (2022) 'Guilty Plea Decisions: Moving Beyond the Autonomy Myth' 85 *Modern Law Review* 133.
Helm, RK, Reyna, VF, Franz, AA and Novick, RZ (2018a) 'Too Young to Plead? Risk, Rationality, and Plea Bargaining's Innocence Problem in Adolescents' 24 *Psychology, Public Policy, and Law* 180.
Helm, RK, Reyna, VF, Franz, AA, Novick, RZ, Dincin, S and Cort, AE (2018b) 'Limitations on the Ability to Negotiate Justice: Attorney Perspectives on Guilt, Innocence, and Legal Advice in the Current Plea System' 24 *Psychology, Crime & Law* 915.
Hood, R (1992) *Race and Sentencing* (Oxford, Oxford University Press).
Johnson, T (2019) 'Fictional Pleas' 94 *Indiana Law Journal* 855.
Jones, S (2011) 'Under Pressure: Women Who Plead Guilty to Crimes They Have Not Committed' 11 *Criminology & Criminal Justice* 77.
Kipnis, K (1976) 'Criminal Justice and the Negotiated Plea' 86 *Ethics* 93.
Kisekka, NG (2020) 'Plea Bargaining as a Human Rights Question' 6 *Cogent Social Sciences* 1818935.
Lammy, D, MP (2017) *Review into the Treatment of and Outcomes for Black, Asian, and Minority Ethnic Individuals in the Criminal Justice System Ministry of Justice*, https://assets.publishing.service.gov.uk/government/uploads/system/uploads/attachment_data/file/643001/lammy-review-final-report.pdf
Lippke, RL (2011) 'Against Trial Penalties' in RL Lippke *The Ethics of Plea Bargaining* (Oxford, Oxford University Press).
Nash, C, Dioso-Villa, R and Porter, L (2021) 'Factors Contributing to Guilty Plea Wrongful Convictions: A Quantitative Analysis of Australian Appellate Court Judgments' *Crime & Delinquency* 00111287211054723.
National Registry of Exonerations (nd) *The Trial Penalty: The Sixth Amendment Right to a Trial on the Verge of Extinction and how to Save it*, www.nacdl.org/Document/TrialPenaltySixthAmendmentRighttoTrialNearExtinct

Nobles, R and Schiff, D (2019) 'Criminal Justice Unhinged: The Challenge of Guilty Pleas' 39 *Oxford Journal of Legal Studies* 100.
—— and —— (2020) 'The Supervision of Guilty Pleas by the Court of Appeal of England and Wales – Workable Relationships and Tragic Choices' 31 *Criminal Law Forum* 513.
Nozick, R (1974) *Anarchy, State, and Utopia* (Oxford, Blackwell).
Olsaretti, S (1998) 'Freedom, Force and Choice: Against the Rights-based Definition of Voluntariness' 6 *The Journal of Political Philosophy* 53.
Peay, J and Player, E (2018) 'Pleading Guilty: Why Vulnerability Matters' 81 *The Modern Law Review* 929.
Reyna, VF (2012) 'A New Intuitionism: Meaning, Memory and Development in Fuzzy-Trace Theory' 7 *Judgment and Decision-Making* 332.
Sentencing Council (2011) *Assault: Definitive Guideline*, www.sentencingcouncil.org.uk/wp-content/uploads/Assault_definitive_guideline_-_Crown_Court.pdf
—— (2017) *Reduction in Sentence for a Guilty Plea: Definitive Guideline*, www.sentencingcouncil.org.uk/wp-content/uploads/Reduction-in-Sentence-for-Guilty-Plea-definitive-guideline-SC-Web.pdf
Shipley, CJ (1986) 'The Alford Plea: A Necessary but Unpredictable Tool for the Criminal Defendant' 72 *Iowa Law Review* 1063.
Testa, A and Johnson, BD (2020) 'Paying the Trial Tax: Race, Guilty Pleas, and Disparity in Prosecution' 31 *Criminal Justice Policy Review* 500.
United States Sentencing Commission (2019) *2019 Sourcebook of Federal Sentencing Statistics*, www.ussc.gov/research/sourcebook/archive/sourcebook-2019
Wertheimer, A (1979) 'The Prosecutor and the Gunman' 89 *Ethics* 269.
Yan, S and Bushway, S (2018) 'Plea Discounts or Trial Penalties? Making Sense of the Trial-Plea Sentence Disparities' 35 *Justice Quarterly* 1226.

Legislation

Canadian Criminal Code
Federal Rules of Criminal Procedure (US)

Cases

United Kingdom

Hamilton and Others v Post Office [2021] EWCA Crim 577
McKinnon v United States [2008] UKHL 59
R v David Caley and others [2012] EWCA Crim 2821
R v Ford [1989] 3 All ER 445 (CA)
R v Goodyear [2005] EWCA Crim 888
R v Howe [1987] AC 417
R v Turner (No 1) [1970] 2 All ER 281

United States

Bordenkirtcher v Hayes 434 US 357 (1978)
Brady v United States 397 US 742 (1970)
Griffin v Illinois 351 US 12 (1956)

European Court of Human Rights

Deweer v Belgium App No 6903/75, 27 February 1980
Natsvlishvili and Togonidze v Georgia App No 9043/05, 29 April 2014

11

Plea Negotiations and Mitigation

MIKE HOUGH AND JESSICA JACOBSON

I. Introduction

This chapter explores the interrelationship between plea negotiation and personal mitigation in the courts system in England and Wales. We argue that in many cases which come before the courts, negotiations over plea and the application of personal mitigation at sentencing can be seen as two phases of a single process in which the offending behaviour is reframed in a manner highly favourable to the offender. As such, they cumulatively and significantly reduce the severity of the sanction the court is likely to impose. This, we contend, raises questions about equity, proportionality and consistency in sentencing outcomes, and the purposes of sentencing more broadly.

A. Plea Negotiations: Historical Background and Scope

Lord Hewitt justified his verdict in a 1923 case with the famous statement that 'Justice should not only be done, but should manifestly and undoubtedly be seen to be done'. The principle has become widely accepted and has done much over time to shape the justice system. It privileges fairness, transparency, certainty, clarity and finality in the resolution of cases. Arguably, however, this concern with what cynics would regard as 'keeping up appearances' also helps to explain the attitudes of the senior judiciary to plea negotiations in the 1970s and 1980s, and their keenness to keep plea bargaining hidden from public view.

The Home Office funded John Baldwin and Michael McConville (1977) to investigate plea bargaining, and their resultant research was intensely critical of the 'backstairs agreements' reached by defence and prosecution counsel. Baldwin and McConville observed the legal profession's apparent refusal to acknowledge the existence and extent of plea bargaining, or to debate the risks of wrongful convictions that arose from inducement to plead. They argued that the senior judiciary on the one hand believed that plea negotiations were 'repugnant to the English system' – largely because of the abuse of due process that the practices involved – but, on the other, were aware that plea bargaining was a pervasive practice reflecting the pragmatism of legal professionals. Senior judges tried to stop the research, driven by concerns about the damage to the legitimacy of the justice system that would flow from exposure of plea negotiation practices.

Since then, these somewhat conflicting judicial attitudes to plea negotiation have shifted, and the judiciary in England and Wales have become more aligned with the American approach, which has recognised for many years the inevitability of routine plea negotiation.[1] Zuckerman (1995) persuasively set out a justification for 'procedural rationing', even if his focus was on the civil rather than criminal law:

> It would be absurd to say that we are entitled to the best possible legal procedure, however expensive, when we cannot lay a credible claim to the best possible health service or to the best possible transport system. Yet it would be equally absurd to suggest that procedure need not strive to achieve any level of accuracy to satisfy the demands of justice. We are therefore entitled to expect procedures, which strive to provide a reasonable measure of protection of rights, commensurable with the resources that we can afford to spend on the administration of justice. (Zuckerman 1995: 160–61)

Accordingly, the virtues of fairness, transparency, finality and clarity are inevitably in tension with affordability throughout the criminal and civil justice systems. We shall argue here that a particular point of tension can be found in arrangements for securing guilty pleas in the criminal courts. For certain, the reality of deals hatched by defence and prosecution does indeed sometimes feel unsavoury, and the potential for innocent defendants to be coerced into pleading guilty is real – especially for vulnerable offenders (*cf* Helm 2019; Chapters 4 and 10). But at the same time, they arguably provide 'good enough' resolution of cases with the benefits of swift justice, economy and minimising the risk of erroneous acquittals. Arguments of this sort have resulted in progressively more open acknowledgement of plea negotiations in England and Wales over the last 40 years. Perhaps the most significant development in formalising the plea negotiation process has been the statutory provision of discounts to sentences for guilty pleas – first included in legislation in 1994.[2] This in essence rewards defendants for preventing the costs of a trial, with the costs understood both in economic terms and in terms of the potential anxiety and distress caused to victims and witnesses who must give evidence at trial. In general, the earlier in the process the defendant pleads guilty, the greater the discount. As set out in the Sentencing Council (2017) guilty plea guideline, those who plead at the earliest opportunity are generally entitled to a maximum sentence discount of one-third.

[1] Gormley and Tata's (2019) discussion of plea bargaining in Scotland shows that the practice is equally endemic north of the border, and that ambivalence towards the process there remains amongst legal professionals.

[2] The 1994 Criminal Justice and Public Order Act first provided a statutory basis for everyday practice, which was restated in the 2003 Criminal Justice Act and carried over into the 2020 Sentencing Code.

At first sight, guilty pleas are simple statements by defendants that they have committed the offence with which they have been charged. Of course, guilty pleas do indeed often involve a straightforward admission of the case brought by the prosecution. However, many guilty pleas can involve the presentation of a version of 'what happened' which is substantially at odds with the initial charge. Both prosecution and defence have vested interests in settling for a guilty plea, and negotiations over this are common. The baseline for such negotiations is the available guilty plea discount, as established by statute and elaborated in Sentencing Council guidelines. But plea negotiations have much wider scope, and can entail three further – often intertwined – types of bargain: in relation to *charge*, where the defence offer to plead guilty to a lesser charge is accepted; *count*, where a guilty plea to one charge is offered conditional on other unrelated charges being dropped; and *facts*, where a guilty plea may be offered contingent on the prosecution accepting a less damning account of the details of the offence of the case. (In 'fact bargaining', the disputed facts might be considered by the judge or magistrates in a Newton Hearing. This is, effectively, a mini-trial – although without a jury if in the Crown Court – at which the judge or magistrates hear evidence to determine whether to sentence in accordance with the prosecution or defence version of events.)

B. Personal Mitigation

It is our contention, in short, that the offences to which defendants plead guilty often have a negotiated, contingent character – because they are the outcome of (largely hidden) processes of charge, count or fact bargaining, or some combination thereof. Moreover, the process of negotiation may *continue* during the formal sentencing hearing, in the sense that the plea in mitigation is an opportunity for the defence to reframe further the offender's actions, circumstances and predisposition. Various important forms of personal mitigation (that is, factors relating to the offender rather than the offence) may in fact be closely intertwined with the guilty plea as they tend to presuppose an open and thoroughgoing admission of guilt on the part of the offender. Remorse, acknowledgement of the causes of the offending behaviour, and demonstrable efforts to address these causes are the obvious examples of this.

We have been forcefully struck by the relationship between guilty pleas and mitigation since we first studied the role of personal mitigation in sentencing (Jacobson and Hough 2007: 44; 2011). Crown Court judges interviewed for that study spoke of this relationship, one of whom, for example, commenting that the defendant who pleads guilty can claim remorse and thus 'engages the court's sympathy much more readily'. However, the position adopted by Sentencing Council guidelines is that the standard sentence discount for a guilty plea (of up to one-third of sentence length) is unrelated to any reductions that can be secured through various forms of personal mitigation. This, it seems, is largely because the justifications for the guilty plea discount are regarded as distinctive from any rationales associated with other forms of mitigation – the former being defined in terms of reduced impact of the crime on victims, saving victims and witnesses from having to testify, and the time and money saved on investigations and trials.[3]

The stepwise approach to sentence decision making that is built into the Sentencing Council guidelines makes clear the distinction between the guilty plea discount and reductions for other forms of mitigation. The three main steps that apply in decision making on most cases are:

- step 1 – determine the sentence 'starting point and category range' by assessing which of three categories of harm and three categories of culpability the offence falls into;
- step 2 – take account of specific aggravating and mitigating factors, to decide where the offence falls within the identified range;
- step 3 – apply the guilty plea discount in accordance with the stage at which the offender pleaded guilty.

This Sentencing Council approach privileges a deserts perspective by emphasising principles of proportionality in assessing offence seriousness as a product of culpability and harm. It treats as second order both the consequentialist aims of sentencing enshrined in legislation (deterrence, rehabilitation, public protection and reparation), and the need to encourage swift and economical justice. Arguably, this approach is a useful heuristic which imposes a simplifying structure on a highly complex process. However, we would suggest that the separation of the statutory discount from personal mitigation, when the *practical reality* is that these are often closely interrelated, can mean that the remorseful offender secures a double discount: the first is for being remorseful, and the second is for offering an early guilty plea. Of course, the impact on the final sentence is greater still if one also takes into account the repercussions of any charge, count or fact bargaining along with the guilty plea discount and personal mitigation.

In other words, personal mitigation – to the extent that it is accepted by the court – interacts with the foregoing process of plea negotiation to produce an account of the offending behaviour that is significantly more favourable towards the offender than would otherwise be the case. And it is this account that is the basis of the sentencing decision. Accordingly, the *effective* impact on sentencing outcome following a guilty plea may greatly exceed the standard 'guilty plea discount' of up to one-third – reflecting the combined effects of the discount, charge/count/fact bargaining, and personal mitigation that builds on the admission of guilt. Whether these cumulative or multiplier effects of plea negotiation and mitigation are problematic is open to question. But it is our view that, at the very least, this is a question that should be asked – which is what this chapter is seeking to do.

[3] www.sentencingcouncil.org.uk/overarching-guides/magistrates-court/item/reduction-in-sentence-for-a-guilty-plea-first-hearing-on-or-after-1-june-2017/.

The main purpose of this chapter is to consider the benefits, tensions and risks associated with current practices of plea negotiation and the interaction between guilty pleas and mitigation. Among the matters at issue here are the undoubted, and widely recognised, advantages of a system which – through the provision of the guilty plea discount and scope for negotiation over plea – delivers *affordable* clarity, finality and relative speed in criminal justice, while simultaneously reducing the *risk of erroneous acquittal*. This brings the added benefit of sparing victims and witnesses the stress of giving evidence in court. However, the sources of anxiety about plea bargaining that the judiciary expressed in the past still remain: what 'actually happened' is not established in open court; rather, the court accepts an account of the offence constructed through informal (and at least partly hidden) negotiations between defence and prosecution. Members of the legal profession and academics alike continue to voice misgivings about the practice (eg Gormley and Tata 2021), including the potential for defendants – especially those with vulnerabilities – to be pressured into pleading guilty against their interests and wishes.

But if there are obvious advantages, as well as risks, to current practices of plea negotiation, what are less obvious are the implications for justice of the interplay between plea negotiations and personal mitigation. It can be argued that this interplay significantly erodes the principle of proportionality[4] and leads to unjustifiably unequal treatment between the offender who pleads guilty and benefits from all impacts on sentencing outcome that this entails, and the offender who exercises their right to maintain their innocence. This issue becomes all the more pressing when one considers differential rates of guilty plea between white and BAME (black, Asian and minority ethnic) defendants (Lammy 2017), and the repercussions for sentencing. On the other hand, a system that strongly rewards offenders who admit their guilt, and alongside this are making efforts to desist from offending, arguably offers wider societal benefits.

C. The Shape of this Chapter

To help us to draw out these issues, we will first present – over Sections II and III – a descriptive account of various forms of plea negotiation and describe the interaction between guilty pleas and mitigation. These accounts are based on the findings of observational research conducted by one of the authors (Jacobson) and colleagues in the Crown Court, adult Magistrates' Courts and the Youth Court over the past 10 years.[5] Following the empirical sections of this chapter,

[4] See Chapter 3 for a full discussion of the tensions between retributivist principles and the practice of discounting sentences to take account of pleas in mitigation and early guilty pleas.

[5] Unless otherwise specified, this empirical material has not been published elsewhere. We should acknowledge the contribution of colleagues who were involved in the observational research: Penny Cooper, Gillian Hunter, Amy Kirby and Emily Setty.

Section IV looks in more detail at what the observed processes and practices mean for equity, proportionality and consistency in sentence decision making, and their implications for how we understand the purposes of sentencing. Finally, Section V concludes the chapter with some brief proposals on how the identified tensions might best be addressed. To anticipate our conclusion, we shall argue that the legitimacy and effectiveness of the criminal justice system would benefit in the long run if processes and decision making were more transparent, and if there were more honesty about the contradictory impulses contained within sentencing policy and practice. And while we have some concerns about the size of the compounded advantages in terms of sentencing outcomes that can be secured by early guilty pleas, plea bargaining and personal mitigation, we would be highly ambivalent about any 'solution' that would entail longer sentences – as anything that will further swell the prison population is unwelcome.

II. Processes of Plea Negotiation

The common-sense presumption about the plea process is that the defendant will know if they are guilty or not, and will plead not guilty either if they 'didn't do it' or if they 'did it' but believe their guilt will not be proven if the case goes to trial. And common sense would again hold that a guilty plea is entered either if they 'did it' and know that there is clear evidence of this or – more rarely – if they 'didn't do it' but judge that a relatively speedy resolution and reduced sentence are preferable to the delays and uncertain outcome of a trial.

These presumptions undoubtedly reflect reality in some cases, but in an unknown but probably large proportion of cases they do not.[6] The more complex reality of a great many cases can be attributed to several factors. Many offences are the result of complex social interactions, that happen quickly, with participants in an emotional state, or drunk or under the influence of drugs – especially when violence is involved. Therefore, precisely 'what happened' may be genuinely unclear to *all* those involved. Secondly, prosecutors are often faced with a choice of charges to bring, often graduated according to the intentions of the defendants and the level of harm caused, as in assaults of various levels of seriousness (causing actual bodily harm (ABH), inflicting grievous bodily harm (GBH)/wounding, and causing GBH with intent). Several charges may simultaneously be laid, partly out of strategic considerations,[7] but equally because the intentions of the defendants are inevitably often opaque to the prosecution and sometimes even to the defendants themselves and defence lawyers.

[6] See Chapter 2 for a more extensive discussion of the practical considerations and the ethics in deciding how to plead.

[7] Including the more serious charges, even when the evidence for the charge is less than overwhelming, may place the prosecution in a good starting position for negotiating a guilty plea for one of the lesser charges.

As a consequence, the need for the defendant to enter a plea in court can often trigger a process of negotiation, involving not only the defendant, but also the sentencer(s), the defence and prosecuting counsel, and – to some extent – the victim(s) of the offence. First, the defendant and their lawyer may seek an indication of sentence, conditional on a guilty plea. In the magistrates' courts, the defendant may simply be told whether they are facing a custodial or non-custodial sentence. In the Crown Court, the judge may give an indication (known as a Goodyear indication) of the maximum sentence they will receive if they plead guilty. These indications of sentence do not, strictly speaking, constitute a bargaining process, but the indication is contingent on a guilty plea and thus reflects the associated discount, and might accordingly help to secure such a plea.

In cases where an indication of sentence is not sought – or if the indicated sentence fails to lead to a guilty plea – this may trigger a genuine bargaining process between the defence and prosecuting lawyers about the precise *facts of the case* to which the defendant will admit, the *level* of charges to which they will plead guilty, and the *number* of charges that can be dropped in return for a guilty plea to others.

Below, we present a number of case studies of plea negotiation. These are intended to be illustrative rather than representative. However, they demonstrate that the negotiation process tends to be highly informal. While parts of the process may occur in open court (these cases were observed by the researchers from the public gallery), this is largely outside the bounds of a formal hearing, and the extent of engagement of lay parties is variable.[8]

A. Successful Charge and Count Bargaining

Our first case study is an example of charge bargaining which produced a guilty plea. Here, defence and prosecution counsel in the Crown Court began the negotiations before the judge or defendant had arrived in the court room.

Case study 1: Successful charge bargain in the Crown Court

The young defendant, Steven, attended court for trial for a section 20[9] assault (inflicting GBH). On arrival in court – in advance of Steven or the judge – the defence advocate commented cheerily that in the 'spirit of Christmas' he wanted to discuss the plea. Prosecution counsel told him that several witnesses had not turned up, but there was CCTV evidence showing Steven punching the complainant.

[8] One aspect of plea bargaining which, unavoidably, is entirely hidden from public view is where the defendant is offered a reduction in sentence in return for assisting the prosecution.

[9] Section 20 of the Offences against the Person Act 1861 created offences where grievous bodily harm was caused, but the level of harm was unintended.

The defence advocate suggested that a guilty plea to affray might be possible, although he had not yet discussed this with Steven (who had been on bail for nearly a year by the date of the trial). The complainant had suffered a broken jaw, but the CCTV footage could not confirm if it was Steven's punch which had caused this injury, since others had become involved in a brawl after the initial punch was thrown.

Defence and prosecution discussed how 'pragmatic' the judge might be, and the maximum sentence for affray. The prosecutor commented that he did not want to 'short-change' the victim. On entering the court, the judge was informed of the discussion, agreed to view the CCTV footage, and said he was happy with the proposal to change the indictment from section 20 assault to affray. He left the courtroom again to allow the prosecution and defence advocates to discuss matters with, respectively, the victim and Steven (who was by now in the dock).

Shortly thereafter, the defence advocate reported Steven's agreement to plead guilty to affray, and the prosecutor stated that the complainant was satisfied – indeed, had said that he did not want Steven to go to prison. On returning to the courtroom, the judge was told of this agreement and that the indictment had been amended accordingly. Only now did the judge address Steven directly: quickly explaining that he would be bailed to appear for sentencing in six weeks' time; that he must comply with probation; that 'all options are open' regarding sentence. 'Got that?' asked the judge. Steven did not speak, but presumably nodded as the judge did not enquire further. To the observer, it was by no means clear that Steven had in fact 'got it'.

Steven left the dock and courtroom, and the judge asked for the jury – who had been waiting for the trial to start – to be brought in. He showed them the CCTV footage and explained that acceptance of the guilty plea to affray was a sensible compromise given the likely difficulty of proving beyond reasonable doubt that it was Steven's punch that had broken the victim's jaw. He told them that the offence of affray could still attract a maximum sentence of three years' imprisonment. He also mentioned the 'door of the court syndrome': namely, that it is when the trial is about to begin that some defendants become more realistic about their options. (We do not know what sentence was subsequently passed in this case.)

Beyond the smoothness of the charge bargaining process in case study 1, and the close, cheerful collaboration it entailed between defence and prosecution, there are other interesting features of the case. While the defendant's role in the process was highly peripheral, and little effort was made to confirm his understanding (reflecting the status of many defendants in court as 'ever-present extras' (Jacobson, Hunter and Kirby 2015)), the prosecuting counsel took care to check that the complainant was aware of, and understood, the charge bargain.[10] Further, the judge went to some lengths to explain to the jury what had happened and why.

Fact bargaining occurs when defendants indicate that they are prepared to plead guilty to the offence with which they have been charged but dispute the prosecution account of the details of what happened. From the prosecution perspective, a guaranteed conviction for the less serious version of the offence may be preferable to a trial in which the defendant could be found not guilty. Case study 2, below, concerns two linked robbery prosecutions in the Youth Court. In each case, the prosecution accepted the defendant's 'basis of plea', according to which the defendant had played a less serious role in the offence than originally alleged.

Case study 2: Fact bargaining in two linked Youth Court hearings

Darren, aged 15, had no previous convictions and was charged with two counts of robbery, committed with three or four others. The victims of the robberies – also young teenagers – had been threatened with a knife; and clothes, cash and phones had been taken from them. Darren pleaded guilty on a basis of plea accepted by the prosecution: that his involvement was relatively brief and that while he had heard the threat to use the knife during the robberies, he did not make the threat himself or produce any weapon.

Adam, another 15-year-old, appeared at a separate Youth Court hearing, having been charged with one of the robberies in which Darren was involved. Unlike Darren, Adam had previous convictions for violent offences: assault, robbery and attempted robbery. At the time of the hearing, he was serving a referral order. Adam also pleaded guilty on an agreed basis of plea: in his case, that he had not known anything about the presence or use of a knife in the robbery.

The group offending, significant psychological harm caused to the young victims (two of whom had made victim personal statements which were read out in court), and the use of the knife were serious aggravating features of the robberies. With regard to Adam, his record of prior offending was significant further aggravation. These features of the offending made a custodial sentence – which would have been a Detention and Training Order, given the offenders' ages – a realistic prospect. Both offenders, however, ultimately received non-custodial penalties, which in part reflected the less serious 'facts' of the offending as agreed with the prosecution.

[10] This was compliant with the *Farquharson Guidelines* on the role of prosecuting advocates, which directs the prosecution to 'consider the consequences of [any decision whether or not to prosecute] for the victim and … take into account any views expressed by the victim or the victim's family', www.cps.gov.uk/legal-guidance/farquharson-guidelines-role-prosecuting-advocates.

The observer of case 2 had no way of assessing the honesty or reliability of the defendants' claims to only marginal involvement in the offence. But such is the 'messy reality' of many cases, especially those involving violent, interpersonal offences, that fact bargaining is necessarily carried out under conditions of considerable uncertainty. Among the various interests being served by this process are, inevitably, those of the justice system in achieving reasonably swift and cost-efficient outcomes.

B. Unsuccessful Charge and Count Bargaining

It is in the nature of negotiation that the outcome is uncertain. The next case study illustrates how charge bargaining can fail to end in a deal. It also shows how charge bargaining and count bargaining are often interlinked – even if in this case the defendant failed to secure either a dropped or reduced charge.

Case Study 3: Unsuccessful plea bargaining in the Crown Court

The defendant Tom, a man in his 20s, faced two charges of dangerous driving, along with charges of harassment and breach of a non-molestation order. Before Tom entered court, his defence counsel proposed to the prosecution that Tom would plead guilty to one careless driving charge in place of the two of dangerous driving. The prosecution advocate left the court to consult on the charges, and the defence lawyer commented to the clerk, 'He's just asked me to do something that's against the grain – I know it's a stupid thing to do.' The clerk stated his sympathy for the lawyer's position, who was bound to do as instructed by his client.

After consulting on the defence proposal, by which time Tom was in the dock, the prosecuting advocate stated that one of the dangerous driving charges must remain, but the second could be dropped to careless driving. The defence advocate spoke to Tom, who rejected the counter-proposal, and said he would continue to plead not guilty to both charges of dangerous driving, claiming mistaken identity.

The judge set a trial date some months later for the dangerous driving offences, and a second date in relation to the harassment and breach orders. Tom responded furiously when told by the judge that nothing could be done to schedule the cases any sooner: 'Go fuck yourself, you're a fucking prick, I'll be in custody for Christmas and won't see my kids.' The judge threatened to find Tom in contempt of court for swearing.

The observing researcher in case 3 later overheard the defence lawyer saying that his defendant was 'the client from hell'. It seems likely that had the defendant been more flexible, his lawyer could have secured him a more favourable result than that for which he was probably heading, having opted for a trial. In a sense this was a case study of a defendant's misjudgements – both in relation to his personal presentation in court, and his lack of realism about the options open to him.

Case study 4 concerns a defendant (unrepresented, in a magistrates' court) who faced two separate charges. The prosecution proposed a plea to the lower charge alone, presumably calculating that a conviction on one of the counts was preferable to a trial and possible acquittal on both. This was rejected by the defendant, whose defence was subsequently accepted by the magistrates.

Case study 4: Defendant's resistance to count bargaining in a magistrates' court

The unrepresented defendant, Julie, was a middle-aged woman and, judging from her clerical collar, a minister of religion. Attending court in a wheelchair, she appeared anxious and flustered. She faced charges of speeding and failure to provide driver details; she was contesting these on the basis that it was her son who had been driving the car, and she had not received the request to provide information because of postal issues at her home address. Before the case opened, the court's legal adviser suggested to Julie that she should have a look on her phone for any evidence from Royal Mail about the postal problem and gave her a few minutes to do so. The prosecuting advocate then explained to her that failure to provide information was worth six penalty points, while speeding was worth three. He said that if she pleaded guilty to the latter charge, the former could be dropped. Julie nevertheless stuck to her not guilty plea, and was acquitted by the magistrates after trial.

In case 4, the prosecutor's offer to drop the most serious charge faced by the defendant can be seen as a perfectly proper way of testing her story and achieving a conviction – but equally, it could be constructed as pressure to secure a wrongful admission of guilt.

C. Plea Bargaining as a Collaborative Process

The next case study, number 5, exemplifies the extensive collaboration that can go into a plea negotiation. In this case, involving a teenage girl charged with assault in the Youth Court, no bargain is explicitly on offer – except in coded terms. In essence, all the legal participants worked to steer the defendant away from a trial.

Case study 5: Active collaboration to achieve guilty plea in the Youth Court

The 16-year-old defendant, Gemma, was charged with an assault by beating[11] of a worker in the care home in which she had been living at the time. The assault had happened shortly after Gemma had self-harmed, and in the context of her ongoing mental health problems and a conflict with a new resident of the home. The district judge hearing the case said to Gemma, 'So we're now in a position to find out if you're pleading guilty or not guilty.' The legal adviser put the charge to Gemma, to which she replied, 'Not guilty.'

The judge commented that he could see from Gemma's face when the charge was put 'how upsetting' a trial would be. He went on to say that the alleged assault seemed to have happened 'in the heat of the moment' and that Gemma might not remember everything about it, but if she were to say 'something' happened, it would be possible for the court to deal with it. 'I'm not trying at all to force anything,' he added, but 'I don't want this to be dragging on.' The defence and prosecution lawyers consulted with each other. The judge asked for information from the Youth Offending Service about mental health support and said it might be possible to 'see an end' to the case today. He then adjourned the hearing for Gemma to talk further with her lawyer.

When the case reconvened, the judge said to the defence lawyer, 'I think we can put the charge again?' The lawyer replied, 'We can – I'm very grateful.' The legal adviser put the same charge of assault by beating to Gemma, who this time replied, 'Guilty.' The judge clarified the 'agreed basis' of the plea, which was that the offence had not involved 'some kicking out'. He then imposed a conditional discharge for three months and wished Gemma 'good luck'. He also asked what she was going to name the two guinea pigs that – as Gemma's social worker had previously explained – she was getting that day. Gemma left the court, smiling and chatting with her social worker.

It is hard to take issue with the decisions made by the legal participants in case 5. Defence, prosecution, district judge, court legal adviser and Youth Offending Service worker all contributed to the process of securing the plea, which all appeared to regard as in the best interests of the girl – especially given that the sentence passed thereafter was a conditional discharge. The case also provides a clear illustration of the increasing prominence of 'case management' as a facet of the judicial role and, indeed, the criminal justice process more broadly (McEwan 2011; 2013; Ward 2017). However, it does lead one to ask why the police and Crown Prosecution Service (CPS) saw fit to proceed to prosecution for such a minor offence committed by a highly vulnerable 16-year-old.

[11] 'Assault by beating' is the usual formulation for the least serious forms of common assault (eg where the victim was pushed, grabbed or spat at, without any significant injury).

Our final case in this section (case study 6) involved a collaborative endeavour between a notably interventionist judge, the prosecutor and the defendant himself – who was unrepresented. There was no charge or fact bargain here, but the judge's Goodyear indication of sentence clearly played a part in encouraging the guilty plea.

Case study 6: Unrepresented defendant's guilty plea in the Crown Court[12]

The unrepresented defendant, Charles, a man in his 40s, had been charged with production of cannabis in his home. At the plea hearing, Charles stated that he was producing cannabis for personal use as a medication for anxiety and Post-traumatic stress disorder; and that he was pleading not guilty on this basis.

The judge explained to Charles the difference between a defence and mitigation, and that what Charles had said about use of cannabis to treat his mental health problems was the latter. The judge checked some details of the charge with the prosecution and asked Charles various questions about his circumstances, his family and a prior conviction for a similar offence. He also asked why Charles was unrepresented. After some further consultation with the prosecutor, including about potential sentence, the judge told Charles that he was going to speak to him as if to a lawyer. He advised him that he would not be sending him to prison whatever the outcome; that the issue was about whether he would plead guilty; and that he should speak to the prosecutor about this, who 'will be fair'.

The case reconvened after a 30-minute adjournment, and Charles pleaded guilty. The judge sentenced him to a low-level community sentence – adding, 'It's not my role to give you lifestyle advice, but heed this: cannabis is not good.'

As with the previous case study, in case 6 it appears that the judge and the prosecution were looking out for the best interests of the defendant. Again, however, wider questions are raised about the justice system – in this case, about the nature and scope of current drug laws. The answers fall well beyond the scope of this chapter, of course.

III. Guilty Pleas and Mitigation

We now turn to look at some examples of how guilty pleas can interact with personal mitigation put forward by the defence. Our first example here, case study 7, is a case in which it was made clear by the judge that certain forms of

[12] This case is also discussed in Jacobson (2020).

personal mitigation were not available to an offender convicted after trial, precisely because of the not guilty plea.

Case 7: Loss of mitigation following a not guilty plea[13]

The 21-year-old defendant, Emmanuel, was charged with inflicting GBH (section 20 assault) on a fellow player at a Sunday morning football match. The assault had occurred in the course of what was variously referred to (by both prosecution and defence counsel and the judge) as a 'mass brawl', 'mass confrontation', 'melee' or 'general hubbub' among many of the players after one had been sent off. There was no dispute that the victim had been severely assaulted – a punch to the side of the face had fractured his skull – or that Emmanuel had been involved; the question for the jury was whether it was Emmanuel who had thrown the damaging punch.

Over two-and-a-half days, seven prosecution witnesses gave evidence about what they had perceived to be the ethnicity, height, build, hairstyle and clothing of the attacker. There was enough inconsistency between these accounts from witnesses for the prosecution counsel to feel compelled to acknowledge it. He told the jury, '[A case doesn't come] in a neat and tidy package with a legal bow on top if it … That is not life … You'll make sensible allowances to reflect that reality'. Nevertheless, the jury found Emmanuel guilty after deliberating for more than a day.

In the sentencing hearing that followed, the defence advocate pointed to various mitigating aspects of Emmanuel's character and circumstances: this was a young man, he said, with no previous convictions, working hard as a plumber, and supportive of and supported by his family. The judge, however, was unimpressed by the mitigation, commenting, 'All of these points would have been good points if he'd pleaded guilty' and that Emmanuel had 'shown no remorse, no empathy'. In a somewhat contradictory fashion, the judge also stated that Emmanuel would not be punished for fighting his case.

In passing a nine-month custodial sentence, the judge commented, 'If ever there was a case where credit for plea was so important, this is it', and said that a guilty plea would have given the court a wider range of options. He reiterated that Emmanuel was being sentenced as a man of 'impeccable good character', which made his decision to plead not guilty 'all the more distressing'.

In case 7, the nine-month sentence would have been reduced to six months had the defendant offered an early guilty plea. This guilty plea would also have enabled his lawyer to enter a much stronger plea in mitigation (or, at least, a plea in mitigation that would have had more traction with the judge), potentially reducing the

[13] This case is also discussed in Jacobson, Hunter and Kirby (2015).

sentence to a high-level community penalty. A contrast can also be drawn with the situation of Steven in case study 1, above, in which a preparedness to plea bargain led to the downgrading of a section 20 charge to a charge of affray. It is to be hoped, of course, that case 7 was a case of a guilty defendant's bad decision about plea rather than a wrongful decision of guilt by the jury.

Case studies 8 and 9 provide striking points of comparison with that of Emmanuel. Both are cases in which there was a guilty plea and illustrate the potential importance of personal mitigation revolving around remorse and a demonstrable keenness to take full responsibility for one's actions.

Case study 8: A young defendant's mitigation focused on remorse and 'progress'

A teenage girl, Lauren, appeared at the Youth Court where she pleaded guilty to charges of robbery and attempted robbery. Her lawyer told the court that Lauren was 'deeply ashamed' of her behaviour and had explained how she was feeling in a letter to the judge.

The lawyer went on to describe the progress Lauren had made since being subject to a secure remand by the Family Court on account of her 'completely out of control' behaviour and vulnerability to criminal and sexual exploitation. Today, the lawyer said, she was drug free, working towards her GCSEs and engaging with therapy and mental health services.

Lauren herself told the district judge that was feeling 'better about myself'. The judge responded, 'It's a good feeling, isn't it, to achieve things?' He went on to pass a non-custodial sentence for the offences, which would, he said, usually merit custody – commenting that hearing about the progress she was making on the secure order was one of the factors in the decision. 'You need to make the most of this opportunity,' he added, to which Lauren replied, 'I will.'

Case study 9: Intensely remorseful offender and sympathetic magistrates

Vincent, an unrepresented defendant in his early 30s, sat with his head in his hands at the start of the hearing. He pleaded guilty to charges of possession of a class A drug (cocaine) and drink driving. The court's legal adviser told the bench that if they thought that Vincent had 'suffered enough' they could give a conditional discharge, although this would be an unusual course of action.

The magistrate asked Vincent what he would like to say about the incident. He told the court that he had been given the wrap of cocaine by a friend during his birthday party and put it in his pocket. He had drunk three pints and was only just over the limit – 'I know it's no excuse.' He went on to say, 'One night and it's lost me my job, everything … I've lost my relationship, my home, everything because of this.' 'It was a bad birthday,' commented the magistrate. Vincent was given a 12-month conditional discharge, at which he thanked the magistrates several times and breathed an audible sigh of relief.

In case studies 8 and 9, guilty pleas and associated mitigation, judged in the round and along with apparent cooperation with the process, provided scope for lenient sentencing. While the sentences given may have been 'constructed' in hindsight to comprise separate stages relating first to personal mitigation and then to the guilty plea discount, we can surmise that in reality, the sentencers reached an overall assessment of the weight to be attached – in combination – both to the evident remorse and the preparedness to accept responsibility for their behaviour as shown by an early guilty plea. What was also clear in those cases was that the offenders 'engage[d] the court's sympathy' – to repeat the quotation above from our early research on mitigation (Jacobson and Hough 2007).

Case studies 10 and 11, drawn from a single day's observation in a magistrates' court, contrast the compliance of a defendant pleading guilty with the vehemence of one opting to contest the case – the former provoking sympathy, and the latter scornful laughter.

Case study 10: Destitute offender pleads guilty before magistrates

The defendant, Dariusz, was a young Polish man who appeared in court from custody (with shaven head and in a prison-issued grey tracksuit), having spent the past six weeks on remand because of previous adjournments of the case. He pleaded guilty to two counts of theft from a supermarket and one assault by beating of the supermarket's assistant manager, who had detained him. The thefts were of low-value items such as chocolate.

The prosecutor described Dariusz as a 'destitute male, homeless, on the streets', whose offences reflected this destitute status. In the plea in mitigation, his lawyer pointed out that Dariusz 'came off worse' from the altercation with the shop manager, having suffered cuts to his face, and was 'deeply remorseful'. The magistrates sentenced Dariusz to a fine, which was 'deemed served' because of the time he had spent on remand. 'So you don't owe the court anything,' the chair reiterated. 'And we wish you luck for the future.' Dariusz replied, 'Thank you, your honour.'

Case study 11: Challenging the magistrate and their authority

A male defendant in his late 20s, Hunter, was charged with breaching a restraining order. The offence related to his ex-partner, with whom he had three children. It was alleged that – against the terms of the order – he had gone to her house. The prosecutor commented that this was the latest of Hunter's 'regular appearances' at court.

Hunter spoke frequently during the plea hearing, mostly asking questions of the court's legal adviser about his legal rights. The magistrates looked on and occasionally commented, with what initially appeared to be mild amusement and later some obvious irritation. When asked how he pleaded, he responded,

> 'Based on how the charge is put to me … A resounding not guilty.' When then asked whether he wished to be tried in the magistrates' or Crown Court, he pondered for a moment and then said, 'I feel like justice would be served in this court. If the wind blows in the right direction.'
>
> After the date was set for the trial, Hunter strode out of the courtroom, saying loudly, 'Carry on the oppression, guys – you're doing great!' As the door to the courtroom swung shut behind him, one of the court officials said, laughing, to Hunter's lawyer, 'Thanks for bringing the entertainment.'

These two cases illustrate the – sometimes overwhelming – impact on court proceedings of defendants' compliance with, or defiance of, the court's authority. Defendants' decisions about their plea can lead to convincing – and often real – 'performances' of compliance; decisions to enter not guilty pleas can equally trigger displays of angry defiance.

IV. Taking Stock of the Cumulative Impact on Sentencing Outcome of Early Plea, Plea Negotiations, and Mitigation

When it comes to the established discount for a guilty plea, and associated processes of charge/count/fact bargaining, many of the tensions between pragmatism and principled justice have been widely discussed. The pragmatists point out that the statutory discount and plea negotiations provide for affordability and speed: the criminal justice process would grind to a halt without them as they provide reasonable incentives for defendants to plead guilty. This reduces court appearances, time spent in court and the costs of both prosecution and State-aided defence. There are real added benefits: avoiding a trial means that victims and witnesses are spared the stress and anxiety associated with giving evidence at court.

On the other side of the balance sheet, there are risks to defendants: there are clear inducements to plead guilty to an offence that they did not commit. These risks are significant for those who are vulnerable in any way and may therefore be more easily pressured to plead guilty (eg Gormley et al 2020; Helm 2019; Chapter 10; Peay and Player 2018). Some victims and complainants may feel that they have been robbed of 'their day in court', and that the offender has secured a milder punishment that the offence deserved.[14] The lack of transparency of the process must inevitably result in inconsistency in practice – as discussed at the

[14] The frustrations of some prosecution witnesses about guilty pleas were noted in research by Jacobson, Hunter and Kirby (2015).

outset of this chapter. Another area of concern about plea negotiations per se is the strict limit on rights to appeal convictions that are based on plea (eg Nobles and Schiff 2020). Finally, the statutory discount and plea negotiations erode the principles of adversarial justice, in favour of a much more managerialist criminal justice process – (eg Ward 2017; Gormley and Tata 2021; Johnston 2020). As Johnston puts it, the dilution of the adversarial system

> ultimately renders the defence lawyer a cog in the criminal justice machine; a stark difference to the gladiator of the accused … The tension created by the managerial agenda from the CrimPR [Criminal Procedure Rules] is clear and the lawyer is required to positively contribute to the efficiency of the system; this is clearly identifiable by having to enter a guilty plea at the first hearing.

The contours of this battleground are fairly well agreed among academics, legal commentators and practitioners, even if there is little agreement about the right balance to strike between pragmatism and principles. However, discussion of plea bargaining in the context of England and Wales rarely looks beyond the above points to consider the *interaction* of guilty plea discounts, plea negotiations and personal mitigation, and the resultant cumulative impact on the eventual outcome of the case.

The key point here is that the impacts on sentencing outcome are not simply combined arithmetically, but are compounded: charge, count or fact bargaining lessens the seriousness of the precise offence(s) of which the offender is convicted; the severity of punishment is then reduced through any plea in mitigation; and the guilty plea sentence discount is then applied on top. How this process operates is best illustrated by a 'worked example', as set out in the box below. This illustrates the potential scale of divergence in outcomes for the offender who pleads not guilty compared to the offender pleading guilty. There are three scenarios, all with the same starting point in which a 30-year-old man is initially charged with a section 20 assault (inflicting GBH), following a late-night, alcohol-fuelled fight in which he is alleged to have punched the victim. The resultant sentence ranges from a medium-level community order to a 12-month custodial sentence, depending on plea and mitigation. The first scenario is reminiscent of case study 7, involving Emmanuel, the Sunday morning footballer who pleaded not guilty to a section 20 charge; the third, of case study 1, in which Steven agreed to plead guilty to affray in place of the assault charge. We should stress that this worked example presents what is by no means an extreme set of scenarios: a reduction in charge wounding/causing GBH with intent (section 18) to unlawful wounding/inflicting GBH (section 20), or from affray to a less serious assault, could lead to an even wider disparity in outcome.

Worked example

Defendant is a 30-year-old male with no previous convictions, initially charged with section 20 assault (inflicting GBH). Accused of committing offence in course of a fight involving several others, following a night's drinking. Victim was punched in the face; suffered badly broken jaw.

SCENARIO 1: Not guilty plea, limited mitigation

Defendant is **found guilty at trial**, having pleaded not guilty (claiming he had only peripheral involvement in the fight and did not throw the punch that caused injury). At sentencing, plea in mitigation focuses on defendant's clean record and part-time employment. Judge comments that mitigation is counter-balanced by aggravating features of offence: it was committed under influence of alcohol, at night, as part of 'unprovoked group attack'. Evident from pre-sentence report that defendant continues to deny offence.

Sentence = **12 months' custody**, which is starting-point sentence for section 20 assault involving category 3 (lesser) harm and category B (medium) culpability.

SCENARIO 2: Full discount for guilty plea, limited mitigation

Defendant **pleads guilty** to original charge at earliest opportunity. At sentencing, plea in mitigation focuses on defendant's clean record and part-time employment. Judge says failure to engage with probation during preparation of pre-sentence report, and 'arrogant' courtroom behaviour, suggest lack of remorse. Judge also says any mitigation is counter-balanced by aggravating features of offence (group attack, at night, under influence of alcohol).

Sentence = **8 months' custody**: early guilty plea reduces what would have been 12-month sentence (as in Scenario 1) by one-third.

SCENARIO 3: Charge bargain, full discount for early guilty plea, substantial mitigation

Defendant indicates willingness to plead guilty to lesser offence at earliest opportunity; ultimately, prosecution accepts **guilty plea to affray** in place of section 20 assault. At sentencing, plea in mitigation focuses on defendant's clean record and part-time employment, along with deep remorse for what happened and concern about victim's welfare. Defendant also said to be actively addressing alcohol and related mental health problems, which he believes to be the cause of his offending. Judge commends him on his progress; says mitigation is substantial and outweighs aggravating features of offence.

Sentence = **medium-level community order**:

- starting point for offence of affray, involving category 2 (medium) harm and category B (medium) culpability = 26 weeks' custody;
- reduced to high-level community order because of mitigation;
- reduced to medium-level community order due to full discount for early guilty plea.

Should we regard as problematic the cumulative impact on sentencing outcomes of charge (or other) bargaining, mitigation and guilty plea discount, as illustrated by the worked example? Not necessarily. Only the strictest of retributionists would refuse to accept *some* modulation around proportionality as the determining factor in the severity of punishment. Consequentialist objectives can be accommodated to a degree, making it possible to reward remorse, reparative gestures and preparedness to address the causes of offending behaviour (*cf* Chapter 3). Received wisdom on the bench – and a reasonable body of research – holds that sentencing practices of this sort can support rehabilitation and desistance, and there is no dispute about the wider societal benefits that rehabilitation and desistance offer. And as we discussed above, the discount for early guilty pleas is justified (in statute and sentencing guidelines) on grounds other than proportionality, as an efficient means both of 'procedural rationing' and of sparing victims and witnesses the burden of giving evidence in court. Equally important, an early guilty plea can be regarded as the first step on a path to taking responsibility for one's actions.

On the other hand, the cumulative impact of the processes we have described may be considered problematic if one considers the vast difference in sentencing outcome that can arise. The *quantum* of the impact has become large enough to undermine the principle of proportionality, which, in theory at least, remains the overarching framework for sentencing in England and Wales. Furthermore, this has happened with a lack of transparency and honesty in relation to plea negotiations and sentencing practice – and with little debate about, or recognition of, the tensions between principles and pragmatism in sentencing.

An additional consideration is whether particular groups of defendants are disadvantaged by current practice in this regard. The Lammy Review on treatment and outcomes for BAME individuals in the criminal justice system (2017) cites several studies that have consistently found lower rates of guilty plea among BAME compared to white defendants (the main cause of which is deemed to lie in differing levels of trust in the system). Lammy points to the implications of this for BAME offenders' access to interventions requiring a guilty plea, and to the guilty plea sentence discount. We would argue that the implications for ethnic disparities in criminal justice outcomes – given the interplay between plea discounts, plea negotiations, and mitigation – are even greater than acknowledged by Lammy.

V. What Is To Be Done?

This chapter has raised more questions than answers, and some of the answers we offer by way of conclusions are very tentative. The most obvious question that arises is whether the disparities in sentencing outcomes between guilty-pleading and not-guilty-pleading offenders should be narrowed.

If the answer to this question is 'yes', on grounds of proportionality and equity, then it would be relatively straightforward to achieve this, but problematic in terms of the net results. A narrowing in disparities could be achieved by reducing the guilty plea discount or reducing sentencers' discretion to mitigate for personal factors. The obvious and significant drawback of such an approach is that it would cause sentence inflation. This would not only breach important principle of penal parsimony, but would also be fiscally irresponsible – however attractive such a development might be to populist politicians. There is the theoretical option of avoiding sentence inflation by reducing the starting points in sentencing guidelines at the same time as reducing the available discounts for guilty plea or personal mitigation. However, the history of penal politics over the last 30 years hardly offers much room for optimism about any politicians' preparedness to go down this road.

We are inclined to offer a different answer to the question of whether the disparities in sentencing outcomes between those pleading not guilty and those pleading guilty should be narrowed. This answer is that such disparities may be an inevitable and potentially justifiable feature of a sentencing system in which the overarching principle of proportionality can, in certain contexts, be overridden by other goals. These goals include not only reducing the cost, time and potential distress to witnesses associated with criminal trials, but also supporting offenders' rehabilitation and desistance from crime, thereby providing wide societal benefits (*cf* Chapters 5 and 7).[15]

However, providing a convincing justification for the disparities demands, on the part of the justice system, far greater honesty and transparency than currently exists about the implications of a plea for sentencing. The existing lack of honesty and transparency means defendants may be entering pleas without full awareness of the repercussions, which is likely to contribute to perceptions of unequal treatment of defendants. As discussed above, a lack of clarity amongst defendants about the implications of not guilty pleas may also contribute to the disparities between ethnic groups in plea rates – with consequent disparities in sentences. And for victims and witnesses also, a lack of information about the plea process, and poor understanding of the meaning of a guilty plea, may lead to discontent with sentencing and delegitimise the courts process in their eyes. How can greater honesty and transparency be achieved? Below, we focus first on options relating to plea negotiations, and then on the relationship between the guilty plea and personal mitigation.

A. Greater Honesty and Transparency in Plea Negotiations

There has been a sea-change over the last 50 years in judicial preparedness to acknowledge the inevitability – and indeed desirability – of plea negotiations.

[15] Consistent with our argument here, Watson (Chapter 7) presents an insightful analysis of the value of a guilty plea – for people who are indeed guilty – as a means of preserving their self-respect in the process of prosecution and conviction. In similar vein, Roberts and Dagan (Chapter 5) argue the case persuasively for recognising the ethical value of a guilty plea, in terms of the value of State recognition of the defendant's autonomy and agency.

However, the need remains for more acknowledgement, visibility and consistency in practices and procedures relating to negotiations over level of charge, number of charges and the agreed facts of the case. Achieving this will require changes at a policy level as well as delivery at a case level. We cannot claim to have developed a full agenda for change – and researchers may not be the best people to do so – but we have in mind such things as encouraging prosecutors to:

- proceed only with those charges which they are confident they can bring to court, in preference to 'charging high' as an opening gambit;
- state clearly the reasons they have for reducing the level of charge or the number of counts;
- ensure that outcomes of negotiations are fully explained to victims and witnesses;
- place plea negotiations on a more formal footing, with agreements formally recorded.

There is also a need to address public misconceptions about plea negotiations. People need to understand that plea negotiations are a key feature of the criminal justice system in England and Wales – and that they have an important and justifiable role to play in delivering justice.

B. Recognising the Interrelationship between Guilty Plea and Personal Mitigation

The key 'compounding' effect of guilty plea on sentence arises because the sentencing guidelines treat mitigating factors and early guilty pleas as conceptually (and psychologically) unrelated. This is reflected in the stepwise sentencing approach set out in sentencing guidelines, whereby mitigation is generally considered at the second step, and the guilty plea discount applied at the third. Clearly there is no logical necessity for an early guilty plea to precede expressions of remorse and a determination to desist from crime, but the reality is that accepting responsibility for one's offending and feeling remorse are – in the vast majority of cases – likely to be intimately intertwined psychological processes. The practical implication of this is that it would make sense for sentencers to treat 'in the round' early guilty pleas and pleas of mitigation associated with expressions of remorse and determination to address offending. Accordingly, the second and third steps of the decision making process could be merged. Doing so would dispense with the legal fiction that the discount for an early guilty plea is *solely* a recognition of the fact that the defendant has saved the court time and money, and has spared victims and witnesses inconvenience, anxiety and distress. It might have the even more significant benefit of recognising formally the guilty plea as the first stage on the road to desistance, and one that should be welcomed and rewarded as a significant consideration in its own right, not just because of pragmatic considerations of efficient case management.

The difficulties that would arise from such a reformulation of the stepwise decision making process are partly practical in that it would entail substantial disruption of the Sentencing Council's guidelines framework, at a stage when they are beginning to bed in very well. Another potential difficulty, as discussed above, is that this could also lead to sentence inflation. Sentencers may feel more comfortable with a series of small discounts to sentence with separate justifications than with offering the same quantum of discount in a single step. But these difficulties could be addressed, in whole or in part, by guidelines that clearly set out the scale of discounts that should be awarded for mitigation, including in the situation where a guilty plea does, and does not, form part of the mitigation.

C. In Conclusion

The main thrust of our argument in this chapter has been that sentencing after a guilty plea is not a straightforward process by which the sentencer determines the penalty for criminal actions that are fully known and agreed upon. Rather, the passing of the sentence is the final step in a process of *creating* a narrative about offence and offender that is acceptable to the court. This narrative will, at least at times, have only a loose relationship to whatever 'really happened'. The proposals for change we have set out above would lead to more open and honest practices around plea negotiation. They would also result in greater recognition of the reality that, in their everyday practice, sentencers subscribe to consequentialist principles in recognising the significance of guilty pleas as an essential starting point on the road to desistance from offending.

References

Baldwin, J and McConville, M (1977) *Negotiated Justice: Pressures to Plead Guilty* (London, Martin Robertson).

Gormley, J and Tata, C (2019) 'To Plead or Not to Plead? "Guilty" Is the Question: Re-thinking Plea Decision-making in Anglo-American Countries' in C Spohn and P Brennan (eds), *Handbook on Sentencing Policies and Practices in the 21st Century* (New York, Routledge).

—— and —— (2021) 'Remorse and Sentencing in a World of Plea-bargaining' in S Tudor, R Weisman, M Proeve and K Rossmanith (eds), *Remorse and Criminal Justice* (London, Routledge).

Gormley, J, Roberts, JV, Bild, J and Harris, L (2020) *Sentence Reductions for Guilty Pleas: A Review of Policy, Practice and Research* (London, Sentencing Academy).

Helm, RK (2019) 'Conviction by Consent? Vulnerability, Autonomy and Conviction by Guilty Plea' 83 *Journal of Criminal Law* 161.

Jacobson, J (2020) 'Observed Realities of Participation' in J Jacobson and P Cooper (eds), *Participation in Courts and Tribunals: Concepts, Realities and Aspirations* (Bristol, Bristol University Press).

Jacobson, J and Hough, M (2007) *Mitigation: The Role of Personal Factors in Sentencing* (London, Prison Reform Trust).
—— and —— (2011) 'Personal Mitigation: An Empirical Analysis in England and Wales' in JV Roberts (ed), *Mitigation and Aggravation at Sentencing* (Cambridge, Cambridge University Press).
Jacobson, J, Hunter, G and Kirby, A (2015) *Inside Crown Court: Personal Experiences and Questions of Legitimacy* (Bristol, Policy Press).
Johnston, E (2020) 'The Adversarial Defence Lawyer: Myths, Disclosure and Efficiency – A Contemporary Analysis of the Role in the Era of the Criminal Procedure Rules' 24 *International Journal of Evidence & Proof*, 58.
Lammy, D (2017) *The Lammy Review: An Independent Review into the Treatment of, and Outcomes for, Black, Asian and Minority Ethnic Individuals in the Criminal Justice System* (London, Ministry of Justice).
McEwan, J (2011) 'From Adversarialism to Managerialism: Criminal Justice in Transition' 31 *Legal Studies* 519.
—— (2013) 'Truth, Efficiency, and Cooperation in Modern Criminal Justice' 66 *Current Legal Problems* 203.
Nobles, R and Schiff, D (2020) 'The Supervision of Guilty Pleas by the Court of Appeal of England and Wales – Workable Relationships and Tragic Choices' 31 *Criminal Law Forum* 513.
Peay, J and Player, E (2018) 'Pleading Guilty: Why Vulnerability Matters' 81 *Modern Law Review* 929.
Sentencing Council (2017) *Reduction in Sentence for Guilty Plea: Definitive Guideline* (London, Sentencing Council).
Ward, J (2017) *Transforming Summary Justice: Modernisation in the Lower Criminal Courts* (London, Routledge).
Zuckerman, AS (1995) 'A Reform of Civil Procedure: Rationing Procedure Rather Than Access to Justice' 22 *Journal of Law and Society* 155.

Legislation

Criminal Justice Act 2003
Criminal Justice and Public Order Act 1994
Offences against the Person Act 1861

12

Guilty Pleas, Fools' Bargains, and Wonderful Justice

LEO ZAIBERT*

It is fitting to begin an essay on guilty pleas with a confession. I thus confess my antipathy toward guilty pleas, and, even more so, toward the system that allows these pleas to be traded, exchanged and negotiated: the plea-bargaining system. Clearly, these are different things: there could be a system that allowed guilty pleas but did not allow bargaining them; but if there existed a system that allowed bargaining pleas that system must (as a matter of logic) allow the pleas in the first place. In any case, I oppose both these things.[1] Part of my antipathy flows from my legal training in a country which embraced the so-called 'inquisitorial' criminal procedure, a legal tradition in which guilty pleas were until very recently virtually non-existent, and where American-style plea-bargaining was seen as an example of a fundamentally primitive and unfair criminal justice system, the so-called 'adversarial' system.[2] As a perceptive critic of plea-bargaining has put it, I am 'alert to my biases' – or at least I try to be (Alschuler 1979: 3). Accordingly, there will be nothing (consciously) autobiographical in what follows.

I. Overview

I will begin, in fact, by considering, at a very abstract level, possible reasons for thinking that a system of pleas and of plea-bargaining is a good thing. I will, however, conclude that those reasons ought to be dismissed. After this brief

* With thanks to Felmon Davis and to the participants in the seminar on guilty pleas held at Worcester College, Oxford University on 25–26 March 2022.

[1] In practice, this one-way conceptual independence between a system of pleas and a system of plea-*bargaining* is unlikely to materialise. If pleas are permitted, then a 'market' for them will probably (invariably?) arise (albeit more or less above ground, more or less formalised, more or less decent, etc). This seems to me analogous to the way in which currency exchange controls invariably generate black markets.

[2] It is not only Anglo-American criminal procedure that scholars from the European tradition (which itself influences many jurisdictions around the globe) tend to see as woefully primitive: their disdain includes substantive criminal law as well. See, eg, Jiménez de Asúa (1963: 1111).

exercise in abstract thinking, I will refer to some chapters in the actual history of guilty pleas and plea-bargaining, with particular emphasis on the different ways in which the 'adversarial' and 'inquisitorial' traditions have embraced (or shunned) these practices. Finally, and since there appears to be some sort of Americanisation of criminal procedure around the globe, in the last two sections of the chapter I discuss some specific – and disturbing – aspects of the development and implementation of the system of guilty pleas and plea-bargaining in the United States.

II. From Owning Up to Pleading Down

There is a perfectly recognisable sense in which *owning up* to our own bad deeds can be morally praiseworthy. Even if the world would have been a better place had the occasion for my owning up to my bad deeds never arisen – ie, because I did nothing wrong – once the bad deed is committed, admitting to it is one good thing I can do about it. This owning up, this admission of guilt – this *confession* – would not of course erase my bad deed, but it could somehow diminish the harm it had caused, and (whether or not it harmed anyone) it may even diminish some of its wrongfulness. In some cases, bad deeds may generate duties of restitution or compensation; in other cases, bad deeds call for repentance, or for apologies, etc. In stressing the value of owning up to our bad deeds I do not wish to undermine the value of these other possible steps that we could or should undertake following our wrongdoing – but I do wish to highlight that the value of owning up can exist independently of the values of those other things.

If we consider two people who committed the exact same bad deed (in the exact same circumstances, etc) except that only one of them owns up to the wrongfulness of what she did, that person is *ceteris paribus* less blameworthy. To admit that owning up can have value independently of other things is not to deny that this value can be exaggerated, manipulated or exploited. The fact that we own up to our bad deeds, even when this is fully sincere and genuinely heartfelt, need not render us completely beyond reproach. Moreover, the owning up can be defeated by other considerations. It is not difficult to think about certain extreme wrongdoers whose owning up may be rather normatively inert. What would an imaginary owning up by, say, Josef Mengele, do to his immense blameworthiness? Call me unforgiving, but I hope that it would do nothing at all.[3] Absolutions, even partial absolutions, should not be secured cheaply. Determining the effects (even in general terms) of owning ups is an important enterprise, but it is not terribly relevant for my purposes here: I am happy to stipulate that, in general, owning up to our bad deeds (just like repenting, apologising, and so on) can be intrinsically good.

[3] My position *at this level of abstraction* need not commit me to any specific position at the more concrete levels of judicial responses or of policy considerations.

Notwithstanding the potential value of owning up (and related phenomena that I have just stipulated), it is difficult to see how these phenomena may survive *systematisation*. For it appears to me that their value depends on their happening spontaneously: the value of my 'owning up' to my bad deed may be called into question if it becomes known that I was forced or even somehow induced to do so, etc.[4] The very idea of systematising these owning ups presents, in and of itself, difficulties. But these general difficulties brought about by any systematisation are further exacerbated in a system as normatively complex as that of criminal justice, where the 'bad deeds' are *crimes*, and when the 'owning ups', 'admissions' and 'confessions' can become *pleas* officially entered into legal proceedings and instruments. Amongst many, I want to focus on two important sources of complexity.

The first one comes to light if we notice that nothing in my initial general formulation of the owning up *mise-en-scene* suggests power differentials of any sort: someone with more power – in whatever way power is conceptualised – can own up to her bad deeds to someone with less power, or vice versa. In contrast, within the context of the criminal justice system, the person who may own up to her bad deeds is typically *immensely* less powerful than the State who hears or accepts her owning up. The second source of complexity flows from the fact that within the criminal justice system the equivalent to the sort of abstract owning up which we are considering is almost always transactional in exactly the way in which the value of owning up would appear to diminish: the *defendant* stands to gain something from her owning up – typically, a less severe (or shortened) sentence, or another diminution in punishment. Again, if the reason why I may own up to some bad deed is that I wish to receive this or that benefit, the value of this owning up is quite different from that value which would flow from an owning up that is the result of honest and disinterested moral reflection.[5]

Not only do these two sources of complexity account for the further erosion of spontaneity[6] that systematisation into the criminal justice system would add to the erosion that any (pre-legal) systematisation of owning up would already generate; they also allow us to highlight a crucial disanalogy between the abstract owning up I have sketched and a guilty plea in a legal system. As it turns out, a guilty plea is much more than an owning up or a confession: a guilty plea is nothing short of an owning up or a confession on steroids. In entering a guilty plea, a defendant – that is, an individual who faces the awesome punitive power of the State (with its dramatic life-altering consequences, including, in some cases, life-*ending* consequences) – rejects all the protections that she could have enjoyed

[4] It is important to stress that the sense of 'spontaneous' at play here is related to 'unforced', 'unbidden', or indeed to 'free' – of originating in the very person: *sua sponte*. Thus, in this sense, a decision may be 'spontaneous' *and* also the result of a very difficult, very protracted and very thoughtful process. I thank several contributors to this volume for suggesting that I clarify the sense in which I use this term.

[5] For similar views and related worries, see Chapters 4 and 10.

[6] 'Spontaneity' in the sense described above.

had she gone to trial. Again, entering a guilty plea is not merely to confess: it is to confess-and-therefore-avoid-trial. Why would anyone want to avoid trial, given that going to trial gives defendants not only all sorts of other protections, but also the opportunity to perhaps be acquitted?

Pleading has to offer something quite attractive to the defendant for her to give up all that the trial offers. And that is exactly what typically happens: the defendant is lured into giving up trial *and its protections* in exchange for a reduced sentence. If this were not bad enough (both in terms of what it says about *justice* and in terms of how it differs from the more abstract sense in which owning up to our wrongdoing can be valuable), the attractiveness of the reduced sentence is often enhanced by the exaggerated initial charge. In other words, prosecutors often over-charge defendants to induce them to plead guilty (Husak 2008: 17–40) and to increase the likelihood that the bargained sentence is (albeit for the wrong kinds of reasons) closer to what the defendants actually deserve. In a perfectly crass way, this is quite reminiscent of offering an item for sale at a particularly high price, hoping that, after bargaining with potential buyers, the final price may be what one realistically expected. Furthermore, this over-charging is related to all sorts of other factors working against defendants: from the over-criminalisation and over-penalisation of conduct to terrifyingly inhumane conditions of imprisonment.

Under these conditions, it is often irrational for a defendant not to accept whatever bargain is offered – nay: throffered (an 'offer' that masks or contains a threat) – to her. Under these conditions, moreover, it is hard to keep a straight face when we are told that these pleas are entered 'voluntarily'. In this context, the use of the term 'voluntary' (and its cognates) is downright dishonest. This type of dishonesty is not an uncommon gambit in the law: for example, after being detained in the United States, undocumented migrants are often said to have 'voluntarily departed', although they only departed in order to avoid the much more dire consequences of deportation (and although they have just risked their and their children's lives to enter the United States in the first place) (Zaibert 2008); employees everywhere 'voluntarily' accept 'separation packages' from employers who would otherwise fire them in much worse conditions, etc. This tendentious use of 'voluntarily' reduces the term to the bare sense of 'consciously', a sense which is, in any event, terribly different from the richer sense of 'freely and deliberately chosen', which is the one we need in this context (particularly if something of the analogy with owning up at the personal level is to be preserved). In fact, the sense of 'voluntarily' at play here is quite like the sense in which I 'voluntarily' hand over my wallet to the robber who, holding a gun against my head, orders me to do so.[7]

For these reasons, it is hard to resist the conclusion that there is just too little in common between the abstract owning ups that may indeed be valuable in some contexts and guilty pleas as they operate in the criminal justice system. Rather

[7] For more on the 'voluntariness' of the typical choice involved in pleading guilty, see Chapter 10.

than a vehicle for mature societies and mature individuals to do the right thing, the transactional – and almost always *bargained* – guilty pleas that have come to altogether dominate adversarial criminal procedure systems such as the United States' – in effect replacing proper trials – are morally objectionable. So, any robust analogy one may have thought was possible between owning up to our wrongdoing in general and guilty pleas in the context of the criminal justice system can be safely discarded.

III. The Adversarial and the Inquisitorial

Although there is no dearth of critics of the system of plea-bargaining (Alschuler 1979; Harvard Law Review 1970; Langbein 1979; Schulhofer 1992; Bibas 2004; Stuntz 2004; 2011), it would appear that the system is unstoppable, and that its taking over the entire world is but a matter of time. Scarcely a decade ago the Supreme Court of the United States recognised that 'Ninety-seven percent of federal convictions and ninety-four percent of state convictions are the result of guilty pleas' (*Missouri v Frye* 2012: 143). Jaw-dropping as these figures are, and despite the fact that there is such miniscule room left for the system of guilty pleas to grow any further, in recent years its near-monopoly of convictions in the United States has become even stronger (Gramlich 2019). The Supreme Court has thus unequivocally – and unabashedly – confessed that 'criminal justice today is for the most part a system of pleas, not a system of trials' (*Lafler v Cooper* 2012: 170). What is perhaps more worrying is that American-style plea-bargaining (and with it, a fortiori, guilty pleas, as we have seen) seems to be all the rage elsewhere too, as the work of noted comparativists shows. Markus Dubber, for example, notes how common they have become in Germany, a place where at least until recently they were anathema (Dubber 1997). Maximo Langer, for his part, talks about a certain 'Americanization' of criminal procedure occurring in a number of other countries – countries not belonging to the tradition of the adversarial criminal procedure (Langer 2004).

One perfectly legitimate reaction to this state of affairs is to conclude, in resignation: well, so much the worse for the current state of criminal procedure. But it is worthwhile to investigate these developments in more depth, probing some connections between some aspects – both historical and analytic – of the inquisitorial and adversarial traditions of criminal procedure and the development and spread of guilty pleas. After all, despite all their efforts to show how plea-bargaining has gone from non-existent to well known in Germany (Dubber's concern) or in a number of other jurisdictions (Langer's concern), both these authors admit to the reticence with which legal scholars and practitioners in the inquisitorial legal tradition react to it.

Dubber's contribution is in a sense humble: he simply wishes to correct John Langbein's view that there is no plea-bargaining in Germany (Langbein 1979).

Independent of that particular debate, Dubber admits that in Germany it is only '20–30 percent' of criminal cases that end with 'some form of bargain' – not necessarily even with *plea* bargains (Dubber 1997: 550). These figures are a far cry from those in the United States, as we have just seen. In another sense, Dubber's contribution is extraordinarily ambitious: he wishes to expose the overall 'hypocrisy' of modern criminal procedure manifested in 'bargaining of all sorts', of which pleas are but one example, and comprising also a number of other ills, many of which revolve around alleged affronts to 'autonomy' (Dubber 1997: 595). While I agree with many of Dubber's general worries about the state of contemporary criminal procedure, I here limit myself to investigating the system of guilty pleas (and their bargaining) in particular.

Something similar is true of Langer (2004): he shows that despite an undeniable growth of American criminal procedure beyond its traditional boundaries, the way in which plea-bargaining has been adopted in other countries is importantly different from (and less problematic than) its American inspiration. As Langer correctly observes,

> the structural differences between the American adversarial conception of criminal procedure and the continental European and Latin American inquisitorial conception of criminal procedure are so deep that individual reforms inspired by American models are unlikely to push these inquisitorial criminal procedures in the direction of the American adversarial system. (Langer 2004: 3)

That is the reason why Langer mobilises the distinction appearing in the very title of his article: whenever adopted in other jurisdictions, American-style plea-bargaining is at most being *translated*, even with 'substantial differences' (Langer 2004: 7), and not merely *transplanted*.

In very general terms, the main source of resistance to American plea-bargaining in those other jurisdictions flows from the view – essential to the inquisitorial tradition – that the point of the trial is to discover the *truth*. Langer suggests, moreover, that truth is taken to be 'more relative and consensual' in the adversarial tradition than in the inquisitorial tradition, where it is 'conceived in more absolute terms' (Langer 2004: 10). It is salutary to underscore that this is not the result of purely epistemological differences between the inquisitorial and the adversarial traditions. In our context, moreover, the concern with truth is not even a purely (ivory tower) epistemological enterprise at all. Rather, it is the result of the fact that in the inquisitorial tradition truth is seen as crucial for criminal trials to arrive at *just* decisions. In our context, even if also intrinsically valuable somehow,[8] truth is also in the service of justice: we are, after all, dealing with *criminal* trials, not with epistemological investigations.

[8] For more on the non-instrumental value of truth in general, see Williams (2002: 206ff) and Thalos (2013). For more on the non-instrumental value of truth in the context of the criminal trial, see Duff et al (2007: 57ff).

It is salutary to keep in mind that 'inquisitorial' relates not only to 'inquisition' as in the awful practice of the Catholic Church, but also to the much more edifying sense of 'inquisitive' and eventually 'inquiring', connected to sustained, systematic investigations. The inquisitorial system thus operates with a robust sense of justice – and of what is involved in the *search* for justice – that applies to *criminal* trials in ways which do not apply to *civil* trials. If, having sued a debtor and thus initiated a trial, a creditor decides (for whatever reason) to settle her dispute out of court, this is something about which the State is essentially indifferent. My creditor may prefer to settle out of court because she prefers to be paid, say, 75 per cent of what I owe her now than to be paid 100 per cent of it in a few years (assuming she prevails in court). Things are importantly different in the criminal context, at least regarding criminal matters of certain gravity. In the inquisitorial tradition, the relatives of someone who killed someone else are, in principle, not allowed to settle matters out of court with the defendant; they are, at any rate, far less free to do this than they would be regarding civil matters – because the *justice* of this decision is crucially important to the State. To put it bluntly, the State could not care less whether my creditor decides to abandon her project of forcing me to pay what I owe her (or whether or not that outcome is 'just'); but the State cares a great deal about *criminals* receiving the punishment that they deserve (and about them being prevented from harming others, etc). Plea-bargaining is too much like an out-of-court civil settlement for those used to (or appreciative of) the inquisitorial criminal procedure tradition to be comfortable with it.[9]

Needless to say, the fact that the inquisitorial tradition may be (as I think it is) preferable to the adversarial tradition *in this regard* does not suggest that it is better overall, or that it does not face all sorts of serious problems that may perhaps not be faced by the adversarial tradition. The point that interests me is the role of justice in the criminal process, and nothing suggests that justice can only (or even better) be realised in one particular tradition. Nothing prevents, either, the possibility of powerful attacks on the American-style plea-bargaining system from scholars neither belonging to nor advocating a turn towards the inquisitorial system. The reason why I pay attention here to the classical opposition between these two traditions in criminal procedure is that there is something in the history of these two traditions, and in the way that certain values have crystallised in each of them, that is particularly illuminating.

IV. Comfort in Fibs, or On Fake Histories

Alschuler begins his highly influential 'Plea Bargaining and Its History' with a wonderfully titled section: 'The Ideological Comforts of History', which is the

[9] For a breezy but illuminating (and entertaining) account of the differences between the inquisitorial and the adversarial systems, see Moskovitz (1995).

inspiration for the title of this section (Alschuler 1979: 1). Essentially (or at least for my purposes here), the comforts of which Alschuler speaks arise within the context of a certain grand narrative whereby plea-bargaining is somehow inevitable, that it is part and parcel of the administration of (criminal) justice, and that it has so been throughout history. Alschuler (1979) offers ample evidence for this view: he quotes many authors who believe that 'plea bargains have accompanied the whole history of this nation's criminal jurisprudence' and even that 'plea agreements are not new; in all probability such bargaining has gone on as long as there have been criminal courts' – going back to Cain and Abel (Alschuler 1979: 2). A couple of decades after Alschuler's article, Justice Antonin Scalia (joined by three other justices), recognised that while he finds it somewhat problematic that the United States has a system of 'plea bargaining aplenty', this is a 'necessary evil' (*Lafler v Cooper* 2012: 185). These views are erroneous – and in fact scandalously so.

Alschuler (1979) is at the forefront of showing how this alleged inevitability is not even true of the United States, plea-bargaining's hotbed: in its early history plea-bargaining did not dominate criminal procedure there in anything remotely like the way in which it does now. Langbein has thoroughly examined legal systems in which neither guilty pleas nor plea-bargaining (in anything like their American versions) are even known – at least not 'for cases of felony or grave misdemeanor' (Langbein 1979: 209).[10] Notwithstanding Dubber's corrections to Langbein, and despite Langbein's expressed emphasis on Germany, much of what he says applies to a number of other jurisdictions – in fact, Langbein sometimes appears to use 'German' and 'continental' interchangeably. It is not only in these other European nations where guilty pleas and plea-bargaining are unknown, but in many other countries as well (Moskovitz 1995; Langer 2004).

In general, guilty pleas and plea-bargaining are either unknown or remarkably unimportant in most countries influenced by that non-common law legal tradition, variously called 'Roman law', 'civil law', the 'Napoleonic' or the 'continental' legal tradition, and so on. The point that Langbein makes about how in Germany, even beyond legal circles, 'American plea bargaining is regarded with astonishment bordering on incredulity' (Langbein 1979: 212) is not only applicable to Germany – and not only applicable to other European countries: similar reactions abound in many countries around the world. Once the usual comforting and self-serving pronouncements of the sort that Alschuler and Langbein cite (and that Moskovitz dramatises) are subjected to even minimal scrutiny, plea-bargaining is exposed as, far from a universal phenomenon, actually a remarkably parochial one – narrowly restricted both geographically and in time.

There is nothing about a criminal justice system, structurally or conceptually, that necessitates a system of guilty pleas (or of its companion system of

[10] As Langbein (1979) points out, regarding very minor infractions, the German 'penal order procedure' may seem as somewhat of an analogue to the American-style plea-bargaining – though, even in that context there are important differences.

plea-bargaining) – much less, as we see in the case of the United States, its almost complete *replacement* with it. But there is a sense in which a particularly *dysfunctional* criminal justice system may need guilty pleas (and aggressive bargaining). Langbein's extraordinary analysis of the parallels between the American adoption of a system of guilty pleas and the European embrace of torture is highly illuminating (Langbein 1976). It is important to emphasise the specific sense of 'torture' at play here: it is torture as a form of gathering evidence, not as a punishment. As Langbein correctly points out, 'no punishment, no matter how gruesome, should be called torture' (Langbein 1976: 3). This is not an abuse of definition – afflictive punishments can be overly severe, they can indeed be torturous – but in a different sense of 'torture'; for Langbein to make this conceptual point is in now way to preclude the normative discussion of punishment's severity or its excesses.

(Continental) Europe had, over centuries, evolved a demanding tariffed process for finding a defendant guilty (of serious crimes). Two general principles that governed the process are important for my purposes here. First, the testimony of two competent eyewitness was necessary for any conviction. Second 'circumstantial evidence, so-called indicia, was not an adequate basis for conviction and condemnation, no matter how compelling' (Langbein 1976: 4). Not even Thoreau's proverbial 'trout in the milk' was deemed enough for conviction of having diluted milk.[11] Circumstantial evidence was, however, not completely ignored; it was just that it could never be *enough* to convict a person.

It should not be difficult to see how this system can quickly run into trouble: what is to be done when there are not two eyewitnesses (even if you had ample circumstantial evidence)? Enter the confession. If the defendant himself confesses to the crime, then he can be convicted – assuming, importantly, that his confession *supplements* the otherwise insufficient evidence: confessions absent corroborating evidence were not only not enough, but the 'interrogation' that may give rise to a confession was not *permitted* unless some independent evidence against the defendant already existed. Whenever evidence existed but was insufficient, then the defendant's own confession could make conviction permissible. The second stage of the problem should be as obvious as the first. What if the defendant, against whom there exists significant but (in light of the demanding tariff) insufficient evidence does not wish to confess? Enter, now, torture.

Langbein is not interested in defending judicial torture. Neither am I. I follow his analyses because the history that he presents reveals that the very tariff on evidence – ie, the demand for two eyewitnesses, the limited role for circumstantial evidence, etc – sought mainly to *protect* defendants from possible abuses arising from unchecked discretion on the part of judges. This protection made it possible for a recalcitrant defendant, who appeared (plausibly) to be guilty, to nonetheless avoid punishment altogether. But then we can see how the reason torture was

[11] The proverb highlights the potentially immense probatory value of 'merely' circumstantial evidence.

introduced into the system was, surprisingly, also to prevent potential abuses in the discretionary power of judges. Torture, part and parcel of the demanding tariff of evidence, came to the rescue of the system.

With this interesting bit of legal history in place, it is worthwhile to briefly discuss the fact that torture was admittedly much less common in England than on the Continent. Quoting Frederick Pollock and Frederic Maitland, Langbein (1976: 77) is sceptical about explaining this by appealing to a comforting (but imaginary) 'unusual degree of humanity or enlightenment' amongst the English.[12] Rather, the explanation relates to the fact that English legal institutions, and in particular its criminal procedure, were 'so crude that torture was unnecessary' (Langbein 1976: 77). Langbein's remark (again echoing Pollock and Maitland) – 'to this day an English jury can convict a defendant on less evidence than was required as a mere precondition for interrogation under torture on the Continent' – should be sobering (Langbein 1976: 78; Pollock and Maitland 1898: 690).[13]

Pollock and Maitland further note that 'luckily for England neither the stringent rules of legal proof nor the cruel and stupid subterfuge [of torture, common in Europe] became endemic [t]here' (Pollock and Maitland 1898: 690). Like Pollock and Maitland, Langbein is perfectly alive to the moral ills of torture and to its potential to be abused as a 'subterfuge'. But the main point remains: despite its being deeply morally offensive, likely to be used disingenuously and cruelly etc, torture was introduced in Europe as part of an effort to *protect* defendants from harms at the hand of an over-zealous criminal procedure that afforded too much discretion to its judges. As Langbein points out, however, the European embrace of judicial torture was, in effect, to 'solve … one problem by creating another' (Langbein 1976: 7). There is, then, a sense in which torture was indeed a 'necessary evil' for the Europeans, but only because of the antecedent (optional) evils that they chose to generate. Given that they adhered to the strict evidentiary tariff just sketched, they did need to supplement it with the use of torture. For, as Langbein put it, 'no society will long tolerate a legal system in which there is no prospect of convicting unrepentant persons who commit clandestine crimes' (Langbein 1976: 7). Evidently, absent the initial adherence, then the 'necessity' of judicial torture would vanish into thin air.

And this is the fascinating parallel that flows from Langbein's (1976) investigation which I wish to pursue: the system of plea-bargaining is a necessary evil in the American criminal justice system, as Scalia (like many others) points out, in

[12] Despite other disagreements with Langbein, Mirjan Damaska similarly rejects any explanation based on the idea that the 'English society of the period was more humane and enlightened than Continental societies'. See Damaska (1978: 864).

[13] Langbein usefully points out how Bentham, too, expressed this view in very similar terms. In one of two manuscripts only very recently made available (to my knowledge, by William Twining in the early 1970s), Bentham wrote: 'there are few if any cases in which a man can be put to the torture under the Roman law, upon less evidence than would be sufficient to convict him by the English' (Twining and Twining 1973: 333).

a parallel way to that in which torture was a necessary evil in past European law. Plea-bargaining is America's procedural subterfuge, just as torture was Europe's subterfuge. There is nothing conceptual or immanent about such necessity. Just like its yesteryear European counterparts, Americans have solved one problem by creating another; and just like yesteryear Europeans, the problematic solution is in many ways worse than the initial problem it sought to solve. Scalia seems right when he asserts that if something like plea-bargaining were to disappear, 'our system of criminal justice would grind to a halt' (*Lafler v Cooper* 2012: 185). But of course, this is only because contemporary criminal law in the United States has been allowed to grow completely out of control in the first place. The United States routinely over-criminalises, over-charges and over-punishes (Husak 2008).

The main conclusion to this discussion of the alleged necessity of plea-bargaining is straightforward: there is no such necessity. It is only against the backdrop of bloated, inhumane and *unnecessary* aspects of the American criminal justice system that plea-bargaining may appear necessary. Things can be made to look as if plea-bargaining is necessary in a robust – albeit 'embarrassing' sense (*Lafler v Cooper* 2012: 186) – only by (irresponsibly) assuming that different problems we have chosen to create (over-criminalisation etc) are also necessary.

Despite the parallels sketched in this section, there is at least one sense in which American plea-bargaining is much worse, or more worrying, than European torture. This is because torture is in and of itself morally repugnant whereas plea-bargaining is not. This difference permits a sort of complacency, or a sort of indifference, towards the latter that is harder to imagine regarding the former.[14] In the next section I will explore ways in which this acquiescing with plea-bargaining has played out in the United States. The lessons I wish to draw from the consideration of the American case are, I hope, of wider value and interest.

V. Institutionalising Vulnerability

The core of the current Supreme Court's position on plea-bargaining can be gleaned from the two recent decisions from which I have quoted already: *Lafler v Cooper* and *Missouri v Frye*. While both were 5–4 decisions (with the conservative justices in the dissenting minority), I will here focus on the dissents. Conservative justices constitute now a clear majority of the Court, and it is hard to imagine the current Supreme Court not advancing the views that Scalia and fellow dissenters[15]

[14] For a similar point, though geared towards the prosecutorial power that plea-bargaining generates, see Stuntz (2011: 295).

[15] For those unfamiliar with the American political scene – or with American jurisprudence – the following note may provide context for the discussion of Scalia in this chapter. Scalia's towering influence in American jurisprudence extends beyond the Supreme Court; it extends beyond jurisprudence itself, since he has become a symbol for 'conservatism'. See, for example, Greene (2016). My discussion of Scalia thus seeks to engage with a rather important and influential current within American jurisprudence.

expressed in these dissents – or worse, as the recent overturning of *Roe v Wade* (1973) in *Dobbs v Jackson Women's Health Organization* (2022) makes painfully clear. Regardless of the current scandalous politicisation of the Supreme Court, however, the dissents illustrate a position shared by a sizeable and influential segment of the American legal establishment, and given the influence that things American seem to have all over the world, the position may find support elsewhere as well.

Steering clear of the carping details of American constitutional theory in *Lafler* and *Frye*, suffice it to say that *Lafler* involves a defendant, Anthony Cooper, who received unquestionably terrible legal advice from his lawyer during the plea-bargaining process. This advice led to Cooper being sentenced to a much longer prison term than would have been the case had he formally accepted a plea bargain offered to him (and which he somehow informally initially accepted although, given the bad advice from his lawyer, he subsequently unaccepted). The majority in *Lafler* sought a way of bringing a measure of relief to Cooper – and thus to many other defendants: again, this is a matter that potentially affects over 97 per cent of all defendants. Scalia, however, was 'saddened' by the majority's decision: saddened by what it says about the Court's 'attitude towards criminal justice', no less (*Lafler v Cooper* 2012: 186).[16] He emphasises two main points: that defendants do not have a 'constitutional right to plea-bargaining' (*Lafler v Cooper* 2012: 180), and that the majority decision absurdly suggests that the 'prejudice' (*Lafler v Cooper* 2012: 178–85) the defendant suffered was 'to receive a full and fair trial' (*Lafler v Cooper* 2012: 176).

This is all remarkably tendentious. I will mention two (closely interrelated) reasons for my assessment. First, objecting to seeing a 'full and fair trial' as a 'harm' (as Scalia claims the majority in *Lafler* is committed to seeing) is surely clever. Scalia's point is not entirely without merit; and taken out of context it may even look compelling. What could possibly be wrong with a full and fair trial? Is it not precisely *that* (together with all the protections that it provides) we want defendants to be able to access? How can *that* be a harm? Once we heed the context, however, things look importantly different. Even if we stipulate that the trial Cooper got was indeed 'full and fair' (a rather problematic stipulation, given that Scalia recognises, as we have seen, that 'criminal justice today is for the most part a system of pleas, not a system of trials'), the fact of the matter is that Cooper had been offered a sentence that was much shorter than he received in the trial. And the only reason he agreed to the trial was the bad legal advice he received from his lawyer. Independently of what trials in general accomplish, or seek to accomplish, *this* particular trial, recommended to this particular defendant by this particular defence lawyer, did cause him an obvious harm.

[16] For ease of exposition, unless otherwise noted, when I refer here to Scalia, I mean to refer to Scalia and his fellow dissenters. As explained in the previous footnote, Scalia's views are shared by many in the United States.

The following analogy may help. Typically, to receive an inheritance is (financially) good. A particular inheritance, however, may be (financially) bad – say, because it contains more debts than credits. For this reason, the law has for centuries recognised the accepting of inheritances 'under benefit of inventory' (the *beneficium inventarii* of Roman law). In an effort to protect people from becoming worse off as a result of receiving an inheritance, the law allows them to accept it on the condition that they are not made worse off. A trial is of course something else, but the principle I seek to capture by the analogy is not terribly different: one could be harmed by something that *in general* is not harmful: an inheritance in one case, a trial in another. The law recognises a protection in the former case, but Scalia wants to deny such protection in the latter.

Second, whether or not defendants have a constitutional right to plea-bargaining is a red herring. We can even stipulate that they do not. Scalia recognises that for all intents and purposes, plea-bargaining has, as a matter of sheer fact, come to replace the trial in the vast majority of criminal cases in the United States. So, even if defendants do not have a constitutional right to it, plea-bargaining is what, as a matter of sheer fact, they get. Should plea-bargaining go on unregulated? ('Regulation', in this context, entails thinking about the forms that the usual protections afforded to defendants in *trials* should take during these bargains so that defendants can be as protected in those contexts as they are in the superseded trials.)[17] As is often the case, Scalia bases his refusal to regulate plea-bargaining on some sort of respect for the separation of powers. Thus, while Scalia admits that 'the plea-bargaining process is a subject worthy of regulation, since it is the means by which most criminal convictions are obtained' (*Missouri v Frye* 2012: 155), he nonetheless rushes to wash his hands, by claiming that it is simply not the Supreme Court's job to do that. Rather, it is the legislative branch's job, which could solve these problems 'in a much more precise and efficient manner' (*Missouri v Frye* 2012: 155).

It is hard not to suspect bad faith here, not only in light of the conceptual acrobatics underwriting Scalia's suggestion that the process of plea-bargaining is somehow *not* part of the trial (so that he can claim that the defendant in *Lafler* somehow received a 'full and fair' trial despite not being treated fairly during the bargaining process), but also in light of his cherry-picking when to endorse political principles. My point is not to deny the importance of respecting the separation of powers. My point is that merely five months after *Lafler* and *Frye*, Scalia and these same dissenters found themselves in the majority in another 5–4 decision that overturned a legislative act which, even in this age of hyper-partisanship, had passed in the House of Representatives by a margin of 390 to 33, and in the Senate

[17] As several contributions to this volume make clear (particularly Chapters 5, 8 and 11), these usual protections are in fact much more common in the United Kingdom than in the United States.

by a margin of 98 to 0 (*Shelby County v Holder* 2013). So much for their alleged respect for the separation of powers.[18]

'The Constitution', Scalia quotes himself claiming (in *Padilla v Kentucky* 2010), 'is not an all-purpose tool for judicial construction of a perfect world' (*Missouri v Frye*: 155). And in cases like this one, Scalia believes that if the Supreme Court recognises protections to defendants, this risks 'swinging a sledge where a tack hammer is needed' (*Missouri v Frye*: 155). Again, this, too, is a facile instance of hand washing and of obfuscating matters. What is the sledge that the majority wielded? Justice in *Lafler* only called for a small step (a tap with a tack hammer?) and not for any 'multi-purpose tool that could construct a perfect world' – to extend the protections afforded to defendants during trial to defendants mired in a process that *all justices* agree has de facto replaced trials. And yet, Scalia refuses to do that modest thing which would have allowed a defendant to serve a considerably shorter sentence than, as a result of his lawyer's bad advice, he ended up sentenced to serve.

In an extraordinary display of cynicism, Scalia claims that the way the criminal justice system treated Cooper is 'wonderfully just' (*Lafler v Cooper* 2012: 187). The remainder of this chapter examines some of the perils of such wonderful justice.

VI. Vulnerability Unleashed: The Colour of Justice

Unlike those deluded by the historical myth whereby plea-bargaining is somehow inseparable from the criminal justice system, Scalia recognises that 'in many – perhaps most – countries of the world, American style plea-bargaining is forbidden in cases as serious as this one' (*Lafler v Cooper* 2012: 185). Scalia, moreover, intimates that those other systems are (in this regard) better than the American system, saddled as the latter is with this 'evil'. Jurisdictions without plea-bargaining, Scalia believes, are after all committed to the 'admirable belief that the law is the law, and those who break it should pay the penalty provided' (*Lafler v Cooper* 2012: 185). The fact that Scalia is aware that criminal justice systems can exist without plea-bargaining makes it hard to understand how he can simultaneously see plea-bargaining as a 'necessary' evil at all. But I will put aside this particular inconsistency and focus instead on a different sort of mistake.

Scalia appears to believe that the wrongfulness of plea-bargaining is mostly a matter of defendants not getting the punishment that the law prescribes. (He appears to presume that the punishment the law prescribes is the punishment that wrongdoers deserve.) Matters are, however, much more complex than Scalia

[18] Even here Scalia is not completely bereft of arguments: he can claim that he is respecting *State* rights from abuses by the federal government. I cannot here address how weak such argument is. The points to emphasise are that Congress had spoken extraordinarily clearly, that Scalia did not care, and that he summarily substituted his own judgement for that of the legislative branch.

countenances. The suite of problems plaguing American criminal justice – again: over-criminalisation, over-charging and over-punishment – makes it highly unlikely that what the law says defendants deserve is what they actually deserve. Scalia fails to mention (or to notice?) that in the vast majority of those countries in which plea-bargaining is either unknown or infrequent punishments are far less severe than in the United States. So, when Scalia mocks the majority decision in *Lafler* for embracing 'the sporting chance theory of criminal law, in which the State functions like a conscientious casino-operator, giving each player a fair chance to beat the house, that is, to serve less time than the law says he deserves' (*Lafler v Cooper* 2012: 186), he unceremoniously dismisses the possibility that the punishments that the plea-bargaining system affords defendants in the United States may be more attuned to what they actually deserve than the punishments that the law provides.

It should by now be perfectly clear that I do not seek to defend the system of plea-bargaining as such: as we have seen, the system can at best be seen as clumsily piling a deeply problematic patch onto other problems. Rather than recognising the initial problems (entirely of our own making) that have rendered plea-bargaining a necessity (in the peculiar and thin sense we have discussed), Scalia reifies those problems, takes them as given, and then complacently makes peace with a second, compounding one. Indeed, one of the problems that the plea-bargaining system seeks to solve is the exorbitantly severe and undeserved punishments that the law in the books prescribes in the first place. Other jurisdictions may not need to turn to plea-bargaining as a mechanism to moderate punishments simply because their punishments do not need that much moderation. What my objection to the homespun simplicity of Scalia's view does seek to underscore is that Scalia either unproblematically assumes that the punishments the law provides are essentially just (in the sense of essentially deserved), or else he is remarkably indifferent to legally prescribed punishments that may be unjust (in the sense of undeserved).

Scalia fails to mention (or to notice?) that the most direct consequence of rejecting the system of plea-bargaining, in those countries that do reject it, is to ensure that defendants' rights are protected. As the authors of an authoritative criminal procedure book point out, defendants' rights 'have been thought so fundamental that [in some jurisdictions] they cannot be waived'; the 'unavailability of the guilty plea [in those jurisdictions is] regarded as a guarantee of defendants' rights' (Campbell, Ashworth and Redmayne 2019: 315). This, of course, flows from the famous liberal fear: fear that the powerful (the State) may take advantage of the weak (the individual – particularly the individual *defendant*). In a passage I have often quoted, Ronald Dworkin (1985) puts it eloquently:

> [I]t would be a mistake to suppose that the liberal thinks that these procedural rights will improve the accuracy of the criminal process, that is, the probability that any particular decision about guilt or innocence will be the right one. Procedural rights intervene in the process, even at the cost of inaccuracy, to compensate in a rough way for the antecedent risk that a criminal process, especially if it is largely administered by one class against another, will be corrupted by the impact of external preferences that cannot be eliminated directly.

In other words, notwithstanding my sympathy toward retributivism – toward the view that there is intrinsic value in giving people what they deserve, even if what they deserve is to suffer – an important goal of criminal procedure is to protect the weak. Quintessentially, the defendant in a trial is the weakest participant in it. Dworkin's observation about criminal procedure is part of his effort to protect the weak from 'the prejudices and external preferences of the majority' (Dworkin 1985: 197). Expanding on this paradigmatic liberal preoccupation, I wish to conclude my discussion of the US system of pleas (and plea-bargaining) by noting the prominent and shameful role that race has played (and continues to play) in the American criminal justice system, and by noting, too, the particular ways in which both the (general) guilty plea system and the more specific plea-bargaining system have contributed to the perpetuation of racist practices and institutions. (The system of guilty pleas has generated racial disparities in other jurisdictions too – but nothing as scandalous or as systematic as in the United States (Campbell, Ashworth and Redmayne 2019: 338–40).)

It is well known that African Americans are grossly overrepresented in the American criminal justice system. (So are other minorities, but predominantly African Americans.) Depressing figures are not hard to come by. Consider statistics compiled by Michelle Alexander:

> [I]n some states, black men have been admitted to prison on drug charges at rates twenty to fifty times greater than those of white men. And in major cities wracked by the drug war, as many as 80 percent of young African American men now have criminal records and are thus subject to legalized discrimination for the rest of their lives. (Alexander 2010: 7; Husak 2008: 4–17)

In light of these figures – and many more like them – it is hard to disagree with Alexander that the criminal justice system treats African Americans as an 'under-caste'.

Making matters much worse, members of this 'under-caste' are actually the descendants of slaves (and earlier on, the 'liberated' slaves themselves). This connection is not coincidental. One last quick glance at history is illuminating. As Alschuler (1979) reminds us, plea-bargaining was 'extremely' rare throughout much of American history. It was only by 'the end of the nineteenth century and beginning of the twentieth' that it became 'a dominant method of resolving criminal cases' (Alschuler 1979: 6). This means that the American love affair with plea-bargaining roughly coincided with a number of other changes in American law in general, and in particular in its criminal law. The general change I have in mind is, of course, the Thirteenth Amendment to the Constitution, in the aftermath of the Civil War. The text of the Thirteenth Amendment is as short as it is shameful:

> Section 1. Neither slavery nor involuntary servitude, *except as a punishment* for crime whereof the party shall have been duly convicted, shall exist within the United States, or any place subject to their jurisdiction. Section 2. Congress shall have power to enforce this article by appropriate legislation.' (emphasis added)

The abolition of slavery in the United States has never been complete: slavery is still legally permitted in the United States, albeit only as punishment for those 'duly convicted' of crimes.

As a result of this 'loophole', postbellum criminal law expanded mightily – above all (though not exclusively) in those jurisdictions in which slavery had been more prevalent. This expansion allowed for the *continued* enslavement of former slaves, except that now they were 'convicted' of crimes. As Douglas Blackmon thoroughly documents, that first wave of over-criminalisation and over-punishment in America consisted of 'arrests for inconsequential charges or for violations of laws specifically written to intimidate blacks – changing employers without permission, vagrancy, riding freight cars without a ticket, engaging in sexual activity – or loud talk – with white women' (Blackmon 2008: 7). Countless convictions in turn led to the 'convict lease' system, whereby 'duly convicted' people were leased as forced labourers, sometimes to their former owners, who would hold them in conditions that, if at all different from the conditions of the 'abolished' slavery, were *worse*: the slave-owners-turned-lessees had far less incentives to be concerned with convicts' welfare than they did when these human beings were their *property*.

A full description of the different expedients put in place to facilitate convictions is beyond the scope of this chapter. But by now their gist should not surprise: immediately after the Thirteenth Amendment, 'uncomplicated adjudication was the key to the system'; 'trials were discouraged'; and '[black] defendants typically would "confess judgment" … before being tried' (Blackmon 2008: 66). Parallels to contemporary American plea-bargaining are as obvious as they are distressing. Under this light, to claim that American-style plea-bargaining is merely a 'subterfuge' is itself a subterfuge: in the United States plea-bargaining has been a tool directly in the service of racist and cruel policies and institutions. When a defendant in the United States pleads guilty and is thereby 'duly convicted' of a crime, he risks, we now can see, being literally and legally *enslaved*.

My claim is not that the system of guilty pleas and plea-bargaining practices *wholly* explains the contemporary over-representation of African Americans throughout the criminal justice system. I need only assert that it has contributed to such over-representation. I do not systematically pursue this assertion here, but considering the evidence presented in Blackmon (2008), Husak (2008) and Alexander (2010), amongst many others, the assertion seems hard to deny. Similarly, I am not claiming that the system of guilty pleas or plea-bargaining is *necessarily* racist, or otherwise discriminatory. Again, I need only highlight how easily it can be used for racist or discriminatory purposes. Actual American history amply reveals how it has *in fact* been used for racist and cruel purposes. America's criminal justice system boasts rates of incarceration that are amongst the highest in the world, and it is amongst the most punitive in many other ways as well. Aided by the system of guilty pleas and their bargaining, the racism and cruelty of the American criminal justice system has facilitated the continued disproportionate incarceration – and possibly the continued *slavery* – of some of the most vulnerable members of society: the descendants of slaves. Whatever else this cautionary tale may turn out to be, it is, contra Scalia (and his fellow dissenters, and presumably his many fellow travellers), most assuredly not 'wonderfully just' (*Lafler v Cooper* 2012: 186).

References

Alexander, M (2010) *The New Jim Crow: Mass Incarceration in the Age of Colorblindness* (New York, New Press).

Alschuler, A (1979) 'Plea Bargaining and Its History' 79 *Columbia Law Review* 1.

Bibas, S (2004) 'Plea Bargaining Outside the Shadow of Trial' 117 *Harvard Law Review* 2463.

Blackmon, D (2008) *Slavery by Another Name: The Re-Enslavement of Black People in America from the Civil War to World War II* (New York, Doubleday).

Campbell, L, Ashworth, A and Redmayne, M (2019) *The Criminal Process* (Oxford, Oxford University Press).

Damaska, M (1978) 'The Death of Legal Torture' 78 *Yale Law Journal* 860.

Dubber, MD (1997) 'American Plea Bargains, German Lay Judges, and the Crisis of Criminal Procedure' 49 *Stanford Law Review* 547.

Duff A, Farmer, L, Tadros, V and Marshall, S (2007) *The Trial on Trial: Towards a Normative Theory of the Criminal Trial*, vol 3 (Oxford, Hart Publishing).

Dworkin, R (1985) *A Matter of Principle* (Cambridge, MA, Harvard University Press).

Gramlich, J (2019) 'Only 2% of Federal Criminal Defendants go to Trial and Most who do are Found Guilty', www.pewresearch.org/fact-tank/2019/06/11/only-2-of-federal-criminal-defendants-go-to-trial-and-most-who-do-are-found-guilty/

Greene, J (2016) 'The Age of Scalia' 130 *Harvard Law Review* 144.

Harvard Law Review (1970) 'The Unconstitutionality of Plea Bargaining' 83 *Harvard Law Review* 1387s.

Husak, D (2008) *Overcriminalization: The Limits of the Criminal Law* (Oxford, Oxford University Press).

Jiménez de Asúa, L (1963) *Tratado de Derecho Penal* (6 vols) (Buenos Aires, Losada).

Langbein, J (1976) *Torture and the Law of Proof: Europe and England in the Ancien Régime* (Chicago, IL, University of Chicago Press).

—— (1979) 'Land Without Plea Bargaining: How the Germans Do It' 78 *Michigan Law Review* 204.

Langer, M (2004) 'From Legal Transplants to Legal Translations: The Globalization of Plea Bargaining and the Americanization Thesis in Criminal Procedure' 45 *Harvard International Law Journal* 1.

Moskovitz, M (1995) 'The O.J. Inquisition: A United States Encounter with Continental Criminal Justice' 28 *Vanderbilt Journal of Transnational Justice* 1121.

Pollock, F and Maitland, F (1898) *The History of English Law Before the Time of Edward I*, vol 2 (Cambridge, Cambridge University Press).

Schulhofer, SJ (1992) 'Plea Bargaining as Disaster' 101 *The Yale Law Journal* 1979.

Stuntz, WJ (2004) 'Plea Bargaining and Criminal Law's Disappearing Shadow' 117 *Harvard Law Review* 2548.

—— (2011) *The Collapse of American Criminal Justice System* (Cambridge, MA, Belknap Press).

Thalos, M (2013) 'Truth Deserves to be Believed' 88 *Philosophy* 179.
Twining WL and Twining, PE (1973) 'Bentham on Torture' 24 *Northern Ireland Legal Quarterly* 305.
Williams, B (2002) *Truth and Truthfulness: An Essay in Genealogy* (Princeton, NJ, Princeton University Press).
Zaibert, L (2008) 'Uprootedness as (Cruel and Unusual) Punishment' 11 *New Criminal Law Review* 384.

Cases

Dobbs v Jackson Women's Health Organization 597 US ____ (2022)
Lafler v Cooper 566 US 156 (2012)
Missouri v Frye 566 US 134 (2012)
Padilla v Kentucky 559 US 356 (2010)
Roe v Wade 410 US 113 (1973)
Shelby County v Holder 570 US 529 (2013)

INDEX

Introductory Note

References such as '178–79' indicate (not necessarily continuous) discussion of a topic across a range of pages. Wherever possible in the case of topics with many references, these have either been divided into sub-topics or only the most significant discussions of the topic are listed. Because the entire work is about the 'self-conviction' and 'guilty pleas', the use of these terms (and certain others which occur constantly throughout the book) as an entry point has been restricted. Information will be found under the corresponding detailed topics.

Milton Keynes UK
Ingram Content Group UK Ltd.
UKHW050920210724
445785UK00003B/51

9 781509 957439